Remember
the new covenant,
even the Book of Mormon . . .

Doctrine and Covenants 84:57

CHRIST
AND
THE NEW COVENANT

The Messianic Message of the Book of Mormon

JEFFREY R. HOLLAND

Deseret Book Company
Salt Lake City, Utah

Library of Congress Cataloging-in-Publication Data

Holland, Jeffrey R., 1940–
   Christ and the new covenant / by Jeffrey R. Holland.
    p.   cm.
   Includes bibliographical references and index.
   ISBN 1-57345-235-1
   1. Jesus Christ in the Book of Mormon. 2. Book of Mormon—
Criticism, interpretation, etc. 3. Jesus Christ—Mormon
interpretations. I. Title.
   BX8627.H65   1997
   289.3'22—dc21   96-48669
                                         CIP

Printed in the United States of America   72082

10 9 8 7 6 5 4 3 2 1

For Pat

Whose light cleaveth unto Light

CONTENTS

APPEARANCE

AFTERWARD

AFFIRMATION

PREFACE

The material bound within these covers has grown out of several years of private study on a subject dear to me since the days of my mission—the central and persuasive presence of Christ (and the wondrous teachings about him) that appear from first page to last throughout the Book of Mormon. Because this has been such a personal project, it is important to understand at the outset some things this book is *not*.

For one thing, it is not a scholarly book in the traditional sense of voluminous source material and exhaustive documentation. This work contains virtually none of that, simply because in compiling these ideas and recording these thoughts I have read almost no material of any kind—scholarly or otherwise—other than the Book of Mormon itself. Where an outside source has been used, it has been cited in an endnote, as have the scriptures. A different book (and, I am quick to acknowledge, probably a better book) would be one referencing everything anyone in or out of the Church has ever said about these passages of scripture. But that would not be this book.

I have had something more personal in mind. This volume is meant to be more like a meditation upon scripture than a work of scholarship. Wherever possible I have let the scriptures speak for themselves without commentary from me. Occasionally those passages are quite lengthy, but to include them has been a conscious decision for which I make no apology. Whenever possible I would rather have the reader focus directly on Book of Mormon language than on someone else's language about it. In saying that, I do not excuse any poor thinking or poor writing on my part. Even a work not intended to be scholarly should still be interesting in its suppositions and intelligent in its observations. I hope this effort does not fall short in either category.

This book is also not a scriptural summary of all the relevant citations in the Standard Works that might shed light on the topic at hand. From the beginning it was intended to be a study of the Book of Mormon's contribution to our understanding of Christ, not a review of the other Standard Works of the Church on that subject. As a rule I have tried to use almost no other scriptural sources, but occasionally a reference to one of the other Standard Works was essential. When it has seemed particularly needful, I have used such a passage. For the most part, however, this is a portrayal of the Book of Mormon view of Christ, and the Book of Mormon view only.

Not that anyone will find it so, but this book is emphatically not a substitute for reading the Book of Mormon itself. In fact, one could make a persuasive argument that no book should be written *about* the Book of Mormon, particularly if reading such a secondary work became an alternative for becoming immersed in the scripture firsthand. No person writing under the limitations of his or her own light, however aided from heaven, could ever begin to duplicate or capture the spiritual splendor of the most extensive and definitive revelation given in this dispensation. This author readily acknowledges that fact, and the shortcoming of this or any other book written about the Book of Mormon is evidence of its truth.

The only real justifications I have felt for producing this work are that the study of Christ and his teachings in the Book of Mormon was wonderfully rewarding to me and that such a book may lead someone to find his or her own insights into the magnificent characterization of the Master contained in this great latter-day witness of him. However limited this book's contribution may be, my prayer is that it will be of some help and encouragement toward reading the Book of Mormon itself and never any barrier to it.

Lastly, this book is not a product of the Council of the First Presidency and Quorum of the Twelve Apostles and is not a doctrinal declaration by or for The Church of Jesus Christ of Latter-day Saints. I alone am responsible for the publication of this work, and I alone am accountable for any errors and limitations it may contain. I can only hope those are relatively few and forgivable.

JEFFREY R. HOLLAND
SALT LAKE CITY, UTAH
1997

ACKNOWLEDGMENTS

I wish to thank Randi Greene and Janet Morley, my secretaries over the past several years in Salt Lake City, Utah, and Solihull, England, respectively, whose talent as well as kindness went into correcting and clarifying of my own primitive word-processing efforts that produced the first drafts of this manuscript. Since then, Randi has, on her own time, been willing to see this through later drafts in which I did so much editing and rewriting. She has also skillfully orchestrated the many logistical and review procedures that are part of getting such a manuscript into the hands of the publisher in final form. I am indebted to her for her skill, her loyalty, and her encouragement to me in pursuing this project.

I am grateful to my brethren of the First Presidency and Quorum of the Twelve Apostles, who bless me with their brotherhood, teach me in our council settings, and give encouragement in sharing the doctrines of the restored gospel. President Boyd K. Packer has given particularly helpful counsel regarding this manuscript, making it better than it would have been even if it is not yet as good as it should be.

I also wish to thank my mission president, Elder Marion D. Hanks, who first introduced me to the profundity of the Book of Mormon and the majesty of Christ that lay hidden there. I know of no one who loves the Book of Mormon more than Elder Hanks, nor of anyone who has taught it with more power and conviction.

I am also grateful to a number of associates at Brigham Young University, particularly my past and present fellow deans of Religious Education there—Daniel H. Ludlow, Robert J.

Matthews, and Robert L. Millet. They have encouraged this work, made invaluable suggestions, and stiffened the author's spine when it did not seem the project was progressing. Dean Millet was particularly kind in undertaking what no friend should ever be forced to endure—reading the manuscript in very early draft form. I am indebted to him for his careful reading of such an incomplete manuscript and his informed response to both its problems and its possibilities. At a later date former deans Ludlow and Matthews gave me the benefit of their singular careers spent writing and editing scriptural studies.

Professor Donald W. Parry was of invaluable assistance on the chapter on Isaiah, sharing generously with me the insights of his own research and writing on this subject. Edward Brandt offered extremely helpful background regarding the chapter on the law of Moses. To these and all others who have offered encouragement and given assistance of any kind, early or late, I express appreciation.

It is almost certain I would not have made the move from personal study project to published book without the prodding and persuasion of first Eleanor Knowles and later Sheri Dew at Deseret Book Company. To them, to Ronald A. Millett, and to their editing, design, and production associates, especially Jack Lyon and Kent Ware, I also express appreciation.

As in all things, my greatest indebtedness is to my wife, Pat, and our three children, who always are and ever have been my encouragement, my solace, and my constant inspiration. They have wanted this book to be published more than I have. I am grateful for their devotion to the Savior, to the scriptures, and to me.

ASSERTION

CHAPTER ONE

"THE NEW COVENANT, EVEN THE BOOK OF MORMON"

f we were to ask casual readers of the Book of Mormon to name the principal character in that book, their responses would undoubtedly vary. Obviously any record covering more than a thousand years of history—with all the persons such a history would include—is unlikely to have a single, central figure emerge over such an extended period of time. Nevertheless, after acknowledging that limitation, perhaps some might list any one of several memorable individuals. Names such as Nephi, the book's early and very recognizable young prophet, or Mormon, the abridger for whom the book is named, or Alma, to whom so many pages are devoted, or Moroni, who concluded the plates and delivered them some fourteen hundred years later to the young Joseph Smith—these would undoubtedly be among the figures mentioned.

All those responses would be provocative, but in terms of the question posed, they would also be decidedly incorrect. The principal and commanding figure in the Book of Mormon, from first chapter to last, is the Lord Jesus Christ. In its unparalleled focus on the Messianic message of the Savior of the world, the Book of Mormon is rightly referred to as God's "new covenant"

with the house of Israel.[1] It is literally a new testament or (to avoid confusion) "another testament" of Jesus Christ. As such the book centers upon that which scriptural testaments have always centered since the days of Adam and Eve—the declaration to all that through the atonement of the Son of God, "as thou hast fallen thou mayest be redeemed, and all mankind, even as many as will."[2]

From the title page to the book's final declaration, this testament reveals, examines, underscores, and illuminates the divine mission of Jesus Christ as recorded in the sacred accounts of two New World dispensations (Jaredite and Lehite) written for the benefit of a third dispensation, the dispensation of the fulness of times. The Book of Mormon has many purposes, but this one transcends all others. Written by prophets and preserved by angels, it was written for the fundamental and eternally essential purpose of "convincing . . . the Jew and Gentile that JESUS is the CHRIST, the ETERNAL GOD, manifesting himself unto all nations." In the course of coming to such conviction about Christ, all who receive this record will also be convinced of "the covenants of the Lord," including his promise that the contemporary remnants of the House of Israel are not "cast off forever."[3]

Thus the Book of Mormon is the preeminent statement of God's covenant with and his love for his children here on earth. It is his definitive latter-day declaration regarding the atoning sacrifice of his Son. It is his great revelation of the greatest Revelation God has ever given us.

ANOTHER TESTAMENT OF JESUS CHRIST

But why is such a record needed? Is not the world quite aware of divine covenants and Christ's centrality to them in the Old and New Testaments? The Book of Mormon speaks to just such an issue and in so doing proclaims its own purpose.

In a remarkable vision recorded early in the Book of Mormon, the young prophet Nephi saw the eventual preparation and circulation of the Holy Bible, "a record of the Jews, which contains the covenants of the Lord, which he hath made unto the house of Israel."[4] But, alarmingly, he also saw the abuse and doctrinal decimation of that book as it moved down through time and passed through many hands.

This Book of Mormon vision foretold that the Bible record would be clear and untarnished in the Meridian of Time. In Jesus' day, it would contain "the covenants of the Lord, which he hath made unto the house of Israel; [which] are of great worth unto the Gentiles." As part of that covenantal clarity, it would also contain and teach "the fulness of the gospel of the Lord," with both Old and New Testaments going "from the Jews in purity unto the Gentiles." But over time, through innocent error as well as malicious design, many saving doctrines and pure principles, especially those emphasizing the covenantal elements of the gospel of Jesus Christ, were lost—sometimes simply willfully expunged—from "the book of the Lamb of God."[5]

Unfortunately, these elements soon missing from the Bible were both "plain and most precious." They were plain in their simplicity and clarity, being easy to "the understanding of . . . men"; they were precious in their purity and profound worth, their saving significance and eternal importance to the children of God. Whatever the reason for the loss of these truths from the biblical record, it has resulted in "pervert[ing] the right ways of the Lord, . . . blind[ing] the eyes and harden[ing] the hearts of the children of men."[6] In painful understatement of the consequences stemming from such a tragic loss of divine truth, Nephi saw in vision that "an exceedingly great many do stumble," honest women and men who would live out their lives less informed of gospel truths and less secure in the salvation of Christ than they deserved to be, all because of the loss of edifying gospel truths from the biblical canon as we have received it.[7]

But in his love for all mankind and with his foreknowledge of such damage to gospel understanding, the Great Jehovah, the premortal Christ, promised Nephi (and all who have received Nephi's record):

"After the Gentiles do stumble exceedingly, because of the most plain and precious parts of the gospel of the Lamb which have been kept back, . . . I will be merciful unto the Gentiles in that day, insomuch that I will bring forth unto them, in mine own power, much of my gospel, which shall be plain and precious, saith the Lamb.

"For, behold, saith the Lamb: I will manifest myself unto thy seed, that they shall write many things which I shall minister unto them, which shall be plain and precious. . . .

"And in them shall be written my gospel, saith the Lamb, and my rock and my salvation."[8]

This promised record, now known as the Book of Mormon, will "make known the plain and precious things which have been taken away from [the Bible]; and shall make known to all kindreds, tongues, and people, that the Lamb of God is the Son of the Eternal Father, and the Savior of the world; and that all men must come unto him, or they cannot be saved.

"And they must come according to the words which shall be established by the mouth of the Lamb; and the words of the Lamb shall be made known in the records of thy seed, as well as in [the Bible]; wherefore they both shall be established in one; for there is one God and one Shepherd over all the earth."[9]

Surely the most plain and precious of all truths lost from the Bible, particularly the Old Testament, are the clear and unequivocal declarations of the mission of Jesus Christ, his foreordained role as Messiah and Savior of the world, and the covenantal elements of his gospel, which have been taught from Adam down through each succeeding dispensation. Thus the Book of Mormon's highest purpose is to restore to the universal family of God that crucial knowledge of Christ's role in the salvation of every man, woman, and child who now lives, has ever lived, or will yet live upon the earth. It is written to the convincing of all who read its pages with "a sincere heart, with real intent" that Jesus is the Christ.[10]

Also lost over this same period of time and for many of the same reasons was, as Nephi noted, an understanding of the nature and fundamental role of divine covenants, sacred promises made between God and his children in prescribing the way to immortality and eternal life. The most sacred moments of man's relationship with divinity have always been marked by the making of such covenants. Soon after being expelled from the garden of Eden, Adam and Eve were taught the principles of the gospel, after which they offered their oblations and sacrifices and made sacred covenants with God, beginning with their own baptisms. Just as immediately Satan tried to blunt those divine covenants and mar the faithfulness of the first family, succeeding in part when he convinced Cain to covenant to do great evil with him, Satan, rather than righteously serving God the Father.[11] So the world has gone ever since that first moment—forces of evil competing with the power of good for the covenantal loyalty of the children of God.

A NEW COVENANT

To help his sons and daughters remember their promises to him—and certainly to help them remember his promises to them—God has directed that the nature and significance of those covenants be recorded. In that process, the texts and documents preserving such promises have also been called "covenants." In fact, the words *testament* and *covenant* are virtually synonymous in their theological usage, the Latin definition of *testamentum* being "a covenant with God, holy scripture." Thus, the Old and New Testaments, as we commonly refer to them, are written testimonies or witnesses (the Latin *testis* meaning "witness") of the covenants between God and man in various dispensations. Furthermore, such covenants always deal with the central issue between perfect, immortal God and imperfect, mortal man— why they are separated and how they can again unite. The Latin root for *covenant* is *convenire,* "to agree, unite, come together." In short, all covenants, all testaments, all holy witnesses since the beginning have essentially been about one thing—the atonement of Jesus Christ, the *at-one-ment* provided every man, woman, and child if they will but receive the witness, the *testi*-mony of the prophets and apostles, and honor the terms of that coming together, that *convenire,* or covenant, whose central feature is always the atoning sacrifice of the Son of God himself.

But even with repeated efforts to teach these truths and re-affirm these promises, God has not always seen his children turn to the gospel of his Son. In our own day he has said, "The whole world lieth in sin, and groaneth under darkness and under the bondage of sin."[12] By and large the modern world has not come unto him, has not accepted the atonement of Jesus Christ, has not received the voice of his prophets, has not made covenants or kept his commandments, has not remembered him always or claimed the promises of exaltation in the kingdom of heaven.

So he has offered us one last covenant, given us one last testament, as part of his final outreach to fallen man. He has offered us one last written witness of his love and his mercy extended for the final time, speaking dispensationally. As one Book of Mormon prophet foresaw it, God is sending laborers into the vineyard one final time, and "then cometh the season and the end."[13] That testament and culminating witness, that "new covenant" offered to the children of men but once more, is the message of the Book of Mormon.

No record teaches more of God's promise to those in the last days. Those promises focus on his Only Begotten Son, on "the merits, and mercy, and grace of the Holy Messiah . . . [who] shall make intercession for all the children of men; and they that believe in him shall be saved."[14]

The task of the children of God in these concluding days of the world's history is to proceed with "unshaken faith in him, relying wholly upon the merits of him who is mighty to save," to "press forward with a steadfastness in Christ, having a perfect brightness of hope, and a love of God and of all men[,] . . . feasting upon the word of Christ, and endur[ing] to the end. This is the way; and there is none other way nor name given under heaven whereby man can be saved in the kingdom of God."[15]

No other book helps us do this so well. No other book was ever divinely produced and protected solely for that purpose. No other book has ever been written with such a full view of the future dispensation to which that record would eventually come. As with Moroni, so too with virtually all the Book of Mormon prophets: "Behold, I speak unto you as if ye were present, and yet ye are not. But behold, Jesus Christ hath shown you unto me, and I know your doing."[16]

The fact that most of this record comes from a period *before* Christ's birth, the fact that it is a record of an otherwise unknown people, the fact that it reaffirms the truthfulness and divinity of the Bible insofar as the latter has been translated correctly, the fact that the Book of Mormon reveals inspiring insights and deep doctrines about Jesus that are found nowhere in the biblical canon (or anywhere else in modern Christendom, for that matter) are just a few of the reasons the book should be considered the most remarkable and important religious text to be revealed since the writings of the New Testament were compiled nearly two millennia ago. Indeed, in its role of restoring plain and precious biblical truths that had been lost, while adding scores of new truths about Jesus Christ and preparing the way for the complete restoration of his gospel and the triumphant day of his millennial return, the Book of Mormon may be considered the most remarkable and important religious text ever given to the world. The prophet who translated the book and then gave his life for the truthfulness of its message said it "was the most correct of any book on earth, and the keystone of our religion, and a man would get nearer to God by abiding by its precepts, than by any other book."[17]

And so it is. The Book of Mormon is the keystone of our religion primarily because it is the most extended and definitive witness we have of the Lord Jesus Christ—of our Alpha and Omega, the True Vine, the Bishop and Shepherd of our Soul, he who is the Key Stone, the Chief Cornerstone of the eternal gospel. Christ is our salvation, and the Book of Mormon declares that message unequivocally to the world. In its message of faith in Christ, hope in Christ, and charity in Christ, the Book of Mormon is God's "new covenant" to his children—for the last time.

ANTECEDENT

CHAPTER TWO

RENDING THE VEIL
OF UNBELIEF

s noted earlier, most of the Book of Mormon account comes from the period before Jesus' birth into mortality. Not surprisingly, then, one of the special contributions of this record is the knowledge it conveys about the regal role of the premortal Christ. Christ as Jehovah, as well as Christ as Jesus, is one of the principal messages of this sacred book.

Latter-day Saint scholars consider the bringing together of the stick of Joseph with the stick of Judah, as prophesied by Ezekiel, one of the great contributions of the Book of Mormon, and so it is.[1] However, in the matter of bringing together disparate records, it is equally important to acknowledge what the Book of Mormon does to unite the Old Testament with the New Testament in a way that is not usually acknowledged and is, in fact, sometimes seen as impossible in other religious traditions.

Many students of the Bible have felt it difficult to reconcile Old Testament theology and the views of Deity portrayed there with what is presented later in the New Testament. Bridging such a perceived gap is yet one more inestimable contribution made by a third testament—the Book of Mormon. This new covenant links the religious worlds of Malachi and Matthew not only by bridging the intervening years between them (commencing, as it does, six hundred years before Christ and ending four hundred years afterward) but, more important, by bringing Old and New Testament texts together in the continuity of doctrine taught and the image of Deity portrayed. Of course, the central role of the premortal, mortal, and postmortal (resurrected) Christ in the Book of Mormon is the unifying thread that ties together all the saving teachings and traditions of the old covenant with the new.

The foreordination of Christ, his premortal divinity, the time and circumstances of his coming, and so many particulars of his mission and message were taught abundantly throughout Book of Mormon history. In approximately 74 B.C. Amulek said to his fellow citizens in the city of Ammonihah, "I think that it is impossible that ye should be ignorant of the things which have been spoken concerning the coming of Christ, who is taught by us to be the Son of God; yea, I know that these things were taught unto you bountifully before your dissension from among us."[2] Chapters 3 through 10 of this book show just how "bountifully" these truths were taught among the Nephites before Christ's birth. But the reader of the Book of Mormon should first consider an earlier and more remarkable account than those.

THE BROTHER OF JARED

One of the greatest prophets in the Book of Mormon goes unnamed in the record that documents his remarkable life. He is identified only as "the brother of Jared." Yet the revelation that unfolded before his eyes was so extraordinary that his life and legacy have become synonymous with bold, consummate, perfect faith.

In the dispersion from the Tower of Babel, the people of Jared arrived at "that great sea which divideth the lands,"[3] where they pitched their tents, awaiting further revelation about crossing the mighty ocean. For four years they awaited divine direction, but apparently they waited too casually, without supplication and exertion. Then came this remarkable encounter: "The Lord came again unto the brother of Jared, and stood in a cloud and talked with him. And for the space of three hours did the Lord talk with the brother of Jared, and chastened him because he remembered not to call upon the name of the Lord."[4]

It is difficult to imagine what a three-hour rebuke from the Lord might be like, but the brother of Jared endured it. With immediate repentance and prayer, this prophet again sought guidance for the journey they had been assigned and those who were to pursue it. God accepted his repentance and lovingly gave further direction for their crucial mission.

For their oceanic crossing, these families and their flocks would need seaworthy crafts similar to the barges they had constructed for earlier water travel—small, light, dish-shaped vessels identical in design above and beneath so they were capable of staying afloat even if overturned by the waves. These "exceedingly tight" crafts were obviously of unprecedented design and capability, made under the direction of him who rules the seas and the winds to the end that the vessels might travel with the "lightness of a fowl upon the water."[5]

As miraculously designed and meticulously constructed as they were, these ships had one major, seemingly insoluble limitation. Such a tight, seaworthy design provided no way to admit light for the seafarers.

"The brother of Jared . . . cried again unto the Lord saying: O Lord, behold I have done even as thou hast commanded me; and I have prepared the vessels for my people, and behold there is no light in them. Behold, O Lord, wilt thou suffer that we shall cross this great water in darkness?"[6]

Then came an extraordinary and unexpected response from

the creator of heaven and earth and all things that in them are, he who boldly declared to Abraham, "Is any thing too hard for the Lord?"[7]

"And the Lord said unto the brother of Jared: *What will ye that I should do* that ye may have light in your vessels?" Then, as if such a disarming inquiry from omnipotent Deity were not enough, the Lord proceeded to articulate the very problems that the brother of Jared knew only too well. He said, "Behold, ye cannot have windows, for they will be dashed in pieces; neither shall ye take fire with you, for ye shall not go by the light of fire.

"For behold, ye shall be as a whale in the midst of the sea; for the mountain waves shall dash upon you. . . .

"*Therefore what will ye that I should prepare for you* that ye may have light when ye are swallowed up in the depths of the sea?"[8]

Clearly the brother of Jared was being tested. God had done his part. Unique, resolutely seaworthy ships for crossing the ocean had been provided. The brilliant engineering had been done. The hard part of the construction project was over. Now the Lord wanted to know what the brother of Jared would do about incidentals.

After what was undoubtedly a great deal of soul-searching, the brother of Jared came before the Lord—perhaps hesitantly but not empty-handed. In a clearly apologetic tone, he said, "Now behold, O Lord, and do not be angry with thy servant because of his weakness before thee; . . . O Lord, look upon me in pity, and turn away thine anger from this thy people, and suffer not that they shall go forth across this raging deep in darkness; but behold these things which I have molten out of the rock."[9]

Things. The brother of Jared hardly knew what to call them. *Rocks* undoubtedly did not sound very inspiring. Here, standing next to the Lord's magnificent handiwork, the impeccably designed and marvelously unique seagoing barges, the brother of Jared offered for his contribution rocks. As he eyed the sleek ships the Lord had provided, it was a moment of genuine humility.

He hurried on: "And I know, O Lord, that thou hast all power, and can do whatsoever thou wilt for the benefit of man; therefore touch these stones, O Lord, with thy finger, and prepare them that they may shine forth in darkness; and they shall shine forth unto us in the vessels which we have prepared, that we may have light while we shall cross the sea.

"Behold, O Lord, thou canst do this. We know that thou art able to show forth great power, which looks small unto the understanding of men."[10]

For all of his self-abasement, the faith of the brother of Jared was immediately apparent—in fact, we might better say *transparent* in light of the purpose for which the stones would be used. Obviously Jehovah found something striking in the childlike innocence and fervor of this man's faith. "*Behold, O Lord, thou canst do this.*" In a sense there may be no more powerful expression of faith spoken in scripture. It is almost as if the brother of Jared was encouraging God, emboldening him, reassuring him. Not "Behold, O Lord, I am sure thou canst do this." Not "Behold, O Lord, thou hast done many greater things than this." However uncertain the prophet was about his own ability, he had *no* uncertainty about God's power. This was nothing but a single, assertive declaration with no hint of vacillation. It was encouragement to him who needs no encouragement but who surely must have been touched by it. "Behold, O Lord, thou canst do this."

What happened next ranks among the greatest moments in recorded history, surely among the greatest moments in recorded faith. It established the brother of Jared among the greatest of God's prophets forever. As the Lord reached forth to touch the stones one by one with his finger—an action coming

in undeniable response to the commanding faith of this man—
"the veil was taken from off the eyes of the brother of Jared,
and he saw the finger of the Lord; and it was as the finger of a
man, like unto flesh and blood; and the brother of Jared fell
down before the Lord, for he was struck with fear."[11]

The Lord, seeing the brother of Jared fall to the earth, commanded him to rise and asked, "Why hast thou fallen?" The
reply: "I saw the finger of the Lord, and I feared lest he should
smite me; for I knew not that the Lord had flesh and blood."

Then came this marvelous declaration from the Lord:
"Because of thy faith thou hast seen that I shall take upon me
flesh and blood; and never has man come before me with such
exceeding faith as thou hast; for were it not so ye could not have
seen my finger. Sawest thou more than this?"

The brother of Jared answered, "Nay; Lord, show thyself
unto me." Following this remarkable exchange and prior to the
full revelation to come, the Lord confronted the brother of Jared's
faith one more time with a most intriguing question: "Believest
thou the words which I shall speak?" he asked him. Not
"Believest thou the words which I have already spoken" but a
much more rigorous request: "Believest thou the words which I
shall speak?"[12]

Preparatory faith is formed by experiences in the past—by
the known, which provides a basis for belief. But redemptive
faith must often be exercised toward experiences in the future—
the unknown, which provides an opportunity for the miraculous. Exacting faith, mountain-moving faith, faith like that of the
brother of Jared, *precedes* the miracle and the knowledge. He had
to believe *before* God spoke. He had to act *before* the ability to
complete that action was apparent. He had to commit to the
complete experience in advance of even the first segment of its
realization. Faith is to agree unconditionally—and in advance—

to whatever conditions God may require in both the near and distant future.

The brother of Jared's faith was complete. Committing to the words God would yet speak, he answered, "Yea, Lord."

Then the Lord removed the veil from the eyes of the brother of Jared and came into full view of this incomparably faithful man.[13]

"Behold," he said, "I am he who was prepared from the foundation of the world to redeem my people. Behold, I am Jesus Christ. I am the Father and the Son. In me shall all mankind have life, and that eternally, even they who shall believe on my name; and they shall become my sons and my daughters.

"And never have I showed myself unto man whom I have created, for never has man believed in me as thou hast. Seest thou that ye are created after mine own image? Yea, even all men were created in the beginning after my own image.

"Behold, this body, which ye now behold, is the body of my spirit; and man have I created after the body of my spirit; and even as I appear unto thee to be in the spirit will I appear unto my people in the flesh."[14]

Understanding the Brother of Jared's Experience

Before examining the doctrinal truths taught in this divine encounter, it will be useful to note two seemingly problematic issues here, issues that seem to have reasonable and acceptable resolutions.

The first consideration rises from two questions the Lord asked the brother of Jared: "Why hast thou fallen?" and "Sawest thou more than this?" It is a basic premise of Latter-day Saint theology that God "knoweth all things, and there is not anything save he knows it."[15] The scriptures, both ancient and modern, are replete with this assertion of omniscience. Nevertheless, God has frequently asked questions of mortals, usually as a way to test their faith, measure their honesty, or develop their knowledge.

For example, he called to Adam in the garden of Eden, "Where art thou?" and he later asked Eve, "What is this that thou hast done?"[16] Yet an omniscient Parent clearly knew the answer to both questions, for he could see where Adam was, and he had watched what Eve had done. Obviously the questions were for the children's sake, giving Adam and Eve the responsibility to reply honestly.

Later, in trying Abraham's faith, God would repeatedly call out about Abraham's whereabouts, to which the faithful patriarch would answer, "Here am I."[17] God's purpose was not to obtain information he already knew but to reaffirm Abraham's fixed faith in confronting the most difficult of all parental tests. Such questions are frequently used by God, particularly in assessing faith, honesty, and the full measure of agency, allowing his children the freedom and opportunity to express themselves as revealingly as they wish, even though God knows the answer to his own and all other questions.

The second issue that requires brief comment stems from the Lord's exclamation "Never has man come before me with such exceeding faith as thou hast; for were it not so ye could not have seen my finger." And later, "Never have I showed myself unto man whom I have created, for never has man believed in me as thou hast."[18]

The potential for confusion here comes with the realization that many (and perhaps all) of the major prophets living prior to the brother of Jared had seen God. How, then, do we account for the Lord's declaration? Adam's face-to-face conversations with God in the garden of Eden can be exempted because of the paradisiacal, pre-fallen state of that setting and relationship. Furthermore, other prophets' visions of God, such as those of Moses and Isaiah in the Bible, or Nephi and Jacob in the Book of

Mormon, can also be answered because they came after this "never before" experience of the brother of Jared.

But before the time of the brother of Jared, the Lord did appear to Adam and "the residue of his posterity who were righteous" in the valley of Adam-ondi-Ahman three years before Adam's death.[19] And we are left with Enoch, who said explicitly, "I saw the Lord; and he stood before my face, and he talked with me, even as a man talketh one with another, face to face."[20] We assume that other prophets between the Fall and the Tower of Babel saw God in a similar manner, including Noah, who "found grace in the eyes of the Lord" and "walked with God,"[21] the same scriptural phrase used to describe Enoch's relationship with the Lord.[22]

This issue has been much discussed by Latter-day Saint writers, and there are several possible explanations, any one—or all—of which may cast light upon the larger truth of this passage. Nevertheless, without additional revelation or commentary on the matter, any conjecture is only that and as such is inadequate and incomplete.

One possibility is that this is simply a comment made in the context of one dispensation and as such applies only to the people of Jared and Jaredite prophets—that Jehovah had never before revealed himself to one of their seers and revelators. Obviously this theory has severe limitations when measured against such phrases as "never before" and "never has man." Furthermore, we quickly realize that Jared and his brother are the fathers of their dispensation, the very first to whom God could have revealed himself in their era.

Another suggestion is that the reference to "man" is the key to this passage, suggesting that the Lord had never revealed himself to the unsanctified, to the nonbeliever, to temporal, earthy, natural man. The implication is that only those who have put off the natural man, only those who are untainted by the world—in short, the sanctified (such as Adam, Enoch, and now the brother of Jared)—are entitled to this privilege.

Some believe that the Lord meant he had never before revealed himself to man in that degree or to that extent. This theory suggests that divine appearances to earlier prophets had not been with the same "fulness," that never before had the veil been lifted to give such a complete revelation of Christ's nature and being.

A further possibility is that this is the first time Jehovah had appeared and identified himself as Jesus Christ, the Son of God, with the interpretation of the passage being "never have I showed myself [as Jesus Christ] unto man whom I have created." That possibility is reinforced by one way of reading Moroni's later editorial comment: "Having this perfect knowledge of God, he could not be kept from within the veil; therefore he saw Jesus."[23]

Yet another interpretation of this passage is that the faith of the brother of Jared was so great he saw not only the *spirit* finger and body of the premortal Jesus (which presumably many other prophets had also seen) but also some distinctly more revealing aspect of Christ's body of flesh, blood, and bone. Exactly what insight into the temporal nature of Christ's future body the brother of Jared could have had is not clear, but Jehovah did say to him, "Because of thy faith thou hast seen that I shall take upon me flesh and blood,"[24] and Moroni said that Christ revealed himself in this instance "in the likeness of the same body even as he showed himself unto the Nephites."[25] Some have taken that to mean literally "the same body" the Nephites would see—a body of flesh and bone. A stronger position would suggest it was only the spiritual likeness of that future body. In emphasizing that this was a spiritual body being revealed and not some special precursor simulating flesh and bone, Jehovah said, "This body, which ye now behold, is the body of my spirit . . . and even as I appear unto thee to be in the spirit will I appear unto my people in the flesh."[26] Moroni also affirmed this, saying, "Jesus showed himself unto this man in the spirit."[27]

A final explanation—and in terms of the brother of Jared's faith the most persuasive one—is that Christ was saying to the brother of Jared, "Never have I showed myself unto man *in this manner, without my volition, driven solely by the faith of the beholder.*" As a rule, prophets are *invited* into the presence of the Lord, are bidden to enter his presence by him and only with his sanction. The brother of Jared, on the other hand, seems to have thrust himself through the veil, not as an unwelcome guest but perhaps technically as an uninvited one. Said Jehovah, "Never has man come before me with such exceeding faith as thou hast; for were it not so ye could not have seen my finger. . . . Never has man believed in me as thou hast." Obviously the Lord himself was linking unprecedented faith with this unprecedented vision. If the vision itself was not unique, then it had to be the faith and how the vision was obtained that was so unparalleled. The only way that faith could be so remarkable was its ability to take the prophet, uninvited, where others had been able to go only with God's bidding.

That appears to be Moroni's understanding of the circumstance when he later wrote, "Because of the knowledge [which came as a result of faith] of this man *he could not be kept from beholding within the veil. . . .* Wherefore, having this perfect knowledge of God, *he could not be kept from within the veil;* therefore he saw Jesus."[28]

This may be one of those provocative examples (except that here it is a real experience and *not* hypothetical) a theologian might cite in a debate about God's power. Students of religion sometimes ask, "Can God make a rock so heavy that he cannot lift it?" or "Can God hide an item so skillfully that he cannot find it?" Far more movingly and importantly one may ask here, "Is it possible to have faith so great that even God cannot resist it?" At first one is inclined to say that surely God could block such an experience if he wished to. But the text suggests otherwise: "This man . . . *could not be kept from beholding within the veil. . . . He could not be kept from within the veil."*

This may be an unprecedented case of a mortal man's desire, will, and purity so closely approaching the heavenly standard that God could not but honor his devotion. What a remarkable doctrinal statement about the power of a mortal's faith! And not an ethereal, unreachable, select mortal, either. This was a man who once forgot to call upon the Lord, one whose best ideas were sometimes focused on rocks, and one who doesn't even have a traditional name in the book that has immortalized his unprecedented experience. Given such faith, we should not be surprised that the Lord would show this prophet much, show him visions that would be relevant to the mission of all the Book of Mormon prophets and to the events of the latter-day dispensation in which the book would be received.

VIEW WITHIN THE VEIL

After the prophet stepped through the veil to behold the Savior of the world, he was not limited in seeing the rest of what the eternal world revealed. Indeed, the Lord showed him "all the inhabitants of the earth which had been, and also all that would be; and he withheld them not from his sight, even unto the ends of the earth."[29] The staying power and source of privilege for such an extraordinary experience was once again the faith of the brother of Jared, for *"the Lord could not withhold anything from him,* for he knew that the Lord could show him all things."[30]

This vision of "all the inhabitants of the earth which had been, and also all that would be . . . even unto the ends of the earth"[31] was similar to that given to Moses and others of the prophets.[32] In this case, however, it was written down in detail and then sealed. Moroni, who had access to this recorded vision, wrote on his plates "the very things which the brother of Jared saw."[33] Then he too sealed them and hid them again in the earth before his death and the destruction of the Nephite civilization. Of this vision given to the brother of Jared, Moroni wrote, "There never were greater things made manifest than those which were made manifest unto the brother of Jared."[34]

Those sealed plates constitute the sealed portion of the Book of Mormon, which Joseph Smith did not translate. Furthermore, they will remain sealed, literally as well as figuratively, until future generations "shall exercise faith in me, saith the Lord, even as the brother of Jared did, that they may become sanctified in me, then will I manifest unto them the things which the brother of Jared saw, even to the unfolding unto them all my revelations."[35]

The full measure of this unprecedented and unexcelled vision—"never were greater things made manifest"—are yet to be made known. But consider what was made known in the course of one man's experience in receiving it, consider that the time was approximately two thousand years before Christ's birth, and consider what is *not* presently contained in the Old Testament canon of that period regarding Jehovah and his true characteristics.

- Jehovah, the God of the pre-Christian era, was the premortal Jesus Christ, identified here by that name.[36]

- Christ has a role as both a Father and a Son in his divine relationship with the children of men.[37]

- Christ was "prepared from the foundation of the world to redeem [his] people,"[38] knowledge that had been shared before with Enoch and would later be shared with John the Revelator.[39]

- Christ had a spirit body in the premortal form of his physical body, "like unto flesh and blood," including fingers, voice, face, and all other physical features.[40]

- In some manner Christ assisted in creating man, a creation ultimately performed by the Father. In that process the bodies of the human family were like unto "the body of [Christ's] spirit."[41]

- With a spirit body and the divinity of his calling, the premortal Christ spoke audibly, in words and language that could be understood by mortals.[42]

- Christ is a God, acting for and with his Father, who is also a God.[43]

- Christ reveals truths to some that are to be kept from others until an appointed time (his "own due time").[44]

- Christ uses a variety of tools and techniques in revelation, including the interpreting power of "two stones" such as those used in the Urim and Thummim.[45]

- Christ had past knowledge of all the inhabitants of the earth who had been and foreknowledge of all who would be, showing all these to the brother of Jared.[46]

- Christ's later atoning, redeeming role was clearly stated even before it had been realized in his mortal life. Furthermore, in a most blessed way for the brother of Jared, it was immediately efficacious: "I am he who was prepared from the foundation of the world to redeem my people," Christ said. "In me shall all mankind have life, and that eternally, even they who shall believe on my name; and they shall become my sons and my daughters."[47]

Then the brother of Jared had his redemption pronounced, as though the Atonement had already been carried out: "Because thou knowest these things ye are redeemed from the fall," Christ promised him, "therefore ye are brought back into my presence; therefore I show myself unto you."[48]

This last statement underscores the eternal nature of the Atonement, its impact reaching out to all who lived before the Savior's birth as well as all who lived after it. All those in Old Testament times who were baptized in Christ's name had the same claim upon eternal life that the brother of Jared had, even though Christ had not yet even been born. In the infinite and eternal matters of the Atonement, as in all other eternal covenants, "time only is measured unto men"[49] and prophets could speak of events yet to be "as though they had already come."[50]

Moroni, in recording the experience of the brother of Jared, added these additional insights and revelations from the same encounter:

- Future disciples would need to be sanctified in Christ to receive all his revelations.[51]

- Those who reject the vision of the brother of Jared will be shown "no greater things" by Christ.[52]

- At Christ's command "the heavens are opened and are shut," "the earth shall shake," and "the inhabitants thereof shall pass away, even so as by fire."[53]

- Believers in the vision of the brother of Jared will be given manifestations of Christ's spirit. Because of such spiritual experience, belief will turn to knowledge, and they will "know that these things are true."[54]

- "Whatsoever thing persuadeth men to do good" is of Christ. Good comes of none except Christ.[55]

- Those who do not believe Christ's words would not believe him personally.[56]

- Those who do not believe Christ would not believe God the Father who sent him.[57]

- Christ is the light, the life, and the truth of the world.[58]

- Christ will reveal "greater things,"[59] "great and marvelous things,"[60] knowledge hidden "from the foundation of the world"[61] to those who rend the veil of unbelief and come unto him.

- Believers are to call upon the Father in the name of Christ "with a broken heart and a contrite spirit" if they are to "know that the Father hath remembered the covenant which he made" unto the house of Israel.[62]

- Christ's revelations to John the Revelator will be "unfolded in the eyes of all the people" in the last days, even as they are about to be fulfilled.[63]

- Christ commands all the ends of the earth to come unto him, believe in his gospel, and be baptized in his name.[64]

- Signs will follow those who believe in Christ's name.[65]

- Those faithful to Christ's name at the last day will be "lifted up to dwell in the kingdom prepared for [them] from the foundation of the world."[66]

In the glow of this revelation comes an appeal to all who will one day receive it. Asking the latter-day reader to pierce the limits of shallow faith, Christ cries:

"Come unto me, O ye Gentiles, and I will show unto you the greater things, the knowledge which is hid up because of unbelief.

"Come unto me, O ye house of Israel, and it shall be made manifest unto you how great things the Father hath laid up for you, from the foundation of the world; and it hath not come unto you, because of unbelief.

"Behold, *when ye shall rend that veil of unbelief* which doth cause you to remain in your awful state of wickedness, and hardness of heart, and blindness of mind, then shall the great and marvelous things which have been hid up from the foundation of the world from you—yea, when ye shall call upon the Father in my name, with a broken heart and a contrite spirit, then shall ye know that the Father hath remembered the covenant which he made unto your fathers, O house of Israel."[67]

The Book of Mormon is predicated on the willingness of men and women to "rend that veil of unbelief" in order to behold the revelations—and the Revelation—of God. The brother of Jared may not have had great belief in himself, but his belief in God was unprecedented. In that there is hope for us all. His faith was without doubt or limit.

"I know, O Lord, that thou hast all power, and can do whatsoever thou wilt for the benefit of man; therefore touch these stones, O Lord, with thy finger."[68] From the moment of that utterance, the brother of Jared and the reader of the Book of Mormon would never again be the same. Once and for all it was declared that ordinary people with ordinary challenges could rend the veil of unbelief and enter the realms of eternity. And Christ, who was prepared from the foundation of the world to redeem his people, would stand in all his glory at the edge of that veil, ready to receive the believers and show them "how great things the Father had laid up" for them at the end of faith's journey.

ANTICIPATION

THREE EARLY WITNESSES: NEPHI

he Lord's manner of teaching and affirming, especially when it involves a covenant, has always provided more than one testimony. His admonition has always been that "in the mouth of two or three witnesses shall every word be established."[1] Indeed, when the Book of Mormon was to come forth through the inspired hand of the Prophet Joseph Smith, it was prophesied that "three shall . . . be shown [the plates] by the power of God. . . . And in the mouth of three witnesses shall these things be established; and the testimony of three, and this work, in the which shall be shown forth the power of God . . . also his word, of which the Father, and the Son, and the Holy Ghost bear record—and all this shall stand as a testimony against the world at the last day."[2]

Those three witnesses were to be Oliver Cowdery, David Whitmer, and Martin Harris. Their experience is recorded in the histories of The Church of Jesus Christ of Latter-day Saints, and their testimony is forever fixed to the opening pages of the Book of Mormon. It will remain there until Lamanite, Jew, and Gentile come to the conviction that Jesus is the Christ, the Eternal God. These men, who in spite of other crises of faith went to their graves affirming their testimonies of the divine origins of the

Book of Mormon, have come into the Latter-day Saint vocabulary simply as "The Three Witnesses."

In keeping with this same covenantal principle, it is interesting to note that there were three earlier witnesses—special witnesses—not only of the divine origins of the Book of Mormon but also of Divinity himself. These early witnesses were Nephi, Jacob, and Isaiah, and it is not by coincidence that their testimonies appear so conspicuously at the beginning of this ancient record.

Their opening testimonies come in the Book of Mormon from what we know as the small plates of Nephi. At least six times in the Book of Mormon, the phrase *for a wise purpose* is used in reference to the making, writing, and preserving of the small plates. One such wise purpose—the most obvious one—was to compensate for the future loss of 116 pages of manuscript translated by the Prophet Joseph Smith from the first part of Mormon's abridgment of the large plates of Nephi.[3]

But there is another "wise purpose" for the inclusion of these smaller plates in the highly edited material that would constitute the Book of Mormon. In Doctrine and Covenants 10:45 the Lord declared to Joseph Smith, "Behold, there are many things engraven upon the [small] plates of Nephi which do throw *greater views* upon my gospel."

All the details and information contained in those first 116 pages of manuscript are not yet known. What *is* known is that most of the "greater views" of the gospel found in the teachings of the small plates of Nephi come from the personal declarations of these three great prophetic witnesses of the premortal Jesus Christ—Nephi, Jacob, and Isaiah. These three doctrinal and visionary voices make clear at the very outset of the Book of Mormon why it is "another testament of Jesus Christ."

In declaring the special preparation these three had for receiving and teaching such "greater views" of the gospel, Nephi revealed the most persuasive qualification of all: They had seen the premortal Jesus Christ.

"And now I, Nephi, write more of the words of Isaiah, for my soul delighteth in his words. For I will liken his words unto my people, and I will send them forth unto all my children, *for he verily saw my Redeemer, even as I have seen him.*

"*And my brother, Jacob, also has seen him* . . . ; wherefore, I will send their words forth unto my children to prove unto them that my words are true. Wherefore, by the words of three, God has said, I will establish my word."[4]

Nephi concluded, "My soul [and he could have said the souls of all three] delighteth in proving unto [our] people the truth of the coming of Christ, . . . that save Christ should come all men must perish."[5]

One could argue convincingly that the primary purpose for recording, preserving, and then translating the small plates of Nephi was to bring forth to the dispensation of the fulness of times the testimony of these three witnesses. Their writings constitute a full 135 of the 145 pages from the small plates. By the time one has read Nephi, Jacob, and Isaiah in these first pages, a strong foundation has been laid for what Nephi called "the doctrine of Christ."[6] It is a foundation conforming perfectly to the title page of the Book of Mormon. After reading these three witnesses from the small plates of Nephi, the reader knows two things in bold relief: that Jesus is the Christ, the Son of the Living God, and that God will keep his covenants and promises with the remnants of the house of Israel. Those two themes constitute the two principal purposes of the Book of Mormon, and they are precisely the introductory themes addressed by Nephi, Jacob, and Isaiah.

Obviously it would be exciting if someone were one day to find the lost 116 pages of the original manuscript of the Book of Mormon. But whatever those pages contain, it could not be more important or more fundamental to the purpose of the Book of Mormon than the teachings of these three prophets recorded on the small plates. Standing like sentinels at the gate of the book, Nephi, Jacob, and Isaiah admit us into the scriptural presence of the Lord.

LEHI

The teaching and testimony of another witness that was, for the most part, lost in that first manuscript material is that of Nephi and Jacob's father, Lehi. Indeed, the first book of that translated material had been entitled the "Book of Lehi."[7] Fortunately, Nephi recorded significant portions of his father's teachings in his own record on the small plates, and that glimpse of Lehi's experience adds to the reader's views of the Savior of the world. The first chapter of the First Book of Nephi begins with Lehi's vision of "One descending out of the midst of heaven, and he beheld that his luster was above that of the sun at noon-day."[8] In this vision the premortal Christ, accompanied by "twelve others," brought forth a book in which Lehi was bidden to read. The book spoke of "many great and marvelous things," including the plain declaration "of the coming of a Messiah, and also the redemption of the world."[9] Thus in the first verses of the first chapter of the first book in the Book of Mormon, the central and undeviating theme is struck.

Even though his contemporaries in Jerusalem rejected Lehi's message, he nevertheless continued his prophecies of "a Messiah, or, in other words, a Savior of the world.

"And he also spake concerning the prophets, how great a number had testified of these things, concerning this Messiah, of whom he had spoken, or this Redeemer of the world.

"Wherefore, all mankind were in a lost and in a fallen state, and ever would be save they should rely on this Redeemer."[10]

Included in Lehi's vision of the coming of Christ to mortality were such revelatory details as the precise time of his coming and the mission of John the Baptist, who "should baptize in Bethabara, beyond Jordan," baptizing the Messiah at the outset of his ministry. "And after he had baptized the Messiah with water, he should behold and bear record that he had baptized the Lamb of God, who should take away the sins of the world."[11] Lehi also saw in vision that the Messiah would be slain and "should rise from the dead, and should make himself manifest . . . unto the Gentiles," providing the first of more than eighty references in the Book of Mormon to the Resurrection. As the brother of Jared had learned before him, Lehi saw what he saw and learned what he learned by power, "received by faith on the Son of God."[12]

Whether it was one of these briefly recorded visions or some other magnificent personal manifestation of Christ we do not know, but Lehi did speak of a singular revelatory experience of the Son of God when he testified to his sons near the end of his life, "Behold, the Lord hath redeemed my soul from hell; *I have beheld his glory,* and I am encircled about eternally in the arms of his love."[13]

This introductory testimony from Lehi as to the birth, mission, death, and divinity of the Savior of the world introduces the reader to the Savior in the first twenty pages of the Book of Mormon. Inasmuch as this impressive but rather limited material is taken from Nephi's account of his father Lehi's vision, it is safe to assume there would be many more of these messianic prophecies in the first 116 pages of translated manuscript that were lost.

NEPHI'S VIEW OF LEHI'S VISION

As limited as Lehi's materials are, we are indebted to him and his visionary experience for the provocation his revelations had upon his son Nephi, for it was Nephi's desire to "see, and hear, and know of [the] things" his father had seen that led him toward his own great manifestations. Desiring such revelations for himself and believing that God could make these same things known to him, Nephi was pondering their meaning when he was caught away in vision. Then, "because [he believed] in the Son of the most high God," he was shown "a man descending out of heaven, . . . the Son of God."[14]

With something of the same detail given to the brother of Jared at the outset of the Jaredite dispensation, Nephi received similar information about the future of his people as the Nephite dispensation began. In a sweeping vision of the future of Joseph's fruitful bough, whose branches were even then running "over the wall,"[15] Nephi was guided by the Spirit of the Lord (and angels sent for that purpose) in foreseeing the Savior's life and ministry, a vision offered because Nephi "believe[d] in the Son of the most high God."[16]

Consider how very extensive and detailed the doctrinal teachings given to Nephi were:

- Nazareth would be the city of Christ's conception.[17]

- The Savior's mother would be "a virgin, most beautiful and fair above all other virgins."[18]

- The virgin mother of the Son of God would be "carried away in the Spirit,"[19] conceiving and giving birth "after the manner of the flesh."[20]

- The child born to the virgin would be "the Lamb of God, yea, even the Son of the Eternal Father!"[21]

- The mother of this child would still be a virgin after the child was born.[22]

- The birth, life, death, atonement, and resurrection of Christ (identified in Nephi's vision of the Tree of Life) were interrelated elements of the love of God shed "abroad in the hearts of the children of men," which was "the most desirable above all things[,] . . . the most joyous to the soul[,] . . . the greatest of all the gifts of God."[23]

- Jesus would be baptized of John the Baptist, and the Holy Ghost would descend from the heavens in the form of a dove.[24]

- Christ would minister "in power and great glory" among the children of men, many of whom would "fall down at his feet and worship him" even as a larger number would "cast him out from among them."[25]

- Christ would choose "twelve others" to assist him, who would be called "apostles."[26]

- Multitudes would gather. Christ would heal the sick and those "afflicted with all manner of diseases, and with devils and unclean spirits."[27]

- The Lamb of God would be "taken by the people" and "judged of the world," culminating in his being "lifted up upon the cross and slain for the sins of the world."[28]

- At the time of the Crucifixion there would be (in the New World) lightning, thunder, earthquakes, a mist of darkness, and "all manner of tumultuous noises," with mountains falling, plains broken up, and cities burning and sinking into the sea.[29]

- After the Crucifixion, the Lamb of God would descend "out of heaven" and appear to people in "the land of promise."[30]

- He would choose "twelve disciples" to minister to the seed of Lehi in the New World as subordinates to the Twelve Apostles in the Old World.[31]

- The Nephite twelve would receive the Holy Ghost, be

ordained, and have their garments "made white in his blood" because of their "faith in the Lamb of God."[32]

- The Savior would promise to bring forth to the Gentiles in the latter days "much of [the] gospel" taught in the New World, which gospel would be "plain and precious."[33]

- The Bible would, at its inception, contain "the fulness of the gospel" and be known as "the Book of the Lamb of God." Later its doctrinal integrity would be violated and many of its "plain and precious" doctrines lost.[34]

- Christ's appearance and teachings in the New World would be recorded, hidden, and brought forth in the Book of Mormon, compensating (along with other latter-day revelations) for the loss of biblical truths.[35]

- "Other books" would come forth by the power of the Lamb of God.[36]

- These other latter-day records (the Doctrine and Covenants and Pearl of Great Price) would, with the Book of Mormon, establish the truth of the first (the Bible), all of which would "make known to all kindreds, tongues, and people, that the Lamb of God is the Son of the Eternal Father, and the Savior of the world; and that all men must come unto him, or they cannot be saved."[37]

- Those who would be saved must come "according to the words" of Christ, words that would be made known in the Book of Mormon and the Bible, both of which would be "established in one; for there is one God and one Shepherd over all the earth."[38]

- In his first advent in the meridian of time, Christ and his message would be declared unto all nations, first to the Jews and then to the Gentiles. In his second coming in the last days, he would reverse that order, his appearance and message first going to the Gentiles and then to the Jews; thus "the last shall be first, and the first shall be last."[39]

- To the Gentiles in the last days, Christ would "manifest himself unto them in word, . . . in power, in very deed, unto the taking away of their stumbling blocks."[40]

- If the Gentiles would repent and harden not their hearts against the Lamb of God and the covenants he has made with his children, they would be "numbered among [adopted into] the house of Israel; and . . . be a blessed people upon the promised land forever . . . and . . . no more be confounded."[41]

- The work by Christ among the Gentiles would be "a great and a marvelous work among the children of men," a work that would be "everlasting," leading to peace and eternal life on the one hand or to temporal and spiritual destruction on the other.[42]

- In the last days there would be "save two churches only," the church of the Lamb of God and the church of the devil. Eventually those who did not belong to Christ's church would, by choice or default, be claimed by the other.[43]

- Although their numbers would be few and their dominions small, the members of the church of the Lamb of God, called "saints," would be found upon all the face of the earth.[44]

- The "mother of abominations" would gather multitudes upon the face of the earth—all the nations of the Gentiles— "to fight against the Lamb of God."[45]

- In response, the power of Christ would descend upon the members of his church, "the covenant people of the Lord," and they would be "armed with righteousness and with the power of God in great glory."[46]

- Under the leadership of Christ, "the work of the Father"

would commence "in preparing the way for the fulfilling of his covenants, which he hath made to his people who are of the house of Israel."[47]

This remarkably detailed vision of Christ's ministry, from his birth and ministry and crucifixion in the Old World to his appearance and teachings in the New World to his role in the latter-day restoration of all things, is all the more impressive coming as it does in the first thirty pages of the Book of Mormon, a concise introduction to the reader of the book's central purpose in declaring that Jesus is the Christ.

But in the spirit of multiple witnesses earlier noted, Nephi followed this magnificent vision with a second, personal, prophetic witness of his own—aided by ancient prophets Zenock, Neum, and Zenos—regarding "the very God of Israel," whom "men trample under their feet" by setting at naught the purity of his life and hearkening not to the voice of his counsels.[48]

NEPHI'S PROPHETIC WITNESS

Reaffirming that Christ would come six hundred years from the time Lehi and his family left Jerusalem, Nephi prophesied that a hostile world, "because of their iniquity, [would] judge [Christ] to be a thing of naught; wherefore they scourge him, and he suffereth it; and they smite him, and he suffereth it. Yea, they spit upon him, and he suffereth it, because of his loving kindness and his long-suffering towards the children of men."[49]

Drawing upon Old Testament history, including the words of three otherwise unknown prophets of that era, Nephi strongly underscored the doctrine revealed to the brother of Jared—that Christ is Jehovah, the God of the Old Testament, as well as Jesus, the Savior of the New Testament.

Earlier Nephi had reprimanded his rebellious brothers by reminding them that the children of Israel had been led out of captivity by "the Lord their God, their Redeemer, going before them, leading them by day and giving light unto them by night."[50] Now he again identified that Old Testament role of the Savior and blended it into the new.

"And the God of our fathers, who were led out of Egypt, out of bondage, and also were preserved in the wilderness by him, yea, the God of Abraham, and of Isaac, and the God of Jacob, yieldeth himself, . . . as a man, into the hands of wicked men, to be lifted up, according to the words of Zenock, and to be crucified, according to the words of Neum, and to be buried in a sepulchre, according to the words of Zenos, which he spake concerning the three days of darkness, which should be a sign given of his death unto those who should inhabit the isles of the sea, more especially given unto those who are of the house of Israel."[51]

Remembering the manifestations of the earth's reaction to the crucifixion as revealed to him in his great vision, Nephi quoted the prophet Zenos:

"The Lord God surely shall visit all the house of Israel at that day, some with his voice, because of their righteousness, unto their great joy and salvation, and others with the thunderings and the lightnings of his power, by tempest, by fire, and by smoke, and vapor of darkness, and by the opening of the earth, and by mountains which shall be carried up. . . .

"And the rocks of the earth must rend; and because of the groanings of the earth, many of the kings of the isles of the sea shall be wrought upon by the Spirit of God, to exclaim: The God of nature suffers."[52]

Nephi—and Zenos—who clearly understood that Christ is the creator and father of the earth, added this marvelous insight as to why his creation reacted so violently to the crucifixion. This was earth's God being crucified, this was creation's benefactor, this was "the God of nature" suffering on the cross, and nature would not receive that injustice passively. It reacted in global groaning and sorrow. It reacted in convulsion and outrage and mourning.

Those contributing to the judgment of crucifixion, those who "turn[ed] their hearts aside, rejecting signs and wonders, and the power and glory of the God of Israel" would for a time be "scourged by all people" and would wander and perish, becoming a "hiss and a by-word," hated among all nations.[53]

But when the day came that they turned their hearts to the Holy One of Israel, all would change: "Then will he remember the covenants which he made to their fathers. . . . And all the earth shall see the salvation of the Lord. . . ; every nation, kindred, tongue and people shall be blessed."[54]

In this context of Old Testament prophets and prophecies and the covenants that would be restored, Nephi quoted two full chapters of Isaiah that underscore the ministry of the Savior. Then he made an important (and unique) commentary on a well-known but not always well-understood verse from the book of Deuteronomy. In that book of the law, Moses had written:

"The Lord thy God will raise up unto thee a Prophet from the midst of thee, of thy brethren, like unto me; unto him shall ye hearken. . . .

"And the Lord said unto me . . . I will raise them up a Prophet from among their brethren, like unto thee, and will put my words in his mouth; and he shall speak unto them all that I shall command him.

"And it shall come to pass, that whosoever will not hearken unto my words which he shall speak in my name, I will require it of him."[55]

In response to that declaration, Nephi explained that he whom Moses foresaw was Christ. He explained, "I, Nephi, declare unto you, that this prophet of whom Moses spake was the Holy One of Israel; wherefore, he shall execute judgment in righteousness. . . .

"And the time cometh speedily that the righteous must be led up as calves of the stall, and the Holy One of Israel must reign in dominion, and might, and power, and great glory.

"And he gathereth his children from the four quarters of the earth; and he numbereth his sheep, and they know him; and there shall be one fold and one shepherd; and he shall feed his sheep, and in him they shall find pasture."[56]

In this passage Nephi not only echoed—and clarified—Moses, but in so doing he also presaged the messianic writings of Malachi[57] and John the Beloved,[58] underscoring the fact that common gospel themes have been taught by all the prophets in all ages, even to the point of commonly revealed language and imagery in some of their messianic teachings.[59]

Indeed, Nephi felt such unity within the brotherhood of the prophets that he generously included in his own text substantial portions of the writings of his younger brother Jacob and the Old Testament prophet Isaiah.

Against the backdrop of those two prophets and their testimonies, Nephi wrote of Jesus' advent among his own people, "When the day cometh that the Only Begotten of the Father, yea, even the Father of heaven and of earth, shall manifest himself unto them in the flesh, behold, they will reject him, because of their iniquities, and the hardness of their hearts, and the stiffness of their necks.

"Behold, they will crucify him; and after he is laid in a sepulchre for the space of three days he shall rise from the dead, with healing in his wings; and all those who shall believe on his name shall be saved in the kingdom of God. Wherefore, my soul delighteth to prophesy concerning him, for I have seen his day, and my heart doth magnify his holy name."[60]

Nephi prophesied of the Messiah's resurrection, Jerusalem's

subsequent destruction, and the scattering of these inhabitants, including their scourging "by other nations for the space of many generations." But the promises of the Book of Mormon to the Jews are as unequaled as they are explicit. Nephi notes that their scourging shall cease and their restoration begin in that day in which "they shall be persuaded to believe in Christ, the Son of God, and the atonement, which is infinite for all mankind—and when that day shall come that they shall believe in Christ, and worship the Father in his name, with pure hearts and clean hands, and look not forward any more for another Messiah, then, at that time, the day will come that it must needs be expedient that they should believe these things.

"And the Lord will set his hand again the second time to restore his people from their lost and fallen state. Wherefore, he will proceed to do a marvelous work and a wonder among the children of men."

That marvelous work will include bringing the Book of Mormon to them "for the purpose of convincing them of the true Messiah, who was rejected by them; and unto the convincing of them that they need not look forward any more for a Messiah to come, for there should not any come, . . . for there is save one Messiah spoken of by the prophets, and that Messiah is he who should be rejected of the Jews. . . . His name shall be Jesus Christ, the Son of God."[61]

Again making an Old and New Testament connection—which would be fundamental to the prophesied understanding and reconciliation of the Jews—Nephi noted that the same power that saved ancient Israel from the poisonous serpents[62] and brought water from the rock at Meribah[63] was the power to save eternal souls. For ancient and modern Israel, he wrote, "There is none other name given under heaven save it be this Jesus Christ, of which I have spoken, whereby man can be saved."[64]

"THAT OUR CHILDREN MAY KNOW"

In this pivotal passage, Nephi stressed the deadness of the law and the life that is in Christ. It is the same lesson every generation of the children of Israel has heard. This ringing declaration of the purpose of the Book of Mormon record deserves to be quoted at length:

"Wherefore, these [writings] shall go from generation to generation as long as the earth shall stand. . . .

"For we labor diligently to write, to persuade our children, and also our brethren, to believe in Christ, and to be reconciled to God; for we know that it is by grace that we are saved, after all we can do.

"And, notwithstanding we believe in Christ, we keep the law of Moses, and look forward with steadfastness unto Christ, until the law shall be fulfilled.

"For, for this end was the law given; wherefore the law hath become dead unto us, and we are made alive in Christ because of our faith; yet we keep the law because of the commandments.

"And we talk of Christ, we rejoice in Christ, we preach of Christ, we prophesy of Christ, and we write according to our prophecies, that our children may know to what source they may look for a remission of their sins. . . .

"Wherefore ye must bow down before him, and worship him with all your might, mind, and strength, and your whole soul; and if ye do this ye shall in nowise be cast out."[65]

Nephi continued this testimony by noting that after Christ had risen from the dead he would show himself unto the Nephites. In spite of the terrible destruction that would accompany the Crucifixion, the faithful—those who "look forward unto Christ with steadfastness for the signs which are given, notwithstanding all persecution—behold, they are they which shall not perish.

"But the Son of righteousness shall appear unto them; and he shall heal them, and they shall have peace with him, until three generations shall have passed away, and many of the fourth generation shall have passed away in righteousness."[66]

With weariness of heart over this testimony—twice he spoke of the pain and anguish of his soul in contemplating such destruction of the wicked—he nevertheless reassured in a wonderful summarizing soliloquy that Christ would do nothing except that which would be for the benefit of the world; "for he loveth the world, even that he layeth down his own life that he may draw all men unto him."[67]

Perhaps no other passage in the Book of Mormon conveys more plainly the breadth of Christ's gift for all people everywhere than those which Nephi then recorded. The gift was given freely and would be denied to no one who came to partake of that mercy and salvation:

"Behold, doth he cry unto any, saying: Depart from me? Behold, I say unto you, Nay; but he saith: Come unto me all ye ends of the earth, buy milk and honey, without money and without price.

"Behold, hath he commanded any that they should depart out of the synagogues, or out of the houses of worship? Behold, I say unto you, Nay.

"Hath he commanded any that they should not partake of his salvation? Behold I say unto you, Nay; but he hath given it free for all men; and he hath commanded his people that they should persuade all men to repentance. . . .

"For he doeth that which is good among the children of men; and he doeth nothing save it be plain unto the children of men; and he inviteth them all to come unto him and partake of his goodness; and he denieth none that come unto him, black and white, bond and free, male and female; and he remembereth the heathen; and all are alike unto God, both Jew and Gentile."[68]

THE DOCTRINE OF CHRIST

In a marvelous final testimony to his people, as well as to the unborn and unseen of the last dispensation yet to come, Nephi made "an end" of his prophesying (including prophesying about the coming forth of the Book of Mormon) and concluded his writing—and his lifetime of teaching—with "a few words . . . concerning the doctrine of Christ."[69]

Although a phrase like "the doctrine of Christ" could appropriately be used to describe any or all of the Master's teachings, nevertheless those magnificently broad and beautiful expressions spread throughout the Book of Mormon, New Testament, and latter-day scriptures might more properly be called "the *doctrines* of Christ." Note that the phrase Nephi used is distinctly singular. In Nephi's concluding testimony, and later in the Savior's own declaration to the Nephites at his appearance to them, the emphasis is on a precise, focused, singular sense of Christ's doctrine, specifically that which the Prophet Joseph Smith declared to be "the first principles and ordinances of the Gospel."[70]

The "doctrine of Christ" as taught by Nephi in his grand, summational discourse focuses on faith in the Lord Jesus Christ, repentance, baptism by immersion, receiving the gift of the Holy Ghost, and enduring to the end. It does not, in this declaration, attempt to cover the entire plan of salvation, all the virtues of a Christian life, or the rewards that await us in differing degrees of heavenly glory. It does not, in this declaration, deal with the offices of the priesthood, the ordinances of the temple, or many other true doctrines. All these are important, but as used in the Book of Mormon, "the doctrine of Christ" is simple and direct. It focuses on the first principles of the gospel exclusively, including an expression of encouragement to endure, to persist, to press on. Indeed, it is in the clarity and simplicity of "the doctrine of Christ" that its impact is found. Nephi knew it would be so. He wrote, "I shall speak unto you plainly, according to the plainness of my prophesying."[71]

Following the Son (Faith in the Lord Jesus Christ). Nephi's appeal, quoting the premortal voice of Christ himself, commands all who would be disciples of Christ and followers of his doctrine to follow him in obedience to the first principles and ordinances of the gospel. Faith in the Lord Jesus Christ ultimately means believing him, trusting him, obeying him, following him.

"Follow me," the voice of Christ commands us through his declaration to Nephi, "and do the things which ye have seen me do."[72] That may be the simplest, clearest, gospel call ever given— the essence of the Christian life expressed in its most understandable terms.

But lest his audience confuse simplicity with ease, Nephi posed this question: "Wherefore, my beloved brethren, can we follow Jesus save we shall be willing to keep the commandments of the Father?"[73]

Noting that even though Jesus was "holy," Nephi stressed that he nevertheless "humble[d] himself before the Father" and witnessed by his faithful obedience that he would keep all of the commandments however strait the gate and narrow the way. By such faith Christ "set the example before [all humankind]."

"And he said unto the children of men: Follow thou me."[74]

Having No Hypocrisy or Deception before God (Repentance). Nephi's call to have faith in and follow Christ would be compelling and memorable if it had ended there. But it did not end there. Nephi went on to teach that to "follow the Son, with full purpose of heart, [means] acting no hypocrisy and no deception before God, but with real intent, repenting of your sins, witnessing unto the Father that ye are willing to take upon you the name of Christ."[75] This call to faith, obedience, and discipleship is not a vague abstraction or a principle of theology left dangling in unanchored discourse. It means to embrace the gospel fully and completely. Faith, by definition, leads to repentance, to a new, resolute way of living.

"Wherefore, do the things which I have told you I have seen that your Lord and your Redeemer should do," Nephi said.[76] That can be done only with a pure and repentant heart. "They draw near to me with their lips, but their hearts are far from me," Christ said to Joseph Smith when the world lay in apostasy and darkness.[77]

Thus Nephi stressed that we can "follow the Son" only by repenting and persisting in that repentance. To follow Christ and have true, efficacious faith in him requires this full purpose of heart, whereby we act with no hypocrisy before men and no deception before God, "but with real intent, repenting of [our] sins."[78]

This doctrine of repentance is so crucial that the Father himself made a declaration on this point. Following Nephi's description of Christ's humility, obedience, and example in being baptized, Nephi recorded:

"And the Father said: Repent ye, repent ye, and be baptized in the name of my Beloved Son."[79]

It has been noted that, for the most part, the voice of the Father has usually been limited in scripture to introducing his Beloved Son and expressing his pleasure in him. But this verse from the stylus of Nephi is revealing in that it gives broader utterance to the Father than that which the biblical canon usually records.

Indeed, the reader is intrigued with the time and location of this powerful commandment to repent, uttered by the Father himself. Was it spoken directly by the Father to Nephi at the time he received this revelation on "the doctrine of Christ"—the sixth century B.C.—or was it spoken at the scene of Christ's baptism in the River Jordan in the meridian of time? If it was spoken at

Christ's baptism, then this important utterance is one of the plain and precious things lost from the New Testament. If it was spoken to Nephi, then his role as a "witness" is enhanced even more than may have been appreciated. This latter seems to be the case, for in the next verse Nephi recorded, "And also, the voice of the Son came unto me,"[80] not an experience suggesting the events of Christ's baptism in the meridian of time. In either case, reinforcement of the commandment to follow the Son by repenting and being baptized came from the Father himself, one of the few declarations so identified in the scriptures.

Baptism by Water. Nephi made a persuasive, prolonged case for baptism with the reasoning that "if the Lamb of God, he being holy, should have need to be baptized by water, to fulfil all righteousness, O then, how much more need have we, being unholy, to be baptized, yea, even by water!"[81]

In this act of submission and humility (though not, in Christ's case, repentance) as he entered into a covenant with his Father and embraced the ordinances representing that covenant, Jesus demonstrated his effort and desire to "fulfil all righteousness." In submitting to John at Jordan, he "showeth unto the children of men that, according to the flesh he humbleth himself before the Father, and witnesseth unto the Father that he would be obedient unto him in keeping his commandments."[82] It was this ordinance of baptism—by immersion and under the hand of one authorized to perform the ordinance—that Christ "showeth unto the children of men the straitness of the path, and the narrowness of the gate, by which they should enter, he having set the example before them."[83] It certainly is a narrow gate leading to a strait—and straight—path if the only perfect being ever to have walked the earth still needed to "fulfil all righteousness" by entering that gate. Only as they are immersed in the waters of baptism can mortals "take upon [them] the name of Christ by baptism—yea, by following [their] Lord and [their] Savior down into the water."[84]

Baptism by Fire and by the Holy Ghost. Nephi prophesied that following Christ's baptism with water, the Holy Ghost would descend upon the Savior in the form of a dove, as of course it did. To Nephi—and all others—Christ underscored that experience by promising, "He that is baptized in my name, to him will the Father give the Holy Ghost, like unto me."[85]

Receiving that doctrine from the Savior of the world, Nephi added his own insight into the redeeming role of the Holy Ghost. He wrote, "Yea, by following your Lord and your Savior down into the water, according to his word, behold, then shall ye receive the Holy Ghost; yea, then cometh the baptism of fire and of the Holy Ghost."[86] The important doctrine proclaimed here is that the ultimate inward remission of sin comes from the cleansing flame of the Holy Spirit *after* the outward, symbolic cleansing of baptism by water has been administered. "For the gate by which ye should enter is repentance and baptism by water," Nephi said, "and *then cometh a remission of your sins by fire and by the Holy Ghost.*"[87]

One of the majestic spiritual promises of such a covenant and cleansing is that "then can ye speak with the tongue of angels," for angels speak by the power of the Holy Ghost, and they speak the words of Christ, giving mortal men and women the ability as well as the vocabulary to "shout praises unto the Holy One of Israel."[88]

But from the voice of Christ himself comes this sobering warning: "After ye have repented of your sins, and witnessed unto the Father that ye are willing to keep my commandments, by the baptism of water, and have received the baptism of fire and of the Holy Ghost, and can speak with a new tongue, yea, even with the tongue of angels, and after this should deny me, it would have been better for you that ye had not known me."[89]

After the faith and repentance, after the water and the Spirit, it is crucial to continue, to persist, to endure. To fall by the wayside then is worse than never having begun the journey at all.

Enduring to the End. This is another "first principle" beyond the four usually listed, taught by the Father himself. Nephi wrote, "I heard a voice from the Father, saying: Yea, the words of my Beloved are true and faithful. He that endureth to the end, the same shall be saved." Nephi then added his own witness, saying, "And now, my beloved brethren, I know by this that unless a man shall endure to the end, in following the example of the Son of the living God, he cannot be saved."[90]

Often one hears trite, sometimes consciously apologetic references to "enduring to the end" as an addition to the first principles and ordinances of the gospel. Nevertheless, the doctrine of faithful endurance is infinitely serious, and it is here declared to be a basic principle of the gospel by the God and Father of us all. "Enduring to the end" is an integral element in the doctrine of Christ, and without it, it would have been better not to have known him.

Following these invitations to faith in the Lord Jesus Christ, repentance, baptism, and receiving the gift of the Holy Ghost, Nephi again eloquently asked for endurance, persistence, and perseverance. Every reader of the Book of Mormon thrills at this summary of the first principles of the gospel, one of the many truly majestic passages in the Book of Mormon! "And now, my beloved brethren, after ye have gotten into this strait and narrow path, I would ask if all is done? Behold, I say unto you, Nay; for ye have not come thus far save it were by the word of Christ with unshaken faith in him, relying wholly upon the merits of him who is mighty to save.

"Wherefore, ye must press forward with a steadfastness in Christ, having a perfect brightness of hope, and a love of God and of all men. Wherefore, if ye shall press forward, feasting upon the word of Christ, and endure to the end, behold, thus saith the Father: Ye shall have eternal life."[91]

On this marvelous note of faith and hope, grace and effort, this holy injunction to press forward in our own determination while relying totally upon the power of Christ to save us, Nephi bore this succinct witness: "And now, behold, my beloved brethren, this is the way; and there is none other way nor name given under heaven whereby man can be saved in the kingdom of God. And now, behold, *this is the doctrine of Christ*, and the only and true doctrine of the Father, and of the Son, and of the Holy Ghost, which is one God, without end. Amen."[92]

His listeners, like some contemporaries, may have given quizzical looks at hearing such simple doctrine. Can this be "the doctrine of Christ"? they may have wondered. Is this the message? Is this the "good news"?

Nephi answered their unspoken questions. "My beloved brethren, I suppose that ye ponder somewhat in your hearts concerning that which ye should do after ye have entered in by the way. But, behold, why do ye ponder these things in your hearts?"[93]

They had no need to worry. It was not more complicated than it sounds. There was no other sandal to drop. They had only to comply with these oft-stated first principles and ordinances and then persist in them with two great safeguards, two unfailing sources of divine direction. As they "press[ed] forward," they were to "feast upon the words of Christ; for behold, the words of Christ [would] tell [them] all things what [they] should do."[94] Then they must live true to the promptings of the Holy Ghost, which would "show unto [them] all things what [they] should do."[95]

Then a third time the declaration came: *"This is the doctrine of Christ."* If Nephi's congregation could not understand, it was because they "ask[ed] not, neither [did they] knock; . . . [and they] must perish in the dark."[96]

This is not easy or whimsical teaching, but it is plain and it is simple. It is not convenient or even comfortable doctrine for some—especially the repentance part—but it is very plain and very precious. The doctrine of Christ is not complicated. It is profoundly, beautifully, single-mindedly clear and complete.

At this crowning moment of his life, Nephi broke off, forbidden by the Spirit to say more "because of the unbelief, and the wickedness, and the ignorance, and the stiffneckedness of men." Some of those men were, presumably, in his immediate audience, but a great many of them were yet to be born later in Nephi's dispensation and in our own. These "will not search knowledge, nor understand great knowledge, when it is given unto them in plainness, even as plain as word can be," he mourned. For these who harden their hearts against the Holy Spirit and cast away the words of Christ, he prayed continually by day and watered his pillow with his tears by night.[97]

But he took hope in his message, believing that even words written in weakness would be made strong by the very message they conveyed, for the message "speaketh of Jesus, and persuadeth them to believe in him, and to endure to the end, which is life eternal. . . . I glory in my Jesus," he said, "for he hath redeemed my soul from hell."[98]

With "great faith in Christ," Nephi declared his love—literally, his "charity," the pure love of Christ—for his people, for the Jews and for the Gentiles. But for none of these could he hope "except they . . . be reconciled unto Christ, and enter into the narrow gate, and walk in the strait path which leads to life, and continue in the path until the end of the day of probation."[99] In short, for none could he hope except they embrace "the doctrine of Christ."

As one of the three early witnesses chosen to introduce the

reader of the Book of Mormon to Christ, Nephi offered beauty and power in his concluding testimony. It is a grand climax to a written record and a perfect epitaph to a faithful life:

"And now, my beloved brethren, and also Jew, and all ye ends of the earth, hearken unto these words and believe in Christ; and if ye believe not in these words believe in Christ. And if ye shall believe in Christ ye will believe in these words, for they are words of Christ, and he hath given them unto me; and they teach all men that they should do good. . . .

"Christ will show unto you, with power and great glory, that they are his words, at the last day; and you and I shall stand face to face before his bar; and ye shall know that I have been commanded of him to write these things, notwithstanding my weakness. . . .

"And now, my beloved brethren, all those who are of the house of Israel, and all ye ends of the earth, I speak unto you as the voice of one crying from the dust: Farewell until that great day shall come."[100]

Surely that day will come, and if the reader does not comprehend it now he or she will surely realize then that the Book of Mormon is indeed a record of the "words of Christ."

CHAPTER FOUR

THREE EARLY WITNESSES: JACOB

s Nephi approached the end of his life, his prophetic role and record-keeping duty were transferred to his younger brother Jacob. Jacob had been well prepared for the task from an early age, having received the spiritual refinement that sometimes comes only from tribulation and testing. Being Lehi and Sariah's first son born after their flight from Jerusalem, he knew the physical rigor and spiritual demands of life in the wilderness. "In thy childhood thou hast suffered afflictions and much sorrow," his father Lehi said of him. "Nevertheless . . . thou knowest the greatness of God; and he shall consecrate thine afflictions for thy gain."[1]

We are grateful for Lehi's teachings that his sons carried into their own records, for it is through Lehi's words we first learn that Jacob saw Christ in vision.

"I know that thou art redeemed, because of the righteousness of thy Redeemer," Lehi told Jacob, "for thou hast beheld that in the fulness of time he cometh to bring salvation unto men.

"And thou hast beheld in thy youth his glory; wherefore, thou art blessed even as they unto whom he shall minister in the flesh."[2]

In every way Jacob was a worthy successor to Nephi and a

well-prepared witness to Christ's divine role in Book of Mormon times and teachings. As he would later say to the anti-Christ Sherem about the divine knowledge and variety of evidence he had received, "I truly had seen angels, and they had ministered unto me. And also, I had heard the voice of the Lord speaking unto me in very word, from time to time; wherefore, I could not be shaken. . . .

"It has been made manifest unto me, for I have heard and seen."[3]

It is indicative of his prophetic stature and spiritual nature that, according to the record we now have, Jacob would be the first of the Nephite prophets to be told (by an angel) that the Messiah would be called "Christ" when he came into mortality.[4]

In light of Jacob's repeated experience with and appreciation for the divine, Nephi gave him "a commandment" to write on the small plates the things Jacob "considered to be most precious." Such "preaching which was sacred, or revelation which was great" he wrote in headline fashion, touching on them in as much detail as time and space allowed, "for Christ's sake, and for the sake of our people."[5]

It is readily understandable why Jacob would write such things for the people's sake. All mortals would need as much sacred preaching and revelation as they could get. The value of such persuasive testimony for the people's sake is obvious.

But that this should (perhaps even more importantly?) be done "for Christ's sake" is intriguing. In what sense could such a record be for the Savior's sake? Surely he doesn't need the reminder of or the motivation for sacred things, he who would become sanctity personified. Surely the Teacher does not need to study the lessons given to the student.

Nevertheless, there do seem to be important ways in which the teachings of a prophet could be for the sake of the Lord. For one thing, Jacob and all other prophets knew that Christ would come to atone for the sins and suffering of all mankind. If that truth were carefully written and powerfully taught—as Jacob surely wrote and taught—perhaps some would avoid sin or cease from it if they had begun. In that sense, any success by the prophets that would prevent some from sinning would bring joy to the Savior, who atoned for all sins.

A second consideration is in the reminder that the Atonement would be infinite and eternal, benefiting all men, women, and children who ever lived. The Savior's mercy and love, including his fairness and justice, would require that *everyone* hear the good news of his gospel. Therefore, those living before Christ's mortal ministry needed to hear the message just as much as those living during and after his mortal ministry. But he cannot spread that message alone. Thus it is for Christ's sake—or in his behalf, if you will—that the gospel must be recorded and testified of in every era, including the Nephite dispensation.

Lastly, we cannot know exactly what the original Hebrew words and thoughts of the Book of Mormon writers were, but at least as it comes to us in English, the word *sake* has its origin in a concept of legal action, in matters of guilt and dispute pursued in a court of law (from the Old English *sacu* and the Old High German *sahha*). In that literal sense, to preach for "Christ's sake" is, in a sense, to stand with him in the heavenly court, reinforcing his role as Mediator and Advocate there. In his intervention for all mankind at the eternal bar of justice, Christ pleads our cause and speaks in our behalf. A prophet's teachings and writings (or those of anyone else speaking "for Christ's sake") will at least symbolically reinforce the message the Master gives there and, in some limited but not unimportant way, add additional voices to the truthful witness being made regarding the Atonement.

A modern revelation reminds us of our joy over any soul we

may have helped toward repentance, but the same passage reminds us also of the joy that comes to Christ on such an occasion:

"Remember the worth of souls is great in the sight of God;

"For, behold, the Lord your Redeemer suffered death in the flesh; wherefore he suffered the pain of all men, that all men might repent and come unto him. . . .

"And he hath risen again from the dead, that he might bring all men unto him, on conditions of repentance.

"And how great is his joy in the soul that repenteth!

"Wherefore, you are called to cry repentance unto this people."[6]

In any case, Jacob seems to have been particularly committed to presenting the doctrine of Christ. Given the amount of space he gave to his witness of the Savior's atonement, Jacob clearly considered this basic doctrine the most sacred of teachings and the greatest of revelations.

"We . . . had many revelations, and the spirit of much prophecy," Jacob said, "wherefore, we knew of Christ and his kingdom, which should come.

"Wherefore we labored diligently among our people, that we might persuade them to come unto Christ. . . .

"Wherefore, we would to God . . . that all men would believe in Christ, and view his death, and suffer his cross and bear the shame of the world."[7]

No prophet in the Book of Mormon, by temperament or personal testimony, seems to have gone about that work of persuasion any more faithfully than did Jacob. He scorned the praise of the world, he taught straight, solid, even painful doctrine, and he knew the Lord personally. His is a classic Book of Mormon example of a young man's decision to suffer the cross and bear the shame of the world in defense of the name of Christ. Life, including those difficult early years when he saw the wickedness of Laman and Lemuel bring his father and mother down to their graves in grief, was never easy for this firstborn in the wilderness.

"We Had a Hope of His Glory"

It was Jacob who gave us the first major Book of Mormon insight into just how extensively the prophets of old knew the gospel and taught of Jesus Christ, even though most of that teaching is now missing from the Old Testament. As his brother Nephi did, so did Jacob also speak repeatedly of Christ, rejoicing in his mercy and prophesying of his coming. He explained why that is so important: "We labor diligently to engraven these words upon plates, hoping that our beloved brethren and our children"—precisely the same audience Nephi addressed—"may know that we knew of Christ, and we had a hope of his glory many hundred years before his coming; and not only we ourselves had a hope of his glory, but also all the holy prophets which were before us.

"Behold, they believed in Christ and worshiped the Father in his name, and also we worship the Father in his name. . . .

"We are not witnesses alone in these things," he reaffirmed, "for God also spake them unto prophets of old."[8]

Through such belief and worship, such revelations and prophesying, Jacob and his people had their hope and faith in Christ so bolstered that they could "command in the name of Jesus and the very trees obey [them], or the mountains, or the waves of the sea."[9]

Such faith in the Savior led Jacob to continual examination of his favorite topic—the atonement and resurrection of Christ. Noting God's power to create and destroy, and the unsearchable depths of his mysteries, Jacob pleaded for mankind to yield, to humble themselves and claim the full measure of the blessings of the Atonement: "Be reconciled unto him through the atonement of Christ, his Only Begotten Son, and ye may obtain a resurrection, according to the power of the resurrection which is in Christ, and be presented as the first-fruits of Christ unto God, having faith, and obtained a good hope of glory in him before he manifesteth himself in the flesh.

"And now, beloved, marvel not that I tell you these things; for why not speak of the atonement of Christ, and attain to a perfect knowledge of him, as to attain to the knowledge of a resurrection and the world to come?"[10]

This admonition by Jacob is an interesting indicator of how firmly the Resurrection had been taught and was understood by Lehi's family. A paraphrasing of Jacob's argument could be, "If you can understand the Resurrection so well and all that it means in the promises of the world to come, shouldn't you be completely conversant with the doctrine of the Atonement, which makes the Resurrection fully efficacious for us?"

Jacob came by his fascination with the Atonement rightly, beginning with his father Lehi's blessing recorded in 2 Nephi 2. In that marvelous blessing, Jacob was in his youth introduced to the grand concepts of the creation of Adam and Eve, the role of moral agency, the inevitability of opposition in all things, the design and purpose of the Fall, the consequence of transgression, the immutability of law, the demands of justice, the gift of mercy and grace, the need for mortality and children, the purpose of probation, and, through it all, the joy of redemption.

Lehi taught Jacob that "the Messiah cometh in the fulness of time, that he may redeem the children of men from the fall," granting unto men and women the chance to "choose liberty and eternal life, through the great Mediator of all men."[11]

In that same blessing Lehi also taught that "redemption cometh in and through the Holy Messiah; for he is full of grace and truth.

"Behold he offereth himself a sacrifice for sin, to answer the ends of the law, unto all those who have a broken heart and a contrite spirit. . . .

"Wherefore, how great the importance to make these things known unto the inhabitants of the earth, that they may know that there is no flesh that can dwell in the presence of God, save it be through the merits, and mercy, and grace of the Holy Messiah, who layeth down his life according to the flesh, and taketh it again by the power of the Spirit. . . .

"Wherefore, he is the firstfruits unto God, inasmuch as he shall make intercession for all the children of men; and they that believe in him shall be saved."[12]

A long chapter on the Atonement provides the centerpiece of this book, a chapter drawing heavily upon Jacob's teachings on the subject. Nevertheless, no segment of such a study devoted specifically to Jacob's role as witness for Christ can pass over those powerful passages without at least some preliminary comment.

The first of Jacob's teachings on Christ and the covenant actually came as inserts into Nephi's writings. Apparently Nephi was so impressed with his younger brother's sermons on these subjects that he asked him to speak for the record. Jacob did that, in part by quoting and clarifying key passages from Isaiah. Those teachings appear as early as the 6th chapter of 2 Nephi. Note the urgent, plaintive tone of Jacob's appeal:

"I speak unto you again; for I am desirous for the welfare of your souls. Yea, mine anxiety is great for you; and ye yourselves know that it ever has been. For *I have exhorted you* with all diligence; and *I have taught you the words of my father;* and *I have spoken unto you concerning all things which are written,* from the creation of the world."[13] That is the formula by which the gospel has always been taught, a process used to this day—personal testimony, the teachings of the living prophets, and the written record of the scriptures. In such a process Jacob was always anxiously engaged. Indeed, he expressed "anxiety" more readily than any other prophet in the Book of Mormon.

Of the Lord's first coming Jacob said, "He . . . has shown unto me that the Lord God, the Holy One of Israel, should manifest himself unto them in the flesh; and after he should manifest himself they should scourge him and crucify him."[14] That rejection would bring severe judgments upon the house of Israel, but following their affliction and suffering—times in which they would be scattered, smitten, and hated—they would be preserved, and "when they shall come to the knowledge of their Redeemer, they shall be gathered together again to the lands of their inheritance."[15]

Such intervention in Israel's behalf (and in behalf of repentant Gentiles, who would also see their covenants with God realized[16]) would culminate in the Lord's second coming, when "the Messiah will set himself again the second time to recover them; wherefore, he will manifest himself unto them in power and great glory, unto the destruction of their enemies, when that day cometh when they shall believe in him; and none will he destroy that believe in him."[17]

THE MIGHTY GOD

Jacob's testimony was that "the Mighty God" will always deliver "his covenant people," and that the Mighty God is, by his own divine declaration, the Lord Jesus Christ, the "Savior and . . . Redeemer, the Mighty One of Jacob."[18]

Jacob reflected on such teachings—especially those contained in the writings of Isaiah—so that his current audience and future readers "might know concerning the covenants of the Lord that he has covenanted with all the house of Israel," giving the parents of every generation cause to "rejoice" and to "lift up [their] heads forever, because of the blessings which the Lord God shall bestow upon [their] children."[19]

At the heart of that covenant and the reason for such rejoicing is the atoning sacrifice of that "Mighty God" who is the Savior and Redeemer of the world. In one of the most definitive sermons on the Atonement recorded in any scripture, Jacob taught this impressive summary of truths on that subject:

- Christ would live among, show himself to, and be crucified by those in Jerusalem.[20]

- It was essential ("expedient") that Christ become "subject unto man in the flesh, . . . that all men might become subject unto him" in the spirit.[21]

- Death passed upon all mankind as part of the Great Creator's "merciful plan."[22]

- Because of Adam and Eve's transgression, a universal fall, including physical death, came upon all men, women, and children born into this world. In merciful response, an infinite (universal) atonement would be made for all, overcoming death by the righteous power of Christ's resurrection.[23]

- If the flesh (body) were not to rise, neither would the spirit, and thus the spiritual fate of all mankind would be "subject to . . . the devil," indeed, to "become devils, angels to a devil, to be shut out from the presence of . . . God."[24]

- Through the power of the resurrection of Christ, temporal death (the grave) and spiritual death (hell) must yield up their "captive bodies" and their "captive spirits," respectively.[25]

- Bodies that were corruptible and mortal before the Resurrection become incorruptible and immortal after the Resurrection.[26]

- The body and the spirit united constitute the "living soul."[27]

- In the Resurrection we will have "perfect knowledge" of our guilt and uncleanliness, or of our repentance and righteous-ness.[28]

• A divine judgment will follow the Resurrection.[29]

• The justice of God demands that "they who are righteous shall be righteous still, and they who are filthy shall be filthy still."[30]

• The righteous, "the saints of the Holy One of Israel," are defined as "they who have believed in the Holy One of Israel, . . . who have endured the crosses of the world, and despised the shame of it." Their inheritance is the kingdom of God, and their joy will be forever.[31]

• The mercy of God delivers the righteous (the repentant) from the grasp of the devil.[32]

• God is omniscient. He "knoweth all things, and there is not anything save he knows it."[33]

• Christ would suffer the pains of "every living creature, both men, women, and children, who belong to the family of Adam," that they might be saved if they would hearken to his voice.[34]

• The Resurrection is universal, passing upon "all."[35]

• The path to salvation in the kingdom of God is "perfect faith in the Holy One of Israel," repentance, baptism in his name, and endurance to the end.[36]

• When no moral law applies (as with little children, the men-tally impaired, those ignorant of the gospel until they are taught it, and so forth), the power of the Atonement "satisfi-eth the demands of . . . justice," and such people are "restored to that God who gave them breath."[37]

• Where the law is known and does apply, however, it is per-ilous for man to waste "the days of his probation."[38]

- The Redeemer's name would be Christ. This information was given to Jacob by an angel and was the first instance we know of in which the Nephite prophets were told what name the Messiah and Holy One of Israel would carry.[39] The personal name *Jesus* was also revealed to these Nephite brothers by an angel, either this angel at this same time or another shortly thereafter.[40]

- No other nation on earth would crucify the Savior if they had witnessed the miracles he performed in Jerusalem.[41]

- Priestcraft and iniquity would be the two primary reasons for the rejection of Jesus in Jerusalem.[42]

- Jehovah "covenanted with their fathers" that scattered Israel would be gathered from the four parts of the earth and the isles of the sea be restored to the lands of their inheritance "when the day cometh that they shall believe in me, that I am Christ."[43]

- The nations of the Gentiles would "be great in the eyes of me, saith God," in fulfilling this covenant promise with the house of Israel.[44]

- It is only "in and through the grace of God" that salvation is obtained.[45]

This is a wonderfully explicit sermon—a sermon that ultimately required two days to deliver—on Christ and his eternal covenant with the human family. Jacob concluded his message of the Atonement and Resurrection with an appeal to his people's desire for "that happiness which is prepared for the saints": "Come unto the Lord, the Holy One," he said. "Remember that his paths are righteous. Behold, the way for man is narrow, but it lieth in a straight course before him, and the keeper of the gate is the Holy One of Israel; and he employeth no servant there; and there is none other way save it be by the gate; for he cannot be deceived, for the Lord God is his name.

"And whoso knocketh, to him will he open; and the wise, and the learned, and they that are rich, who are puffed up because of their learning, and their wisdom, and their riches— yea, they are they whom he despiseth; and save they shall cast these things away, and consider themselves fools before God, and come down in the depths of humility, he will not open unto them. . . .

"Come, my brethren, every one that thirsteth, come ye to the waters; and he that hath no money, come buy and eat; yea, come buy wine and milk without money and without price. . . .

"How great the covenants of the Lord, and how great his condescensions unto the children of men. . . .

"Wherefore may God raise you from [physical] death by the power of the resurrection, and also from everlasting [spiritual] death by the power of the atonement, that ye may be received into the eternal kingdom of God, that ye may praise him through grace divine. Amen."[46]

It is a stunning thing for the contemporary Christian world to consider that the plan of salvation, with its pivotal doctrines of moral agency, the fall of man, and the atonement of Christ, was taught in such detail and precision—as in this two-day sermon by Jacob—so many generations before Christ came in mortality. Surely this is one of the clearest of Book of Mormon contributions, a contribution noted in Jacob's reminder that "none of the prophets have written, nor prophesied, save they have spoken concerning this Christ."[47]

THE WOUNDED SOUL

As one of the great prophets testifying of the Savior, Jacob, even as a young man, was always forthright in his teachings,

sobered by his responsibilities, and anxious in the extreme for
the welfare and salvation of his people. He referred to working
with "faith and great anxiety" for his people, of being "weighed
down" with "desire and anxiety" for the welfare of their souls.[48]
He spoke often of "the wounded soul," and so his soul seemed
to be—wounded by the transgression of others, wounded by the
daggers of sorrow and suffering that wounded the Savior himself.[49] In his wilderness experience he came to know the power
and importance of the redeeming blood of Christ, and he taught
that truth with "much boldness of speech."[50]

In one of the most vivid images of pulpit oratory on record,
we see Jacob's faith and fervor in declaring the word of Christ to
his people:

"O, my beloved brethren, remember my words. Behold, I
take off my garments, and I shake them before you; I pray the
God of my salvation that he view me with his all-searching eye;
wherefore, ye shall know at the last day, when all men shall be
judged of their works, that the God of Israel did witness that I
shook your iniquities from my soul, and that I stand with brightness before him, and am rid of your blood.

"O, my beloved brethren, turn away from your sins; shake
off the chains of him that would bind you fast; come unto that
God who is the rock of your salvation."[51]

In an important explanation of being a covenant people,
Jacob explained (as Nephi had done) why the Nephites kept the
law of Moses even though they knew the fuller light of the
gospel of Jesus Christ. He says it was partly as a matter of obedience, the law "pointing [their] souls to [Christ]," just as it was
for "Abraham in the wilderness to be obedient unto the commands of God in offering up his son Isaac, which is a similitude
of God and his Only Begotten Son."[52]

The story of Abraham and Isaac has long been recognized
and loved for its symbolic parallel to the willingness of God the

Father to offer his Only Begotten Son, but Jacob was, so far as we know, the first prophet to declare that similitude in scripture.[53]

Fearing that his contemporaries in the Old World branch of the house of Israel would not recognize such messianic symbolism, including the symbolism in the law of Moses, Jacob saw that the Jews would look "beyond the mark" and stumble in their search for the Holy One of Israel, this literal Son of God to be known as Jesus Christ: "By the stumbling of the Jews they will reject the stone upon which they might build and have safe foundation.

"But behold, according to the scriptures, this stone shall become the great, and the last, and the only sure foundation, upon which the Jews can build."[54]

In answer to the rhetorical question "How is it possible that these, after having rejected the sure foundation, can ever build upon it, that it may become the head of their corner?" Jacob quoted the Prophet Zenos' allegory of the tame and wild olive trees, the longest scriptural parable in the Book of Mormon. He did so to reveal "the mystery" of Christ's eventual redemption of the Jews.[55]

As Jacob confronted and defeated Sherem, the first great anti-Christ in the Book of Mormon, his concluding testimony remains with us as an echo of the allegory of the olive tree. It is crucial counsel to all: "Behold, after ye have been nourished by the good word of God all the day long, will ye bring forth evil fruit, that ye must be hewn down and cast into the fire?

"Behold, will ye reject . . . the words of the prophets; and will ye reject all the words which have been spoken concerning Christ, after so many have spoken concerning him; and deny the good word of Christ, . . . and make a mock of the great plan of redemption, which hath been laid for you? . . .

"O be wise; what can I say more?"[56]

Jacob the unshaken and unshakable—born in affliction, refined in service, triumphant in Christ. His question to his brethren is his question to us, a question stemming from his prophetic calling in which the redemption of Christ was the preeminent and preoccupying fact of his life and service:

"Wherefore, beloved brethren, be reconciled unto [God] through the atonement of Christ, his Only Begotten Son, . . . having faith, and [having] obtained a good hope of glory in him before he manifesteth himself in the flesh. . . . Why not speak of the atonement of Christ, and attain to a perfect knowledge of him . . . ?"[57]

Why not, indeed?

CHAPTER FIVE

THREE EARLY
WITNESSES:
ISAIAH

n an effort to persuade
his rebellious brothers, the family of Lehi generally, and ulti-
mately all of the house of Israel to "remember the Lord their
Redeemer," Nephi (so weary from the spiritual burden of this
task that his very joints were weak) taught from the great
prophets recorded on the precious plates of brass. He cited
Zenock and Neum and Zenos, prophets lost from the current
biblical record, and lost to the modern reader were it not for the
Book of Mormon references to them. He also read to them many
things from the writings of Moses contained on those plates. But
most powerfully of all he taught from the prophet Isaiah. To the
future reader of his record, Nephi wrote, "That I might more
fully persuade them to believe in the Lord their Redeemer I did
read unto them that which was written by the prophet Isaiah."[1]

Isaiah is by every standard *the* messianic prophet of the Old
Testament and as such is the most penetrating prophetic voice in
that record. He, more than any other witness in the Old World,
saw and wrote and prophesied of the Savior's coming both in
the meridian of time and again in the latter days. He is quoted
more often in the New Testament, Book of Mormon, Doctrine

and Covenants, and contemporary documents such as the Dead Sea Scrolls than any other Old World prophet.

A useful footnote to 2 Nephi 12:2 in the current edition of the LDS scriptures indicates that some 433 verses of Isaiah—roughly a third of the entire book—are quoted in the Book of Mormon.[2] One student of Isaiah documents that no less than 391 of those verses refer to the attributes, appearance, majesty, and mission of Jesus Christ.[3] Another scholar has pointed out that Isaiah provided at least sixty-one names and titles of the Father and of the Son in his writings, most of those referring to some aspect of the mission of Christ. Those sixty-one titles are found 708 times in the Book of Isaiah, making an average appearance of once every 1.9 verses.[4]

Surely it is because of this consuming messianic focus—messianic preoccupation, we might more properly say—that Isaiah was of such interest and importance to Nephi and the record he and his Nephite descendants were to keep. It can be said that Nephi taught to his people virtually every major messianic message given by this Old Testament witness of Christ's ministry. Isaiah's messianic record was of crucial importance not only to these Nephite children of Israel wandering in their New World wilderness but also to those who would see the covenants of Abraham, Isaac, and Jacob restored in the latter days.

"Wherefore, hearken, O my people, which are of the house of Israel, and give ear unto my words," wrote Nephi, "for because the words of Isaiah are not plain unto you, nevertheless they are plain unto all those that are filled with the spirit of prophecy. . . .

"Yea, and my soul delighteth in the words of Isaiah, . . . [and] they are of worth unto the children of men, and he that supposeth that they are not, unto them will I speak particularly, . . . for I know that they shall be of great worth unto them in the last days; for in that day shall they understand them; wherefore, for their good have I written them."[5]

Certainly the words of this majestic prophet brought delight to Nephi's soul, for 352 of the Isaiah verses quoted in the Book of Mormon—more than 80 percent of the total number in the entire book—come from Nephi's two books! Even a major portion of the Isaiah material quoted by Jacob in chapters 6 through 8 in 2 Nephi were included in the record because they were, as Jacob wrote, "the words which my brother [Nephi] . . . desired that I should speak unto you."[6]

In this admiration for Isaiah, Nephi and Jacob have sacred company. It was, after all, the Savior himself who said, after quoting to the Nephites the entire 54th chapter of Isaiah, "Ye ought to search these things. Yea, a commandment I give unto you that ye search these things diligently; for great are the words of Isaiah.

"For surely he spake as touching all things concerning my people which are of the house of Israel."[7]

One of the reasons Nephi felt so strongly about Isaiah's words and the special merit of his witness has already been noted. Isaiah not only wrote of Christ, but he had also seen him and his ministry in vision:

"I, Nephi, write more of the words of Isaiah, for my soul delighteth in his words. For I will liken his words unto my people, and I will send them forth unto all my children, for he verily saw my Redeemer. . . .

"Wherefore, I will send their words forth unto my children to prove unto them that my words are true. . . .

"And now I write some of the words of Isaiah, that whoso of my people shall see these words may lift up their hearts and rejoice for all men. Now these are the words, and ye may liken them unto you and unto all men."[8]

It would seem even from Isaiah's name ("Jehovah saves" or

"The Lord is salvation") that he was prepared at birth—or, more accurately, from before birth—to testify of the Messiah, bearing witness of the divinity of Christ in anticipation of both his first and second comings. Because he did focus on the Savior so repeatedly in his writings, and because he did freely mix and interchange material relating to his own day, to the meridian of time, and to the latter days, it is important to remember that many of Isaiah's prophecies can be, have been, or will be fulfilled in more than one way and in more than one dispensation.

These parallel prophecies with application in more than one age create much of the complexity in Isaiah, but they also provide so much of the significance and meaning that his writings contain. In light of such complexity, it goes without saying that the prophecies of Isaiah are opened more widely to the eye and heart of the modern reader because of the restoration of the gospel. Latter-day scriptures, key portions of which provide crucial clarification, commentary, and dispensational distinctions not otherwise found in the Isaiah text of the Old Testament—or anywhere else, for that matter—are as unprecedented as they are invaluable in understanding his writings.

Much could be said about virtually every Isaianic verse that refers to the Savior—entire books have been written on the subject—but consider at least the teachings of Isaiah recorded in the Book of Mormon that cluster conveniently into five categories.

CHRIST'S BIRTH AND MORTAL MINISTRY

In the 17th chapter of his second book, Nephi recorded the great Immanuel prophecy of Isaiah. In verses 14 and 15 he wrote, "The Lord himself shall give you a sign—Behold, a virgin shall conceive, and shall bear a son, and shall call his name Immanuel.

"Butter and honey shall he eat, that he may know to refuse the evil and to choose the good."[9]

This sign was given to the Old Testament King Ahaz, encouraging him to take his strength from the Lord rather than the military might of Damascus, Samaria, or other militant camps. Ahaz was slow to hear that counsel, but the Lord gave it anyway, declaring one of the signs to be a virgin's conception and birth of a son whose name would be called Immanuel.

There are plural or parallel elements to this prophecy, as with so much of Isaiah's writing. The most immediate meaning was probably focused on Isaiah's wife, a pure and good woman who brought forth a son about this time, the child becoming a type and shadow of the greater, later fulfillment of the prophecy that would be realized in the birth of Jesus Christ. The symbolism in the dual prophecy acquires additional importance when we realize that Isaiah's wife may have been of royal blood, and therefore her son would have been royalty of the line of David. Here again is a type, a prefiguration of the greater Immanuel, Jesus Christ, the ultimate son of David, the royal King who would be born of a literal virgin.[10] Indeed, his title *Immanuel* would be carried forward to the latter days, being applied to the Savior in section 128 verse 22 of the Doctrine and Covenants.

A related scripture in 2 Nephi 19 can also have multiple meanings and may be applied in several ways, including as the coronation of a king or messiah. But its most traditional and celebrated application is to Christ's birth. Everyone responds to the moving power of the lines written by Isaiah and made famous throughout the musical world by George Frideric Handel: "Unto us a child is born, unto us a son is given; and the government shall be upon his shoulder; and his name shall be called, Wonderful, Counselor, The Mighty God, The Everlasting Father, The Prince of Peace.

"Of the increase of government and peace there is no end, upon the throne of David, and upon his kingdom to order it, and to establish it with judgment and with justice from henceforth, even forever. The zeal of the Lord of Hosts will perform this."[11]

One of the beautiful reminders in this magnificent passage, even with its splendor and royalty and sense of triumph, is the gentle declaration that through all of his power and majesty, Christ is still "the Son"—the Son as taught by Abinadi and other Book of Mormon prophets—humble, obedient, submissive, willing to yield to the demands of mortality, doing all this that he might ultimately order the government of temporal beings (the flesh) after the higher laws of divine transcendence (the spirit). We are reminded here that he is, gloriously, the Son of God, a child of heaven.

The fact that the government would eventually be upon his shoulders affirms what all the world will one day acknowledge—that he is Lord of lords and King of kings and will one day rule over the earth and his Church in person, with all the majesty and sacred vestments belonging to a holy sovereign and a high priest. All can take comfort from the fact that because the government—and the burdens thereof—will be upon his shoulders, they will be lifted in great measure from our own. This is yet another reference in Isaiah to the Atonement, the bearing away of our sins (or at very least in this reference, our temporal burdens) on the shoulders of Christ.

As "Wonderful Counselor," he will be our mediator, our intercessor, defending our cause in the courts of heaven. "The Lord standeth up to plead, and standeth to judge the people," Isaiah (and Nephi) reminded earlier.[12] Note the wonderful compassion of our counselor and spokesman in this passage of latter-day scripture:

"Listen to him who is the advocate with the Father, who is pleading your cause before him—

"Saying: Father, behold the sufferings and death of him who did no sin, in whom thou wast well pleased; behold the blood of thy Son which was shed, the blood of him whom thou gavest that thyself might be glorified;

"Wherefore, Father, spare these my brethren that believe on my name, that they may come unto me and have everlasting life."[13]

Of course, as noted by Isaiah, Christ is not only a mediator but also a judge.[14] It is in that role of judge that we may find even greater meaning in Abinadi's repeated expression that "God himself" will come down to redeem his people.[15] It is as if the judge in that great courtroom in heaven, unwilling to ask anyone but himself to bear the burdens of the guilty people standing in the dock, takes off his judicial robes and comes down to earth to bear their stripes personally. Christ as merciful judge is as beautiful and wonderful a concept as that of Christ as counselor, mediator, and advocate.

"Mighty God" conveys something of the power of God, his strength, omnipotence, and unconquerable influence. Isaiah sees him as always able to overcome the effects of sin and transgression in his people and to triumph forever over the would-be oppressors of the children of Israel.

"Everlasting Father" underscores the fundamental doctrine that Christ is a Father—Creator of worlds without number, the Father of restored physical life through the Resurrection, the Father of eternal life for his spiritually begotten sons and daughters, and the One acting for the Father (Elohim) through divine investiture of authority. All should seek to be born of him and become his sons and his daughters.[16]

Lastly, with the phrase "Prince of Peace," we rejoice that when the King shall come, there will be no more war in the human heart or among the nations of the world. This is a peaceful king, the king of Salem, the city that would later become Jeru-Salem. Christ will bring peace to those who accept him in mortality in whatever era they live, and he will bring peace to all those in his millennial and postmillennial realms of glory.

CHRIST VISITS THE SPIRITS IN PRISON

In the 21st chapter of 1 Nephi, verses 6–9, we read this passage:

"I will also give thee for a light to the Gentiles, that thou mayest be my salvation unto the ends of the earth.

"Thus saith the Lord, the Redeemer of Israel, his Holy One, to him whom man despiseth, to him whom the nations abhorreth, to servant of rulers: Kings shall see and arise, princes also shall worship, because of the Lord that is faithful.

"Thus saith the Lord: In an acceptable time have I heard thee, O isles of the sea, and in a day of salvation have I helped thee; and I will preserve thee, and give thee my servant for a covenant of the people, to establish the earth, to cause to inherit the desolate heritages;

"That thou mayest say to the prisoners: Go forth; to them that sit in darkness: Show yourselves. They shall feed in the ways, and their pastures shall be in all high places."[17]

Christ brought freedom to mortal beings imprisoned by ignorance, sin, apostasy, and death. He also brought deliverance to those on the other side of the veil who had not heard the gospel but would receive it in their spirit prison. Peter taught this clearly,[18] and the whole of section 138 of the Doctrine and Covenants is devoted to this glorious doctrine.

In teaching this to his people, Nephi might well have included the only other major messianic passage from Isaiah that is not recorded in the Book of Mormon—Isaiah 61.

"The Spirit of the Lord God is upon me; because the Lord hath anointed me to preach good tidings unto the meek; he hath sent me to bind up the brokenhearted, to proclaim liberty to the captives, and the opening of the prison to them that are bound;

"To proclaim the acceptable year of the Lord, and the day of vengeance of our God; to comfort all that mourn;

"To appoint unto them that mourn in Zion, to give unto them beauty for ashes, the oil of joy for mourning, the garment of praise for the spirit of heaviness; that they might be called trees of righteousness, the planting of the Lord, that he might be glorified."[19]

On both sides of the veil, the captives rejoice and praise their God as Christ throws wide the prison doors.

CHRIST SHOWS KINDNESS TO AND PRESERVES ZION IN THE LAST DAYS

1 Nephi 21:13–16 contains a beautiful passage from the first two of Isaiah's chapters quoted in the Book of Mormon, the two chapters Nephi chose to read to his belligerent brothers that he "might more fully persuade them to believe in the Lord their Redeemer."[20] This poetic and moving language underscores Christ's redeeming, atoning care for the children of Israel, both ancient and modern:

"Sing, O heavens; and be joyful, O earth; for the feet of those who are in the east shall be established; and break forth into singing, O mountains; for they shall be smitten no more; for the Lord hath comforted his people, and will have mercy upon his afflicted.

"But, behold, Zion hath said: The Lord hath forsaken me, and my Lord hath forgotten me—but he will show that he hath not.

"For can a woman forget her sucking child, that she should not have compassion on the son of her womb? Yea, they may forget, yet will I not forget thee, O house of Israel.

"Behold, I have graven thee upon the palms of my hands; thy walls are continually before me."[21]

This poetic passage provides yet another reminder of Christ's saving role, that of protective, redeeming parent to Zion's children. He comforts his people and shows mercy when they are afflicted, as any loving father or mother would toward a child, but, as Nephi here reminds us through Isaiah, much more than any mortal father and mother could do. Although a mother may forget her sucking child (as unlikely as any parent might think that could be), Christ will not forget the children he has redeemed or the covenant he has made with them for salvation in Zion. The painful reminders of that watch care and covenant are the marks of the Roman nails graven upon the palms of his hands, a sign to his disciples in the Old World, his Nephite congregation in the New World, and to us in latter-day Zion that he is the Savior of the world and was wounded in the house of his friends.[22]

This protective, redemptive relationship of a loving Father is carried over to 2 Nephi 7, where Christ speaks to the children of Israel *as* children:

"Have I put thee away, or have I cast thee off forever? For thus saith the Lord: Where is the bill of your mother's divorcement? To whom have I put thee away, or to which of my creditors have I sold you? Yea, to whom have I sold you? Behold, for your iniquities have ye sold yourselves, and for your transgressions is your mother put away.

"Wherefore, when I came, there was no man; when I called, yea, there was none to answer. O house of Israel, is my hand shortened at all that it cannot redeem, or have I no power to deliver?"[23]

These children will have a happy home and sealed parents yet. In the last days that bill of divorcement against their mother will be set aside, and so will the demands of any creditors. The Lord is in debt to no one, so neither will his children be. He alone can pay the price for the salvation of Israel and the establishment of Zion. His wrath is turned away, and he will not cast off his bride or allow her children to be sold into slavery.

As for the shortening of his hands, the scriptures repeatedly testify that the reach of God's arm is more than adequate, the extent of his grace entirely sufficient. He can always claim and embrace the Israel that he loves. In spite of their unfaithfulness, his hand remains constant, not shortened or slackened or withheld.

The Savior himself would say to the Nephites, quoting Isaiah, "In a little wrath I hid my face from thee for a moment, but with everlasting kindness will I have mercy on thee, saith the Lord thy Redeemer."[24]

THE MILLENNIAL CHRIST

On the subject of Christ's role in the fullness of times and his millennial reign, Isaiah provided one of the most important passages in the entire Old Testament, a favorite for Latter-day Saints, a chapter rich with Restoration meaning—Isaiah 11.

"There shall come forth a rod out of the stem of Jesse, and a branch shall grow out of his roots.

"And the Spirit of the Lord shall rest upon him, the spirit of wisdom and understanding, the spirit of counsel and might, the spirit of knowledge and of the fear of the Lord;

"And shall make him of quick understanding in the fear of the Lord; and he shall not judge after the sight of his eyes, neither reprove after the hearing of his ears.

"But with righteousness shall he judge the poor, and reprove with equity for the meek of the earth; and he shall smite the earth with the rod of his mouth, and with the breath of his lips shall he slay the wicked.

"And righteousness shall be the girdle of his loins, and faithfulness the girdle of his reins."[25]

It is clear from the Book of Mormon[26] and the Doctrine and Covenants[27] that the principal character in this passage is Jesus Christ. Joseph Smith, recalling the visit of the angel Moroni on the night of September 21, 1823, wrote that Moroni "quoted the eleventh chapter of Isaiah, saying that it was about to be fulfilled."[28]

The imagery of the tree in this passage is a natural continuation of the figure used in relationship to Christ and the children of Israel throughout the scriptures and discussed in several portions of this book. Heaven's Forester carefully trims his trees (consider Zenos' allegory quoted by Jacob) and in this manner cleans out the evil of his forest. With God's cleansing of Israel—cutting down boughs here, leveling thickets there, especially the lofty and arrogant ones—all that remains of the people of covenant at this reading is a stump. This prepares the way for flourishing new shoots to come out of the heritage of Jesse.[29]

Elder Bruce R. McConkie said this about the "branch" in this passage: "The king who shall reign personally upon the earth during the millennium shall be the Branch who grew out of the house of David. He shall execute judgment and justice in all the earth because he is the Lord Jehovah, even him whom we call Christ.

"Through Zechariah the Lord spoke similarly: 'Thus saith the Lord of Hosts[:] . . . I will bring forth my servant the BRANCH. . . . I will remove the iniquity of that land in one day. In that day, saith the Lord of hosts, shall ye call every man his neighbour under the vine and under the fig tree.'[30] Of that glorious millennial day the Lord says also: 'Behold the man whose name is The BRANCH; and he shall grow up out of his place, and he shall build the temple of the Lord: Even he shall build the temple of the Lord; and he shall bear the glory, and shall sit and rule upon his throne.'[31]"

Elder McConkie concluded: "That the branch of David is

Christ is perfectly clear. . . . He is a new David, an Eternal David, who shall reign forever on the throne of his ancient ancestor. . . . David's temporal throne fell long centuries before our Lord was born, and that portion of Israel which had not been scattered to the ends of the earth was in bondage to the iron yoke of Rome. But the promises remain. The eternal throne shall be restored in due course with a new David sitting thereon, and he shall reign forever and ever. . . .

"How glorious shall be the coming day when the second David, who is Christ, reigns on the throne of the first David; when all men shall dwell safely; when the earth shall be dotted with temples; and when the gospel covenant shall have full force and validity in all the earth!"[32]

There is warning for all in the language here that speaks of God smiting the earth with the rod of his mouth and the very breath of his lips slaying the wicked. Nephi, near the end of his life, quoted this verse again when he warned, "With righteousness shall the Lord God judge the poor, and reprove with equity for the meek of the earth. And he shall smite the earth with the rod of his mouth; and with the breath of his lips shall he slay the wicked."[33] In that day the Word will come with power, and there will be incomparable power in his words. In those last days Christ's judgment will be the truth he speaks and an acknowledgment of that truth from all who hear him.

In that millennial moment the Messiah will usher in the peace for which all the righteous have wished, worked, and waited:

"The wolf also shall dwell with the lamb, and the leopard shall lie down with the kid, and the calf and the young lion and fatling together; and a little child shall lead them.

"And the cow and the bear shall feed; their young ones shall lie down together; and the lion shall eat straw like the ox.

"And the sucking child shall play on the hole of the asp, and the weaned child shall put his hand on the cockatrice's den.

"They shall not hurt nor destroy in all my holy mountain, for the earth shall be full of the knowledge of the Lord, as the waters cover the sea.

"And in that day there shall be a root of Jesse, which shall stand for an ensign of the people; to it shall the Gentiles seek; and his rest shall be glorious. . . .

"And he shall set up an ensign for the nations, and shall assemble the outcasts of Israel, and gather together the dispersed of Judah from the four corners of the earth."[34]

In equally triumphant language and comparable latter-day importance, Nephi reminds us (through Isaiah) of temples being built in the tops of the mountains near the headquarters of the kingdom of God on earth, where Christ will rule and reign as Lord of lords and King of kings:

"And it shall come to pass in the last days, when the mountain of the Lord's house shall be established in the top of the mountains, and shall be exalted above the hills, and all nations shall flow unto it.

"And many people shall go and say, Come ye, and let us go up to the mountain of the Lord, to the house of the God of Jacob; and he will teach us of his ways, and we will walk in his paths; for out of Zion shall go forth the law, and the word of the Lord from Jerusalem.

"And he shall judge among the nations, and shall rebuke many people: and they shall beat their swords into plow-shares, and their spears into pruning-hooks—nation shall not lift up sword against nation, neither shall they learn war any more.

"O house of Jacob, come ye and let us walk in the light of the Lord; yea, come, for ye have all gone astray, every one to his wicked ways."[35]

THE CRUCIFIXION AND ATONEMENT

Perhaps no more beautiful passages have ever been written about the Savior's atonement and crucifixion than those written by Isaiah. We have already noted the first three verses of the 61st chapter of Isaiah, the passages with which Christ announced his Messiahship to what must surely have been a startled synagogue in the tranquil village of Nazareth.[36] Those verses would rank among the most moving and meaningful ever written, particularly in light of their true Messianic meaning and the use that the Savior himself made of them.

There are other passages from Isaiah that add greatly to our understanding of the Master's mission. For example, something of the scorn and vilification of Christ's arrest and trial was taught in this passage written by Isaiah more than seven centuries before the event and recorded by Nephi on his plates nearly six centuries before those fateful days:

"The Lord God hath opened mine ear, and I was not rebellious, neither turned away back.

"I gave my back to the smiter, and my cheeks to them that plucked off the hair. I hid not my face from shame and spitting.

"For the Lord God will help me, therefore shall I not be confounded. Therefore have I set my face like a flint, and I know that I shall not be ashamed."[37]

But surely the most sublime, the lengthiest and most lyrical declaration of the life, death, and atoning sacrifice of the Lord Jesus Christ is that found in the 53rd chapter of Isaiah, quoted in its entirety in the Book of Mormon by Abinadi as he stood in chains before King Noah.[38] Abinadi was, of course, a prefiguration, a type and shadow of the Savior, a fact that makes his moving tribute to Christ even more powerful and poignant (if that is possible) than when Isaiah wrote it. Members of The Church of Jesus Christ of Latter-day Saints have been invited to seek everything that is "virtuous, lovely, or of good report or praise-worthy," a fitting description of the Holy One of Israel as declared by Isaiah and Abinadi in their testimonials of him. Consider these elements of his life, love, and gift to all:

"For he shall grow up before him as a tender plant, and as a root out of a dry ground."[39] Sometimes we forget that Christ was born into mortality not only to die for us but also to live like us. He experienced his infancy, childhood, teenage years, and adulthood so that he might more fully understand the challenges associated with life spent in a world that is not our home. Under the watchful eye of his Heavenly Father, he was "tender" in at least two ways—he was young, pure, innocent, and particularly vulnerable to the pain of sin all around him, and he was caring, thoughtful, sensitive, and kind—in short, tender. In his childhood and youthful years with Joseph and Mary, at which time he was only a plant, he was to anchor himself and become a mighty root;[40] then he would grow to become the Tree of Life. (The tree of life as a symbol includes the tree on which he would be slain for the sins of the world.)[41] This would all be accomplished within a few square miles of dry and rocky terrain in ancient Palestine, and in a climate of dry and sterile Judaic legalism that had long since choked out the lifegiving strength of earlier gospel dispensations.

"He hath no form nor comeliness; and when we shall see him, there is no beauty that we should desire him."[42] We have no reason to believe that Christ was unattractive physically, but this verse may suggest that he was plain—as in "plain and precious." In any case we know that his power was an inner, spiritual gift, and that as the son of a mortal mother, he did not stand out in any distinctive physical way, leading his surprised and offended contemporaries of the day to say of him and his messianic announcement, "Is not this Joseph's son?"[43] He certainly did not come to them in a way that filled the people's traditional hopes

and views of a Messiah who would be striking in visage or powerful in politics.

"He is despised and rejected of men; a man of sorrows, and acquainted with grief: and we hid as it were our faces from him; he was despised, and we esteemed him not. Surely he hath borne our griefs, and carried our sorrows: yet we did esteem him stricken, smitten of God, and afflicted."[44] Ultimately Christ was rejected by the people to whom he had come, with even some of his closest disciples growing fearful and (at least temporarily) abandoning him in the end. When he was cursed, vilified, mocked, and spat upon, no one stepped forward to protect or defend him. This was, of course, according to divine decree that the full weight of the Atonement would be borne by Christ and Christ alone. Certainly as he bore the sins and sadness, the heartbreak and hurt of every man, woman, and child from Adam to the end of the world, it is an understatement to say he was "a man of sorrows, and acquainted with grief."

Part of the pain here is the fact that some thought this man of Galilee was getting what he deserved, being "smitten of God." The Savior's most piercing cry may have added to that misunderstanding: "Eli, Eli, lama sabachthani? that is to say, My God, my God, why hast thou forsaken me?"[45] Then, as today, many thought that if there is suffering, there surely must be guilt. Indeed, there was plenty of guilt here—a whole world of it—but it fell upon the only utterly sinless and totally innocent man who had ever lived.

"But he was wounded for our transgressions, he was bruised for our iniquities: the chastisement of our peace was upon him; and with his stripes we are healed. All we like sheep have gone astray; we have turned every one to his own way; and the Lord hath laid on him the iniquity of us all."[46] In a way that is as monumentally merciful as it is beyond our ability to comprehend, in a way that fills us with as much wonder as it does gratitude, Christ personally took upon himself,

beginning in the garden of Gethsemane and continuing on to the cross at Calvary, both the spiritual and physical burden of the transgressions and iniquities of everyone in the human family, for all "like sheep have gone astray." Every accountable person who ever lived—except Jesus—has sinned "and come short of the glory of God."[47] Furthermore, we know that Christ took upon himself other lesser but still painful burdens as well—sicknesses and afflictions, sorrows and discouragements and infirmities of every kind—that these sufferings might be lifted along with the suffering for sin and disobedience.[48]

He who most deserved peace and was the Prince of Peace had peace taken from him. He who deserved no rebuke, let alone physical abuse, went under the lash that his taking of such stripes might spare us such pain if only we would repent. The total cost of such combined spiritual and physical suffering is incalculable. Yet the iniquities, including the sorrows and sadness, of every mortal being who ever has lived or will live in this world were laid across one lonely set of shoulders. In the most magnificent display of strength ever known in the world of human endeavor, they were carried until full payment had been made.

"*He was oppressed, and he was afflicted, yet he opened not his mouth: he is brought as a lamb to the slaughter, and as a sheep before her shearers is dumb, so he openeth not his mouth.*"[49] Here the image of wayward sheep in verse 6 (the human family) is shifted in verse 7 to that of an innocent sheep (Christ), who goes to the slaughter without utterance. When confronted by the high priest Caiaphas, Jesus "held his peace."[50] Later Herod "questioned with him in many words; but he answered him nothing."[51] Finally with Pilate, the one man who could have spared his life, Jesus "gave him no answer."[52] He was the Lamb of God prepared from before the foundation of the world for this ultimate and infinite sacrifice. In his sacrifice he was giving millennia of meaning to the untold number of lambs that had been offered on an untold number of altars in anticipation and similitude of this final blood offering of God's Firstborn. Here was at long last the Holy Lamb without spot or blemish that would again (and in a much more universal way) permit the destroying angels to pass over those of the covenant.[53]

"He was taken from prison and from judgment: and who shall declare his generation? for he was cut off out of the land of the living: for the transgression of my people was he stricken. And he made his grave with the wicked, and with the rich in his death; because he had done no violence, neither was any deceit in his mouth."[54] Christ was taken prisoner by soldiers who entered the garden of Gethsemane expressly to seize him, and he spent the rest of his remaining hours in bondage and judgment at the hands of Pilate. He was then "cut off out of the land of the living." He died with the wicked, crucified between two thieves, and found a burial place at the hand of the wealthy Joseph of Arimathea. Christ was the embodiment of truth, with no deceit of any kind ever having passed his lips. Nor would he do evil (even in word) in his time of greatest injustice, praying in the last hours of his life that his Father would forgive those involved, "for they know not what they do."[55]

"Yet it pleased the Lord to bruise him; he hath put him to grief: when thou shalt make his soul an offering for sin, he shall see his seed, he shall prolong his days, and the pleasure of the Lord shall prosper in his hand."[56] Certainly it did not "please" the Father to bruise his Son, as we currently understand and use that word. Modern translations of Isaiah render these opening lines "it was the will of the Lord" rather than "it pleased the Lord." That gives a clearer meaning of what was meant by the word *pleased* when Joseph Smith translated this passage early in the nineteenth century. Furthermore, acknowledging Christ's submission to the will of the Father in Mosiah 14 is consistent with and sets the stage for the very teaching Abinadi was about to give to King Noah and his people in Mosiah 15. Indeed, Abinadi would give a

succinct definition of those who are Christ's seed. They are those whose sins he has borne and for whom he has died.[57] His soul truly was "an offering for sin," bringing the joy of a glorious heavenly reunion with "his seed," a reunion nowhere more movingly described than in President Joseph F. Smith's vision of the righteous dead.[58] All of this is, indeed, a "pleasure" to the Lord.

"He shall see of the travail of his soul, and shall be satisfied: by his knowledge shall my righteous servant justify many; for he shall bear their iniquities. Therefore will I divide him a portion with the great, and he shall divide the spoil with the strong; because he hath poured out his soul unto death: and he was numbered with the transgressors; and he bare the sin of many, and made intercession for the transgressors."[59] Christ certainly did know and feel the "travail of his soul," an anguish commencing in the garden of Gethsemane, where he "began to be sorrowful and very heavy . . . even unto death."[60] He prayed so earnestly through the depths of that agony that his sweat became "as it were great drops of blood falling down to the ground."[61] Later he would describe the experience of that suffering: "[It] caused myself, even God, the greatest of all, to tremble because of pain, and to bleed at every pore, and to suffer both body and spirit—and would that I might not drink the bitter cup, and shrink."[62]

But he was faithful to the end, "satisfied" in its most literal, legal sense, having made reparation and restitution sufficient to appease the demands of justice. Because he "poured out his soul unto death" bearing the "sin of many," he received the inheritance of the great, sitting on the right hand of God, where all that the Father has was given him.[63] True to his nature and true to his covenant, Christ will share that divine inheritance with all others who will be strong in keeping the commandments, thus making them "heirs of the kingdom of God" in precisely the way Abinadi declared this doctrine to King Noah.[64]

For such merciful protection and glorious promises we must never again "hide our faces from him and esteem him not."

CHAPTER SIX

"WE KNEW OF CHRIST"

he testimonies of Nephi,
Jacob, and Isaiah have been given as the three great early wit-
nesses who stand at the gateway to the Book of Mormon, declaring their testimony of Christ. However, the coming of Christ and
the beauty of his message were "taught . . . bountifully" through
the entire course of the Book of Mormon.[1] Indeed, Nephi, Jacob,
and Isaiah had their own testimonies bolstered by the declaration of other prophets before them. Obviously, prophets coming
later had their affirmations strengthened by these three, and so
the reinforcing, prophetic declarations of Christ unfold throughout the Book of Mormon.

In fact, the theme "Jesus is the Christ," which runs throughout the Book of Mormon, suggests that one way of reading and
remembering this sacred record is to move, in effect, from one
teaching about the Savior to the next. Those discourses come
with such regularity, like a series of mountaintop sightings to a
needy traveler, that they elevatingly lead the reader through the
Book of Mormon from beginning to end. Having already introduced that idea with the teachings of four major prophets, it
seems useful to combine here in one summary section the
remaining teachings and sermons, large or small, which speak

of the Savior up to the time of his appearance in the New World, stressing just how widely the ancient prophets knew "the doctrine of Christ" and how very broadly it was taught. The title for this coalescing chapter—"We Knew of Christ"—is taken from the testimony of these witnesses themselves, with the sermons or subsections identified by the priests and teachers who gave them to us—the prophets of the small plates, King Benjamin, Abinadi, Alma the Elder, Alma the Younger, Amulek, the Sons of Mosiah, Captain Moroni, the later Nephi and Lehi, and Samuel the Lamanite.

THE PROPHETS OF THE SMALL PLATES

As already noted in great detail in chapter three of this book, Nephi's writings document the shared purpose and common practice of Book of Mormon prophets who bore testimony of Christ and his ministry. He recorded the Savior's ministry, including the painful details of the crucifixion, for the express purpose that his people might know fully of Christ and accept his teachings: "I, Nephi, have written these things unto my people, that perhaps I might persuade them that they would remember the Lord their Redeemer. . . .

"For behold, I have workings in the spirit, which doth weary me even that all my joints are weak, for those who are at Jerusalem; for had not the Lord been merciful, to show unto me concerning them, *even as he had prophets of old,* I should have perished also.

"And he surely did show unto *the prophets of old* all things concerning them."[2]

Jacob and Nephi—in that order—spoke of the name the Messiah would carry,[3] but Nephi was quick to acknowledge that other ancient prophets knew the name as well: "*According to the words of the prophets,* the Messiah cometh in six hundred years from the time that my father left Jerusalem; and *according to the words of the prophets,* and also the word of the angel of God, his name shall be Jesus Christ, the Son of God."[4]

Nephi's brother Jacob—whose teachings of the Savior have been thoroughly reviewed in chapter four—followed that acknowledgment with a testimony of the breadth of revelation and widespread knowledge of Christ that had been given to these ancient prophets. He wrote, "For this intent have we written these things, that they may know that we knew of Christ, and we had a hope of his glory many hundred years before his coming; and not only we ourselves had a hope of his glory, but also *all the holy prophets which were before us.*

"Behold, they believed in Christ and worshiped the Father in his name, and also we worship the Father in his name. And for this intent we keep the law of Moses, it pointing our souls to him. . . .

"Wherefore, we search the prophets, and we have many revelations and the spirit of prophecy; and having all these witnesses we obtain a hope, and our faith becometh unshaken, insomuch that we truly can command in the name of Jesus and the very trees obey us, or the mountains, or the waves of the sea."[5]

In that bold and persuasive spirit Jacob pleaded with his brethren, "*Behold, will ye reject these words? Will ye reject the words of the prophets; and will ye reject all the words which have been spoken concerning Christ, after so many have spoken concerning him;* and deny the good word of Christ, and the power of God, and the gift of the Holy Ghost, and quench the Holy Spirit, and make a mock of the great plan of redemption, which hath been laid for you?"[6]

But soon enough one came doing exactly those things. Sherem, the first of the anti-Christs noted in the Book of Mormon, came declaring "that there should be no Christ" and in every way attempted to "overthrow the doctrine of Christ."[7] Knowing that Jacob "had faith in Christ who should come," Sherem made a particularly perverse effort to confront and challenge him about the practice of what Sherem called his "preaching that which ye call the gospel, or the doctrine of Christ." With "a perfect knowledge of the language of the people," including flattery and distinctly powerful speech, Sherem based his argument on the tediously predictable reasoning of all the anti-Christs in the Book of Mormon that "no man knoweth of such things; for he cannot tell of things to come."[8]

In picking up that gauntlet, Jacob asked, "Believest thou the scriptures?"

Sherem answered, "Yea."

"Then ye do not understand them," Jacob replied, "for they truly testify of Christ. *Behold, I say unto you that none of the prophets have written, nor prophesied, save they have spoken concerning this Christ.*[9]

It is some tribute to him that Sherem ultimately acknowledged his fatal dishonesty. Literally on his deathbed he "denied the things which he had taught . . . and confessed the Christ, and the power of the Holy Ghost, and the ministering of angels. . . .

"And he said: I fear lest I have committed the unpardonable sin, for I have lied unto God; for *I denied the Christ, and said that I believed the scriptures; and they truly testify of him.*"[10]

Shortly thereafter, Jacob's son Enos had a memorable spiritual experience because of his faith in Christ, a being, the heavenly voice told him, "whom thou hast never before heard nor seen."[11] Likewise Enos's son Jarom noted that the prophets (plural) of the Lord labored at "persuading them to look forward unto the Messiah, and believe in him to come as though he already was."[12] Jarom's great-great nephew Amaleki delivered his record to King Benjamin, "exhorting all men to come unto . . . Christ, who is the Holy One of Israel, and partake of his salvation, and the power of his redemption. Yea, come unto him, and offer your whole souls as an offering unto him."[13]

These passages mark the conclusion of the small plates of Nephi, completed some 130 years before the birth of Christ. As the transition is made to Mormon's abridgment of the large plates of Nephi, the emphasis on Christ, his doctrines, his teachings, and the certainty of his mortal ministry continues unabated, though in a more temporal context and a more highly edited format.

KING BENJAMIN

In the first of the sermons recorded by Mormon (in the Book of Mormon as we now have it), King Benjamin gave a magnificent discourse on Christ's suffering and atonement, the role of justice and mercy, and the need to take upon ourselves the name of Christ in a covenantal relationship—truths delivered to him "by an angel from God."[14] He also stressed again that all the holy prophets have taught this, and that they, like Jarom, taught the "eternal present" of the Savior's life.

Consider these truths from King Benjamin's singular sermon:

- Christ, who reigns "from all eternity to all eternity" would "come down from heaven among the children of men, and . . . dwell in a tabernacle of clay."[15]

- Christ would work "mighty miracles," including healing the sick and raising the dead; causing the lame to walk, the blind to receive their sight, and the deaf to hear; and curing all manner of diseases and casting out the evil spirits that "dwell in the hearts of the children of men."[16]

- The Savior would suffer temptations, hunger, thirst, fatigue, and "pain of body"—more than a man can suffer "except it be unto death."[17]

- In his atoning anguish, blood would come from every pore, so great would be his anguish over the sins and suffering of mankind.[18]

- He would be called Jesus Christ, the Son of God, the Father

of heaven and earth, the creator of all things from the beginning.[19]

- His mother would be called Mary.[20]

- His own people would reject him, considering him only "a
man." They would accuse him of having an evil spirit, a
devil, and would scourge and crucify him.[21]

- He would rise from the dead on the third day.[22]

- He would stand to judge the world with a righteous judgment, for which "all . . . things are done."[23]

- Christ's blood would atone for those who sin and are ignorant of "the will of God concerning them."[24]

- Repentance is required of all others who sin knowingly and
"rebelleth against God."[25]

- Many "signs, and wonders, and types, and shadows" would
be given to the house of Israel, including the law of Moses,
pointing the people toward Christ's coming. Nevertheless,
they would harden their hearts and stiffen their necks, fail-
ing to understand that the law of Moses "availeth nothing
except it were through the atonement of [Christ's] blood."[26]

- There would be "no other name given nor any other way nor
means" by which salvation could come. It comes only in and
through "the name of Christ, the Lord Omnipotent."[27]

As revelatory and detailed as these teachings are, King
Benjamin linked his strongest doctrinal application of Christ's
teaching to the state and circumstance of little children, those
who served as such ideal objects of Christ's love and such pure
examples of his humility.

Little children are not capable of sinning, King Benjamin
taught, but they suffer the effects of the fall of Adam along with
the rest of the mortal family. Nevertheless, Christ atones for that

fall and overcomes death in their behalf: "The infant perisheth not that dieth in his infancy," King Benjamin said. Indeed, adults will be punished unless they humble themselves and become as little children, believing that "salvation was, and is, and is to come, in and through the atoning blood of Christ, the Lord Omnipotent."[28]

Then King Benjamin declared in a memorable passage the childlike humility and trust required of every disciple of Christ: "The natural man is an enemy to God, and has been from the fall of Adam, and will be, forever and ever, unless he yields to the enticings of the Holy Spirit, and putteth off the natural man and becometh a saint through the atonement of Christ the Lord, and becometh as a child, submissive, meek, humble, patient, full of love, willing to submit to all things which the Lord seeth fit to inflict upon him, even as a child doth submit to his father.

"And moreover, I say unto you, that the time shall come when the knowledge of the Savior shall spread throughout every nation, kindred, tongue, and people.

"And behold, when that time cometh, none shall be found blameless before God, except it be little children, only through repentance and faith on the name of the Lord God Omnipotent."[29]

King Benjamin reminded his listeners that these were not new truths, even in the second century before Christ. "*The Lord God hath sent his holy prophets among all the children of men,*" the prophet said, "*to declare these things to every kindred, nation, and tongue,* that thereby whosoever should believe that Christ should come, the same might receive remission of their sins, and rejoice with exceedingly great joy, *even as though he had already come among them.*"[30]

It is little wonder that those hearing the king's candid message fell to the earth and cried, "O have mercy, and apply the atoning blood of Christ that we may receive forgiveness of our sins, and our hearts may be purified; for we believe in Jesus Christ, the Son of God, who created heaven and earth, and all things; who shall come down among the children of men." Their earnest prayer was heard and they were filled with joy, received a remission of their sins, and found peace of conscience "because of the exceeding faith which they had in Jesus Christ who should come."[31]

As is always the case with the honest in heart, such a powerful witness of Christ evoked an honest response, and these believers sought to establish a covenant with their Savior. Expressing a "mighty change" in their hearts, they had "no more disposition to do evil, but to do good continually." They were willing, they declared, "to enter into a covenant with our God to do his will, and to be obedient to his commandments in all things that he shall command us, all the remainder of our days."[32]

King Benjamin was delighted with this response from the congregation and informed them that in this covenant-making process, they had become "children of Christ, his sons, and his daughters." "For behold," he told them, "this day he hath spiritually begotten you; for ye say that your hearts are changed through faith on his name; therefore, ye are born of him and have become his sons and his daughters."[33]

More will be said later of Christ's role as "Father," but this is one way in which that title is appropriately applied to him who is customarily referred to as "Son." He is the Father of redeemed, restored, spiritual life—in short, eternal life. The faithful are born again—of Christ and by Christ and through Christ—when this mighty change wrought by him comes into their hearts. As is appropriate at the time of a new birth, a name is given, and the name the redeemed take upon themselves is "the name of Christ," evidence that all such have entered into a covenant with

God that they would be obedient to the gospel to the end of their lives.

King Benjamin said of this new life and identity, "I would that ye should remember to retain the name written always in your hearts, . . . that ye hear and know the voice by which ye shall be called, and also, the name by which he shall call you." That such a name would have binding power in eternity through covenants made in mortality is made clear in this final declaration by the worthy king:

"Therefore, I would that ye should be steadfast and immovable, always abounding in good works, that Christ, the Lord God Omnipotent, may seal you his, that you may be brought to heaven, that ye may have everlasting salvation and eternal life, through the wisdom, and power, and justice, and mercy of him who created all things, in heaven and in earth, who is God above all."[34]

That this sermon carried a spiritual power beyond the clarity of the written word is undeniable, for following the close of the discourse and wishing to take "the names of all those who had entered into a covenant," this mighty servant of God realized "there was not one soul, except it were little children, but who had entered into the covenant and had taken upon them the name of Christ."[35] Oh that we might have more such sermons, and, even more important, that all who hear them might make such honest and binding covenants as a result.

ABINADI

Abinadi, that prophetic prefiguration of Christ whose sermon will be addressed in detail later, underscored the fact that in his ministry he was doing only what his predecessors and contemporaries had done:

"For behold, did not Moses prophesy unto them concerning

the coming of the Messiah, and that God should redeem his people? Yea, and even *all the prophets who have prophesied ever since the world began*—have they not spoken more or less concerning these things?

"Have they not said that God himself should come down among the children of men, and take upon him the form of man, and go forth in mighty power upon the face of the earth?

"Yea, and have they not said also that he should bring to pass the resurrection of the dead, and that he, himself, should be oppressed and afflicted?"[36]

In another of those consummate sermons on the Savior laced throughout the Book of Mormon, Abinadi made these declarations about the Son of God:

- "God himself" would atone for the sins and iniquities of his people.[37]

- Christ would play mortal roles as Father and as Son.[38]

- The law of Moses was to be a type and shadow, a prefiguration of Christ who would come.[39]

- Christ would dwell in the flesh and suffer temptation but not yield to it.[40]

- The Savior would suffer himself to be mocked, scourged, cast out, and disowned by his own people.[41]

- He would work "many mighty miracles" only to be led without resistance to the crucifixion.[42]

- His "intercession for the children of men" reflecting his mercy and compassion would allow him to stand "betwixt" these people and the demands of justice.[43]

- In this atoning process he would break the bands of death, take upon himself the the transgressions of all, satisfy the demands of justice, and redeem his people.[44]

- Christ's "seed" (the "children of Christ" spoken of by King Benjamin) would be those who have believed the prophets and looked forward to Christ for a redemption of their sins. These are they whose sins Christ would bear and for whom his death would be wholly efficacious.[45]

- Were it not for this redemption and resurrection, all mankind would perish.[46]

- Christ would bring a "first resurrection" that would include the faithful who lived and died before Christ's death, including little children and those in their maturity who died without any saving knowledge of the gospel.[47]

- There would be no resurrection of the willfully rebellious at the time of Christ's (or "the first") resurrection.[48]

These truths, he testified, have constituted "the words of the prophets, *yea, all the holy prophets who have prophesied concerning the coming of the Lord.*"[49] Abinadi then concluded his masterful sermon with this declaration: "If Christ had not come into the world, *speaking of things to come as though they had already come,* there could have been no redemption.

"And if Christ had not risen from the dead, or have broken the bands of death that the grave should have no victory, and that death should have no sting, there could have been no resurrection.

"But there is a resurrection, therefore the grave hath no victory, and the sting of death is swallowed up in Christ.

"He is the light and the life of the world; yea, a light that is endless, that can never be darkened; yea, and also a life which is endless, that there can be no more death. . . .

"Teach . . . that redemption cometh through Christ the Lord."[50]

ALMA THE ELDER

Out of Abinadi's heroic—and ultimately fatal—declaration to the wicked King Noah came one crucial convert, a young priest in the king's court named Alma. Hearing Abinadi's witness of Christ and fleeing into the wilderness to record the message and repent of his sins, Alma began baptizing all who wished to make a covenant with Christ. He asked that they "serve [God] and keep his commandments, that he may pour out his Spirit more abundantly" upon them. These new disciples would also demonstrate their faith by:

- Coming into the fold of God.[51]

- Being called his people.[52]

- Bearing one another's burdens.[53]

- Mourning with those that mourn.[54]

- Comforting those who stand in need of comfort.[55]

- Standing as witnesses of God at all times and in all things and in all places.[56]

- Entering into a covenant to serve God and keep his commandments.[57]

This declaration by Alma at the Waters of Mormon still stands as the most complete scriptural statement on record as to what the newly baptized commit to do and be.

This baptismal experience for such a large group led to the formation of a church in the wilderness, known from that time forward as "the church of Christ." These early organizations were known among the ancients as "churches of anticipation" when they arose (as they regularly did) before the mortal ministry of Christ. Before long there were several branches of the church in the land, with as many as seven in the immediate area of Zarahemla. These multiple congregations "did assemble themselves together in different bodies, being called churches; every church having their priests and their teachers, and every priest preaching the word according as it was delivered to him by the mouth of Alma." Regardless of the number of branches established, they "were all one church, yea, even the church of God; for there was nothing preached in all the churches except it were repentance and faith in God." Those who joined were to "take upon them the name of Christ, or of God"[58]

The doctrine taught was, as noted, centered on "repentance and faith on the Lord, who had redeemed his people." They were to be united in their hearts, with no contention in their sociality or their doctrine, "having their hearts knit together in unity and in love one towards another." They were to keep the Sabbath day holy and give thanks to the Lord every day. Their priests were to labor with their own hands for their support, and the whole church was to gather together to worship at least one day a week. The people were to impart of their substance "every one according to that which he had; if he have more abundantly he should impart more abundantly; and of him that had but little, but little should be required; and to him that had not should be given. And thus they should impart of their substance of their own free will and good desires towards God." In this manner they were to walk "uprightly before God, imparting to one another both temporally and spiritually according to their needs and their wants."[59]

ALMA THE YOUNGER

As this Nephite "church of anticipation" began to flourish, Alma's son Alma and his associates, the sons of Mosiah, were disrupting the work of the prophets. In that circumstance a great revelation came to the distraught father from "the voice of the Lord," clearly the voice of the premortal Christ. Of the church and those who are baptized into it, the voice said: "Blessed is this people who are willing to bear my name; for in my name shall they be called; and they are mine. . . .

"For behold, this is my church. . . . And whomsoever ye receive shall believe in my name; and him will I freely forgive.

"For it is I that taketh upon me the sins of the world; for it is I that hath created them; and it is I that granteth unto him that believeth unto the end a place at my right hand.

"For behold, in my name are they called. . . .

"And then shall they know that I am the Lord their God, that I am their Redeemer."[60]

The conversion that then came to Alma the Younger in this period of the church's development in Zarahemla is one of the most dramatic and influential in all of the Book of Mormon.

Being confronted and ultimately confounded by an angel of the Lord, Alma fell to the earth and was speechless and helpless for three days and three nights. For two of those days and nights, his high priest father and the other faithful of Zarahemla fasted and prayed that strength would return to this young man, for his father "knew that it was the power of God" that had overcome him.[61] When his strength returned, he stood and spoke of the mighty change that had come to him through Christ. He said to those gathered around him:

"I have repented of my sins, and have been redeemed of the Lord; behold I am born of the Spirit.

"And the Lord said unto me: Marvel not that all mankind, yea, men and women, all nations, kindreds, tongues and people, must be born again; yea, born of God, changed from their carnal and fallen state, to a state of righteousness, being redeemed of God, becoming his sons and daughters;

"And thus they become new creatures; and unless they do this, they can in nowise inherit the kingdom of God. . . .

"After wading through much tribulation, repenting nigh

unto death, the Lord in mercy hath seen fit to snatch me out of an everlasting burning, and I am born of God."

The personal pain of that repentance and rebirth was further described by this newly converted son: "My soul hath been redeemed from the gall of bitterness and bonds of iniquity. I was in the darkest abyss; but now I behold the marvelous light of God. My soul was racked with eternal torment; but I am snatched, and my soul is pained no more.

"I rejected my Redeemer, and denied that which had been spoken of by our fathers; but now that they may foresee that he will come, and that he remembereth every creature of his creating, he will make himself manifest unto all.

"Yea, every knee shall bow, and every tongue confess before him. Yea, even at the last day, when all men shall stand to be judged of him, then shall they confess that he is God; then shall they confess, who live without God in the world, that the judgment of an everlasting punishment is just upon them; and they shall quake, and tremble, and shrink beneath the glance of his all-searching eye."[62]

Years later, recounting this dramatic event for the benefit and caution of his son Helaman, Alma said. "My soul was harrowed up to the greatest degree and racked with all my sins," he explained. Remembering every sin and iniquity left him feeling the torments and pains of hell. Feeling that he had spiritually "murdered" many of the faithful followers of Christ whom he had led away from the church, Alma confessed, "The very thought of coming into the presence of my God did rack my soul with inexpressible horror."

"Oh," thought he for three tormented days, "that I could be banished and become extinct both soul and body, that I might not be brought to stand in the presence of my God, to be judged of my deeds."[63]

It was while racked with such torment, harrowed up by the

memory of his many sins, that Alma remembered that his father had prophesied to the people "concerning the coming of one Jesus Christ, a Son of God, to atone for the sins of the world."

"Now, as my mind caught hold upon this thought," he said, "I cried within my heart: O Jesus, thou Son of God, have mercy on me, who am in the gall of bitterness, and am encircled about by the everlasting chains of death."[64]

When Alma thought of Christ—simply had the *thought* of Christ—his torment was lifted and his pains were eased. He was harrowed up by the memory of his sins no more, and his physical strength returned.

Of this marvelous example of the mercy of Christ and the power of clinging to his atonement even if only in thought, Alma said to Helaman: "What joy, and what marvelous light I did behold; yea, my soul was filled with joy as exceeding as was my pain! . . .

"Yea, and from that time even until now, I have labored without ceasing, that I might bring souls unto repentance; that I might bring them to taste of the exceeding joy of which I did taste; that they might also be born of God, and be filled with the Holy Ghost. . . .

"For because of the word which he has imparted unto me, behold, many have been born of God, and have tasted as I have tasted, and have seen eye to eye as I have seen; therefore they do know of these things of which I have spoken, as I do know; and the knowledge which I have is of God."[65]

Perhaps only those who have known such anguish can fully appreciate the merciful redemption of which Alma spoke. But everyone has had such fearful and harrowing moments; everyone has had hours of affliction and "inexpressible horror." To all such—the "vilest of sinners" or the everyday disciple who wishes only to get through life's journey—Alma speaks to the heart.

At the beginning of his teaching to Helaman he said, "I do know that whosoever shall put their trust in God shall be supported in their trials, and their troubles, and their afflictions, and shall be lifted up at the last day."[66]

In conclusion, he ended as he began: "And I have been supported under trials and troubles of every kind, yea, and in all manner of afflictions; yea, God has delivered me from prison, and from bonds, and from death; yea, and I do put my trust in him, and he will still deliver me."[67]

Of course Alma the Younger's troubles had begun when he denied what had been so bountifully taught by his own father, and what was always so bountifully taught throughout the Book of Mormon era. "I rejected my Redeemer," he said, "and *denied that which had been spoken of by our fathers;* but now that they may foresee that he will come, and that he remembereth every creature of his creating, he will make himself manifest unto all."[68]

At his father's death, the newly converted Alma assumed the prophetic mantle, and, it is instructive to note, preached Christ to members of his own congregation as well as to those who were not members of the Church. Pleading for "a mighty change" to come to his baptized brethren in Zarahemla, Alma warned of the unconverted life: "I ask of you, my brethren of the church, have ye spiritually been born of God? Have ye received his image in your countenances? Have ye experienced this mighty change in your hearts?

"Do ye exercise faith in the redemption of him who created you? . . .

"There can no man be saved except his garments are washed white; yea, his garments must be purified until they are cleansed from all stain, through the blood of him *of whom it has been spoken by our fathers,* who should come to redeem his people from their sins. . . .

"Behold, I say unto you, that the good shepherd doth call

you; yea, and in his own name he doth call you, which is the name of Christ; and if ye will not hearken unto the voice of the good shepherd, to the name by which ye are called, behold, ye are not the sheep of the good shepherd. . . .

"I say unto you, that I know that Jesus Christ shall come, yea, the Son, the Only Begotten of the Father, full of grace, and mercy, and truth. And behold, it is he that cometh to take away the sins of the world, yea, the sins of every man who steadfastly believeth on his name."[69]

In the same spirit Alma went to preach to the church that had been established in the valley of Gideon, "according to the revelation of the truth of the word which had been spoken by his fathers, and according to the spirit of prophecy which was in him, according to the testimony of Jesus Christ, the Son of God, who should come to redeem his people from their sins, and the holy order by which he was called."[70]

Alma taught these people that of the many things to come, there was "one thing . . . of more importance than they all." "For behold," he said, "the time is not far distant that the Redeemer liveth and cometh among his people."[71]

Alma acknowledged with prophetic candor that he did not know exactly when Christ's appearance in the New World would be, but the Spirit instructed him to "cry unto this people, saying—Repent ye, and prepare the way of the Lord, and walk in his paths, which are straight; for behold, the kingdom of heaven is at hand, and the Son of God cometh upon the face of the earth."[72]

Reaffirming not only the virgin birth but also that that virgin's name would be Mary, Alma gave one of the book's most revealing and encouraging statements about the breadth of the Atonement and the range of ills and heartaches it would cover.

Of this divine Son of Mary, Alma said, "He shall go forth, suffering pains and afflictions and temptations of every kind;

and this that the word might be fulfilled which saith he will take upon him the pains and the sicknesses of his people.

"And he will take upon him death, that he may loose the bands of death which bind his people; and he will take upon him their infirmities, that his bowels may be filled with mercy, according to the flesh, that he may know according to the flesh how to succor his people according to their infirmities. . . .

"The Son of God suffereth according to the flesh that he might take upon him the sins of his people, that he might blot out their transgressions according to the power of his deliverance."[73]

This doctrine led Alma to invite his audience to lay claim to these blessings by being baptized unto repentance "that ye may be washed from your sins, that ye may have faith on the Lamb of God, who taketh away the sins of the world, who is mighty to save and to cleanse from all unrighteousness."[74]

Note the kinds of problems Alma said the Atonement would remedy—pain, affliction, sickness, sorrow, temptation, and infirmities of every kind, as well as spiritual sin and physical death. This doctrine is central to the full meaning of the mission and ministry of the Lord Jesus Christ. Most Christians believe that, based upon repentance, the atonement of Christ will redeem humankind from the final consequences of sin and death. But only those who receive the restored gospel, including the Book of Mormon, know how thoroughly the Atonement heals and helps with so many more categories of disappointment and heartache here and now, in time as well as in eternity. In this life as well as the next, Christ "restoreth my soul" and administers "goodness and mercy . . . all the days of my life."[75]

ALMA AND AMULEK (PART 1)

From a marvelous missionary companionship who are likened unto "two lions," we learn a great deal about the Savior in their words to the people of Ammonihah. Picking up the elements of their missionary discussions—particularly those directed to the adversarial Zeezrom—we are taught the following:

- The Savior will come in his glory, the glory of the Only Begotten of the Father, in "not many days" (this prophecy was given in approximately 82 B.C.).[76]

- He would be full of grace, equity, and truth; full of patience, mercy, and longsuffering. He would be quick to hear the cries of his people and to answer their prayers.[77]

- He would redeem those who would be baptized unto repentance, through faith on his name.[78]

- Christ cannot save people "in their sins," although he can save them "from their sins," for no unclean thing can inherit the kingdom of heaven.[79]

- Christ can rightfully be called "the very Eternal Father of heaven and of earth, and all things which in them are." He is "the beginning and the end, the first and the last."[80]

- He would come into the world to redeem his people, the only ones for whom the Atonement can have full effect being those "who believe on his name."[81]

- Except for the universal gift of resurrection, the wicked remain "as though there had been no redemption made."[82]

- In the Resurrection, the spirit and body will be reunited "in its perfect form; both limb and joint shall be restored to its proper frame." Not so much as "a hair of their heads [will] be lost."[83]

- At the time of judgment, we will have a "bright recollection of all our guilt."[84]

- We will never die again physically after the Resurrection. The spirit and body will be forever united, "never to be divided."[85]

- At the day of judgment, our words, our works, and our thoughts will condemn us.[86]

- The wicked will experience a "second death," a spiritual death pertaining unto things of righteousness, and will be under the power and captivity of Satan, tormented as if in a lake of fire and brimstone.[87]

- Their circumstances will be painful, for they will not be able to be redeemed in their sins, and they will not be able to die, for their spirits and bodies will be forever reunited.[88]

- After the fall of Adam, this life became "a probationary state; a time to prepare to meet God."[89]

- Death is a necessary step in full repentance, redemption, and the joy of the Resurrection, for if Adam and Eve had partaken of the fruit of the tree of life after their transgression, "they would have been forever miserable, having no preparatory state."[90]

- Because all need to know these things, God has "conversed with men" from the beginning, according to their faith, repentance, and holy works, making known unto them the plan of redemption prepared from the foundation of the world.[91]

- After having made known the plan of redemption, God gave commandments whereby the blessings of the plan could be obtained.[92]

- God calls on his children yet, "in the name of his Son," to repent and claim the promises available only through his "Only Begotten Son."[93]

- If people continue to transgress and thus provoke God, the result will be [a second] death, just as it was "in the first provocation."[94]

- God has ordained priests "after the order of his Son" to teach these things to the people. They have been ordained in a way that serves as a type and shadow of Christ, letting the people know in what manner they may look forward to the Son of God for redemption.[95]

- The gospel is taught in "plain terms" so there can be no misunderstanding or reason for error.[96]

- Angels are employed to spread these glad tidings, including the declaration of Christ's coming.[97]

This is a significant amount of information about the Savior's ministry, especially when we realize it was given in very hostile circumstances and to a very threatening audience. Indeed, following these teachings, Alma and Amulek were forced to watch innocent women and children, followers of Christ, cast to a fiery death. Furthermore, they themselves were confined in prison, bound with strong cords, denied food and water, spat upon, and mocked by their assailants. In that cruel and violent circumstance, it was faith in Christ that gave Alma and Amulek their strength: "Alma cried, saying: How long shall we suffer these great afflictions, O Lord? O Lord, give us strength according to our faith which is in Christ, even unto deliverance."

At that declaration their bonds were broken and the walls of the prison were rent in two, with Alma and Amulek coming out of the prison unhurt, "for the Lord had granted unto them power, according to their faith which was in Christ. And they straightway came forth out of the prison; and they were loosed from their bands; and the prison had fallen to the earth, and every soul within the walls thereof, save it were Alma and Amulek, was slain."[98]

To new convert Zeezrom, devastated by feverish guilt for his resistance to the truth and his implicit guilt in the deaths of so many innocent people, Alma said: "Believest thou in the power of Christ unto salvation?"

Zeezrom said that he did. Alma continued: "If thou believest in the redemption of Christ thou canst be healed."

Zeezrom affirmed that belief as well.

"And then Alma cried unto the Lord, saying: O Lord our God, have mercy on this man, and heal him according to his faith which is in Christ.

"And when Alma had said these words, Zeezrom leaped upon his feet, and began to walk; and this was done to the great astonishment of all the people; and the knowledge of this went forth throughout all the land of Sidom.

"And Alma baptized Zeezrom unto the Lord; and he began from that time forth to preach unto the people."[99]

With such dramatic manifestations of both good and evil, time was quickly moving toward the coming of Christ: "The Lord did pour out his Spirit on all the face of the land to prepare the minds of the children of men, or to prepare their hearts to receive the word which should be taught among them at the time of his coming." They were taught about "holding forth" to the people the safety of the gospel—"things which must shortly come; yea, . . . the coming of the Son of God, his sufferings and death, and also the resurrection of the dead.

"And many of the people did inquire concerning the place where the Son of God should come; and they were taught that he would appear unto them after his resurrection; and this the people did hear with great joy and gladness."[100]

The Sons of Mosiah

Even as Alma and Amulek were having such success with the Nephites, the sons of Mosiah were teaching the same truths about Christ to the Lamanites. In a dramatic exchange with King Lamoni and his people, Ammon taught "the plan of redemption, which was prepared from the foundation of the world; and he also made known unto them concerning the coming of Christ, and all the works of the Lord did he make known unto them."[101]

It is in response to this testimony of Christ that King Lamoni cried out in much the same manner that the converted young Alma did: "O Lord, have mercy; according to thy abundant mercy which thou hast had upon the people of Nephi, have upon me, and my people."[102] Sinking to the earth as if dead, Lamoni was unconscious for two days and nights until Ammon restored him by the power of the priesthood. From that experience King Lamoni arose saying, "Behold, I have seen my Redeemer; and he shall come forth, and be born of a woman, and he shall redeem all mankind who believe on his name."[103] His wife, the queen, arose from her spiritual experience crying, "O blessed Jesus, who has saved me from an awful hell! O blessed God, have mercy on this people!"[104]

Ammon delighted in this experience because he knew "the dark veil of unbelief" had been cast away from these prominent but now deeply humble Lamanite leaders. The light coming to their minds was that which always overcomes darkness—"the light of the glory of God, which was a marvelous light of his goodness." This illumination infuses such joy into the souls of men and women that every cloud of darkness is dispelled and the promise of everlasting life prevails in the human heart.[105]

It is unfortunate that during this mission the wearisome theme of the anti-Christs—that one cannot know of things to come—was presented by those of the order of Nehor formed among the Amalekites and the Amulonites, apostate Nephites who lived among the Lamanites to whom the Sons of Mosiah had been preaching.

"Now Aaron said unto [one of the Amalekites]: Believest

thou that the Son of God shall come to redeem mankind from their sins?

"And the man said unto him: We do not believe that thou knowest any such thing. We do not believe in these foolish traditions. We do not believe that thou knowest of things to come, neither do we believe that thy fathers and also that our fathers did know concerning the things which they spake, of that which is to come.

"Now Aaron began to open the scriptures unto them concerning the coming of Christ, and also concerning the resurrection of the dead, and that there could be no redemption for mankind save it were through the death and sufferings of Christ, and the atonement of his blood."[106]

The scriptures Aaron was using are still from an "Old Testament" era, yet the sacred writings speak clearly of Christ's coming, his atonement and resurrection—further evidence of the loss of plain and precious truths from our present Bible. To king Lamoni's father "Aaron did expound . . . the scriptures from the creation of Adam, laying the fall of man before him, and their carnal state and also the plan of redemption, which was prepared from the foundation of the world, through Christ, for all whosoever would believe on his name.

"And since man had fallen he could not merit anything of himself; but the sufferings and death of Christ atone for their sins, through faith and repentance, and so forth."[107]

Even a group such as the Anti-Nephi-Lehies—so wicked in their past and so newly introduced to the truth—understood the doctrine of Christ and his atonement. Following his conversion King Anti-Nephi-Lehi said to his people, "I . . . thank my God, yea, my great God, that he hath granted unto us that we might repent of these things, and also that he hath forgiven us of those our many sins and murders which we have committed, and taken away the guilt from our hearts, through the merits of his Son."[108]

Fearful that the stain of more blood upon their weapons might place them beyond the redeeming "blood of the Son of our great God," which was to be shed for the atonement of their sins, these faithful converts refused to take up arms again.[109]

These Anti-Nephi-Lehies, once a hardened and bloodthirsty people, accepted the gospel totally and became "distinguished for their zeal towards God, and also towards men; for they were perfectly honest and upright in all things; and they were firm in the faith of Christ, even unto the end.

" . . . And they never did look upon death with any degree of terror, for their hope and views of Christ and the resurrection; therefore, death was swallowed up to them by the victory of Christ over it."[110]

ALMA AND AMULEK (PART 2)

In the meantime Alma had met Korihor, the most diabolical of all the anti-Christs in the Book of Mormon, who "began to preach unto the people against the prophecies which had been spoken by the prophets, concerning the coming of Christ. . . .

"And this Anti-Christ . . . began to preach unto the people that there should be no Christ. And after this manner did he preach, saying:

"O ye that are bound down under a foolish and a vain hope, why do ye yoke yourselves with such foolish things? Why do ye look for a Christ? For no man can know of anything which is to come. . . .

"Behold, ye cannot know of things which ye do not see; therefore ye cannot know that there shall be a Christ."[111] Korihor taught that such a deranged quest for a remission of sins was "the effect of a frenzied mind." There could be "no atonement made for the sins of men," he taught, but rather "every man fared in this life according to the management of the creature." Every person prospered according to his own cleverness and conquered according to his own strength. Then moving beyond the realm of either civil or moral law into anarchy, Korihor concluded that "whatsoever a man did was no crime." Thus with "great swelling words" Korihor ridiculed the "foolish . . . [and] silly traditions" of believing in a Christ who should come.[112]

Korihor's arguments sound very contemporary to the modern reader, but Alma used a timeless and ultimately undeniable weapon in response—the power of personal testimony. Angry that Korihor and his like were essentially against happiness, Alma asked, "Why do you teach this people that there shall be no Christ, to interrupt their rejoicings."[113] "I know there is a God," he declared, "and also that Christ shall come. . . . I have all things as a testimony that these things are true." The unequivocal reference to "all things" in this prophetic reply is surely an intentional echo by Alma of that doctrine taught throughout the Book of Mormon that "all things which have been given of God from the beginning of the world, unto man, are the typifying of [Christ]."[114] The forces of nature and of history, as well as of spirit, are ultimately always on the side of the disciple of Christ.

Korihor was overcome by Alma's testimony of Christ and finally smitten by the very power of the God he had denied. Nevertheless, his brand of teaching inevitably had its influence among some of the less faithful who, like the neighboring Zoramites, were already given to "perverting the ways of the Lord."

Zoram and his followers are one of the most memorable apostate groups mentioned in the Book of Mormon primarily because they considered themselves so unusually righteous and anything but unfavored of God. Once a week they stood atop a prayer tower called a Rameumptom and, using always "the self-same prayer," thanked God that they were better than everyone else, "a chosen and a holy" people "elected" by God to be saved while all around them were equally "elected" to be cast down to hell. In the reassuring safety of all this, they were also spared any belief in such "foolish traditions" (evidence of Korihor's legacy emerging here) as a belief in a Savior, for it had been "made known" to them there should be no Christ.

After that unabashed public performance once every seven days, the Zoramites returned to their homes, "never speaking of their God again" until they ascended the Rameumptom the next week. Little wonder that when Alma and his missionary brethren witnessed this self-righteous spectacle they were "astonished beyond all measure."[115]

Alma lost little time in countering such unholy prayer and its equally unholy theology with his own prayer for divine assistance against this form of self-serving iniquity that made him literally sick at heart.

"O Lord, wilt thou give me strength, that I may bear with mine infirmities," he prayed. "For I am infirm, and such wickedness among this people doth pain my soul.

"O Lord, my heart is exceedingly sorrowful; wilt thou comfort my soul in Christ . . . and give unto me success, and also my fellow laborers . . . that they may have strength, that they may bear their afflictions."

"Wilt thou comfort their souls in Christ . . . [and] grant unto us that we may have success in bringing [the Zoramites] again unto thee in Christ."[116]

In response to such a selfless prayer—the pure antithesis of the Zoramite offering—"the Lord provided for them that they should hunger not, neither should they thirst; yea, and he also gave them strength, that they should suffer no manner of afflictions, save it were swallowed up in the joy of Christ."[117]

To those of the Zoramites who responded to his message,

Alma quoted the previously mentioned but otherwise unknown prophets Zenos and Zenock. Indeed, he quoted an unknown sermon on prayer by Zenos, who said, "Thou didst hear me because of mine afflictions and my sincerity; and it is because of thy Son that thou hast been thus merciful unto me, therefore I will cry unto thee in all mine afflictions, for in thee is my joy; for thou hast turned thy judgments away from me, because of thy Son."[118]

With that prayerful phrasing in mind, Alma said, "Now behold, my brethren, I would ask if ye have read the scriptures? If ye have, how can ye disbelieve on the Son of God?

"For it is not written that Zenos alone spake of these things, but Zenock also spake of these things—

"For behold, he said: Thou art angry, O Lord, with this people, because they will not understand thy mercies which thou hast bestowed upon them because of thy Son."

Alma continued, "And now, my brethren, ye see that a second prophet of old has testified of the Son of God. . . .

"But behold, this is not all; these are not the only ones who have spoken concerning the Son of God.

"Behold, he was spoken of by Moses; yea, and behold a type was raised up in the wilderness. . . .

"Cast about your eyes and begin to believe in the Son of God, that he will come to redeem his people, and that he shall suffer and die to atone for their sins; and that he shall rise again from the dead, which shall bring to pass the resurrection, that all men shall stand before him, to be judged at the last and judgment day, according to their works. . . .

"Then may God grant unto you that your burdens may be light, through the joy of his Son."[119]

Amulek immediately added his testimony as one newly called to the work: "My brethren, I think that it is impossible that ye should be ignorant of the things which have been spoken concerning the coming of Christ, who is taught by us to be the Son of God; yea, I know that these things were taught unto you bountifully before your dissension from among us. . . .

"The great question which is in your minds is whether the word be in the Son of God, or whether there shall be no Christ.

"And ye also beheld that my brother has proved unto you, in many instances, that the word is in Christ unto salvation."[120]

Amulek, even though a new missionary, had a stunning grasp of theology, for he had been tutored by an angel,[121] had the influence of the Holy Spirit, and had labored at the side of Alma. Taking his lead from Alma's marvelous sermon on "the word" being likened to a seed—a metaphor Alma continued through the staff (tree) Moses raised in the wilderness on to the "tree" springing up to everlasting life—Amulek asked the people of Zoram to have enough faith to "plant the word in [their] hearts, that [they might] try the experiment of its goodness."[122]

After hearing the testimony of Alma, Zenos, Zenock, and Moses, Amulek said, "And now, behold, I will testify unto you of myself that these things are true."[123] From such a forthright testimony of a new convert we are taught that:

- Christ shall come among the children of men, taking upon himself the transgressions of his people and atoning for the sins of the world.[124]

- Because all are hardened, fallen, and lost, all mankind "must unavoidably perish" except for the atonement of Christ.[125]

- The Atonement must be a "great" sacrifice as well as a "last" sacrifice. It cannot be a sacrifice of fowl or beast. It must be "infinite and eternal."[126]

- No mortal can sacrifice his or her own blood and have it redemptively atone for the sins of another. Thus the Atonement must be infinite not only in its scope but also in the godly being of the one making it.[127]

- This great and last sacrifice would be divine. It would be the Son of God who, like his sacrifice, would himself be "infinite and eternal."[128]

- With this sacrifice the law of Moses would be fulfilled, and symbolic blood sacrifice would end.[129]

- The whole meaning of the law of Moses was to point toward Christ, "that great and last sacrifice."[130]

- The intent of this last sacrifice would be to "bring about the bowels of mercy, which overpowereth justice," providing a way for mortals to have "faith unto repentance."[131]

- Prayer is the way we begin to exercise faith unto repentance. We begin by calling upon God to have mercy upon us.[132]

- That prayer for mercy from God will be in vain if we "do not remember to be charitable" to those who need mercy from us—the needy, the naked, the sick, and the afflicted.[133]

- Those who do not procrastinate the day of their repentance will have "their garments . . . made white through the blood of the Lamb."[134]

- The holy scriptures testify of these things, providing "so many witnesses."[135]

Amulek concluded his testimony declaring to non-believers that they should work out their salvation with fear before God, no more denying the coming of the Savior. They should, he said, "contend no more against the Holy Ghost, but . . . receive it, and take upon you the name of Christ."[136]

ALMA TO HIS SONS

Most of Alma's commission to his sons is included in material examined elsewhere in this book, but in addition, Alma did direct Helaman to "preach unto [the people] repentance, and faith on the Lord Jesus Christ; teach them to humble themselves and to be meek and lowly in heart; teach them to withstand every temptation of the devil, with their faith on the Lord Jesus Christ."[137]

To Shiblon he said, "I was three days and three nights in the most bitter pain and anguish of soul; and never, until I did cry out unto the Lord Jesus Christ for mercy, did I receive a remission of my sins. But behold, I did cry unto him and I did find peace to my soul. . . .

"Ye may learn of me that there is no other way or means whereby man can be saved, only in and through Christ. Behold, he is the life and the light of the world. Behold, he is the word of truth and righteousness."[138]

And to Corianton he stressed, "I would say somewhat unto you concerning the coming of Christ. Behold, I say unto you, that it is he that surely shall come to take away the sins of the world; yea, he cometh to declare glad tidings of salvation unto his people. . . .

"And now I will ease your mind somewhat on this subject. Behold, you marvel why these things should be known so long beforehand. Behold, I say unto you, is not a soul at this time as precious unto God as a soul will be at the time of his coming?

"Is it not as necessary that the plan of redemption should be made known unto this people as well as unto their children?

"Is it not as easy at this time for the Lord to send his angel to declare these glad tidings unto us as unto our children, or as after the time of his coming?"[139]

Whatever else the Book of Mormon makes clear, it makes clear that every soul in every dispensation is precious to God, and therefore no age or era was—or is—left without its witness of Christ. Surely it is "necessary that the plan of redemption should be made known to [all] people."

CAPTAIN MORONI

Following the departure of Alma, problems increased in Nephite society, and the adversary's influence became more and more manifest prior to Christ's advent among them. As a military leader, Captain Moroni built an entire military philosophy around his unwavering commitment to Christ. To his dissenting antagonist Amalickiah, Moroni said, "Ye behold that the Lord is with us; and ye behold that he has delivered you into our hands. And now I would that ye should understand that this is done unto us because of our religion and our faith in Christ. And now ye see that ye cannot destroy this our faith.

"Now ye see that this is the true faith of God; yea, ye see that God will support, and keep, and preserve us, so long as we are faithful unto him, and unto our faith, and our religion; and never will the Lord suffer that we shall be destroyed except we should fall into transgression and deny our faith."[140]

In faithful response to his religious belief and military duty, Captain Moroni prayed mightily unto his God for the blessings of liberty to rest upon his brethren, so long as a band of Christians should remain to possess the land—

"For thus were all the true believers of Christ, who belonged to the church of God, called by those who did not belong to the church.

"And those who did belong to the church were faithful; yea, all those who were true believers in Christ took upon them, gladly, the name of Christ, or Christians as they were called, because of their belief in Christ who should come."

Of these Moroni said, "Surely God shall not suffer that we, who are despised because we take upon us the name of Christ, shall be trodden down and destroyed, until we bring it upon us by our own transgressions. . . .

"Rending their garments in token, or as a covenant, that they would not forsake the Lord their God; or, in other words, if they should transgress the commandments of God, or fall into transgression, and be ashamed to take upon them the name of Christ, the Lord should rend them even as they had rent their garments."

As in other battles in other lands, many of these men died and "went out of the world rejoicing,"[141] knowing firmly that their souls had been redeemed by the Lord Jesus Christ, whose name they had taken upon themselves and whose gospel they had tried to defend.

NEPHI AND LEHI

Soon two marvelous brothers—great-grandsons of Alma the Younger—introduced an era of tremendous growth in faith prior to Christ's birth, a period when "tens of thousands" joined the church. Reading as he did of Nephi and Lehi's success, Mormon editorialized regarding the resolute "man [or woman] of Christ," they who grasp the iron rod and safely walk the way of life, triumphing over Lucifer's deception and efforts to destroy, claiming in the end the principalities and powers promised to the heirs of the covenant.

In this stirring passage he wrote, "Thus we see that the gate of heaven is open unto all, even to those who will believe on the name of Jesus Christ, who is the Son of God.

"Yea, we see that whosoever will may lay hold upon the word of God, which is quick and powerful, which shall divide asunder all the cunning and the snares and the wiles of the devil, and lead the man of Christ in a strait and narrow course across that everlasting gulf of misery which is prepared to engulf the wicked—

"And land their souls, yea, their immortal souls, at the right hand of God in the kingdom of heaven, to sit down with

Abraham, and Isaac, and with Jacob, and with all our holy fathers, to go no more out."[142]

Although others were lifted up in pride and the great success of the church began to falter, nevertheless Nephi and Lehi "did fast and pray oft, and did wax stronger and stronger in their humility, and firmer and firmer in the faith of Christ, unto the filling their souls with joy and consolation, yea, even to the purifying and the sanctification of their hearts, which sanctification cometh because of their yielding their hearts unto God."[143]

As a constant reminder and guide for their actions, these brothers had in their hearts the words of their father, Helaman, who, in the spirit of the "man of Christ" declaration, had reminded them that "there is no other means whereby man can be saved, only through the atoning blood of Jesus Christ, who shall come; yea remember that he cometh to redeem the world. . . .

"Remember that it is upon the rock of our Redeemer, who is Christ, the Son of God, that ye must build your foundation; that when the devil shall send forth his mighty winds, yea, his shafts in the whirlwind, yea, when all his hail and his mighty storm shall beat upon you, it shall have no power over you to drag you down to the gulf of misery and endless wo, because of the rock upon which ye are built, which is a sure foundation, a foundation whereon if men build they cannot fall."[144]

As the advent of Christ approached, social disorder increased, with burgeoning warfare, murder, and political disarray. To counter this trend and give hope, Nephi invoked the ancient teachings his people knew so well, testifying of these problems and the coming of the Messiah who would resolve them.

To the corrupt judges who were steadily destroying Nephite society, Nephi gave an overview and summary of just how extensively the early prophets "knew of Christ." He said, "Ye not only deny my words, but *ye also deny all the words which have been spoken by our fathers, and also the words which were spoken by this man, Moses,* who had such great power given unto him, yea, the words which he hath spoken concerning the coming of the Messiah.

"Yea, did he not bear record that the Son of God should come? And as he lifted up the brazen serpent in the wilderness, even so shall he be lifted up who should come.

"And as many as should look upon that serpent should live, even so as many as should look upon the Son of God with faith, having a contrite spirit, might live, even unto that life which is eternal.

"*And now behold, Moses did not only testify of these things, but also all the holy prophets, from his days even to the days of Abraham.*

"Yea, and behold, Abraham saw of his coming, and was filled with gladness and did rejoice.

"Yea, and behold I say unto you, that Abraham not only knew of these things, but there were many before the days of Abraham who were called by the order of God; yea, even after the order of his Son; and *this that it should be shown unto the people, a great many thousand years before his coming, that even redemption should come unto them.*

"And now I would that ye should know, that even since the days of Abraham *there have been many prophets that have testified these things;* yea, behold, the prophet Zenos did testify boldly; for the which he was slain.

"And behold, also Zenock, and also Ezias, and also Isaiah, and Jeremiah. . . .

"Our father Lehi was driven out of Jerusalem because he testified of these things. Nephi also testified of these things, and also *almost all of our fathers, even down to this time; yea, they have testified of the coming of Christ,* and have looked forward, and have rejoiced in his day which is to come."[145]

SAMUEL THE LAMANITE

The degree to which social and religious disorder had come to the Nephites is evidenced by the appearance of a Lamanite—traditionally the people who had been the object, not the source, of such preaching—to call the Nephite people to repentance. Openly rejected in the land of Zarahemla, Samuel responded to the voice of the Lord, climbed upon the wall surrounding the city, and "prophesied unto the people whatsoever things the Lord put into his heart."[146]

One of the things the Lord put into his heart was to warn the people of a "heavy destruction" that awaited them if they did not change their ways. "Nothing can save this people," Samuel shouted from his place upon the wall, "save it be repentance and faith on the Lord Jesus Christ, who surely shall come into the world, and shall suffer many things and shall be slain for his people."[147]

Of this coming—then just five years away—Samuel prophesied of signs and wonders to attend the event, signs and wonders that would be a matter of life and death for the faithful Nephites who would, at the peril of their life, watch for the fulfillment of these promises.[148]

Samuel prophesied that at the time of Christ's birth a new star would appear in the heavens over the New World, just as it would in the Old, but that there would be additional signs and wonders for these Nephites. "There shall be great lights in heaven," Samuel said, "insomuch that in the night before he cometh there shall be no darkness, insomuch that it shall appear unto man as if it was day." This would be so vivid, Samuel promised, that the people would watch the rising and the setting of the sun but "the night [would] not be darkened," so that a day, a night, and a second day would be uninterrupted by any dimming of the light. This was to be the principal manifestation in a time of "many signs and wonders in heaven" that the Light of the World, the Bright and Morning Star, he whose glory is above the brightness of the sun, had been born into mortality.[149]

Although the unbelieving Nephites did not take kindly to this bold Lamanite, nevertheless Samuel continued with his message, a message with even more portent for the wicked. Having prophesied of the wonders of Christ's birth and the opportunity "Jesus Christ, the Son of God, the Father of heaven and of earth, the Creator of all things from the beginning" would bring for a remission of sins "through his merits," Samuel spoke more ominously of Christ's death.

That death would be necessary so that "salvation [might] come; yea, it behooveth him and becometh expedient that he dieth, to bring to pass the resurrection of the dead, that thereby men may be brought into the presence of the Lord[,] . . . redeem[ing] all mankind from the first death—that spiritual death . . . the fall of Adam."[150]

Lest a second, spiritual death then come after the Resurrection, a final judgment upon the unrepentant that would see them "cut off again as to things pertaining to righteousness,"[151] Samuel pleaded for a change of heart among the people. If there was no change, he warned, then the signs and wonders of Christ's death would have even more fateful meaning for them than the signs and wonders of his birth.

As the Light and Life of the world was extinguished, Samuel prophesied, "the sun [would] be darkened and refuse to give his light."[152] So too would the moon and the stars be hidden. For the three days of the Savior's death and entombment, there would be no light upon the face of the New World. At the actual moment of his death, there would be thunderings and lightnings for the space of many hours. The earth would shake and tremble. Rocks above and beneath the earth—even those formations considered to be a solid mass—would be fractured.

Mountains would be laid low like valleys, and valleys would become mountains of great height. Highways would be broken up and cities be made desolate. Women with child would find no place of refuge; they would "be heavy and cannot flee; therefore, they [would] be trodden down and . . . left to perish."[153] As the prophet Zenos had said of such destruction in his own prophecy long before Samuel's, "The God of nature suffers."[154]

Some few Nephites believed Samuel's words (at least partly because they could not seem to hit him with their stones and arrows) and slipped away to be baptized by Nephi, who was still busy "baptizing, and prophesying, and preaching, crying repentance unto the people, showing signs and wonders, working miracles among the people, that they might know that the Christ must shortly come."[155] But the greater part of the people in Zarahemla rejected the prophet and his message, and there was, in a marvelous line from Mormon, "but little alteration in the affairs of the people."[156]

So in the shadow of Christ's advent, the mission that was to bring One to do what no living man, woman, or child could do for themselves, the rebellious among the Nephites and Lamanites began to do exactly what the atonement of Christ declared they should not do—they "began to depend upon their own strength and upon their own wisdom. . . .

"And they began to reason and to contend among themselves, saying . . . it is not reasonable that such a being as a Christ shall come."[157]

Worse than not being "reasonable" (which, by definition, miracles never can be), the prophecy of Christ's coming struck at an even more painful part of the Nephite psyche—their vanity. "This is a wicked tradition," they said, "which has been handed down unto us by our fathers, to cause us that we should believe in some great and marvelous thing which should come to pass, *but not among us,* but in a land which is far distant, a land which we know not; therefore they can keep us in ignorance, for we cannot witness with our own eyes that they are true."[158]

This was all a plot, a scheme by a group of unpatriotic renegades who "may have guessed right" on a few miracles, they said. These prophetic enemies of reason and local pride wanted to work "some great mystery" that they could not understand, that would keep them in bondage and ignorance and dependence upon them forever, they said. "And many more things did the people imagine up in their hearts, which were foolish and vain."[159]

Imaginations? Foolishness? Vanity? And so the pre-advent of Christ closes in the Book of Mormon with the realization of Father Lehi's dream that began it. In an endless sequence of prophetic declarations of Christ—declarations of "all the holy prophets" for "a great many thousand years before his coming"[160]—the Book of Mormon makes the repeated and divine assertion that Jesus is the Christ, that he is the way of salvation and no other, that his gospel "is the most desirable above all things . . . yea, and the most joyous to the soul." "We knew of Christ," all these ancient prophets said, and yet, from 600 B.C. and Lehi's flight from Jerusalem to the very eve of the birth of Christ 406 pages later, the challenge to safety and salvation, to faith and righteousness and the fruit of the tree of life is the same:

"The multitude of the earth was gathered together; and I beheld that they were in a large and spacious building. . . . And the angel of the Lord spake unto me again, saying: Behold the world and the wisdom thereof. . . . I saw and bear record, that the great and spacious building was the pride of the world[,] . . . vain imaginations and the pride of the children of men."[161]

CHAPTER SEVEN

TYPES AND SHADOWS:
THE LAW OF MOSES

In an early declaration of his prophetic purpose, Nephi wrote, "We did observe to keep the judgments, and the statutes, and the commandments of the Lord in all things, according to the law of Moses. . . . Behold, my soul delighteth in proving unto my people the truth of the coming of Christ; *for, for this end hath the law of Moses been given; and all things which have been given of God from the beginning of the world, unto man, are the typifying of him.*"[1]

Later, when Nephi was moving toward his final testimony with its majestic declaration of "the doctrine of Christ," he emphasized the fundamental role the law of Moses had among his people and the commitment they had made to live it, even though they knew the gospel of Christ in great detail and taught it to their children unceasingly.

"Notwithstanding we believe in Christ, we keep the law of Moses," he said, "and look forward with steadfastness unto Christ, until the law shall be fulfilled.

"For, for this end was the law given; wherefore the law hath become dead unto us, and we are made alive in Christ because of our faith; yet we keep the law because of the commandments.

"And we talk of Christ, we rejoice in Christ, we preach of

Christ, we prophesy of Christ, and we write according to our prophecies, that our children may know to what source they may look for a remission of their sins.

"Wherefore, we speak concerning the law that our children may know the deadness of the law; and they, by knowing the deadness of the law, may look forward unto that life which is in Christ, and know for what end the law was given. And after the law is fulfilled in Christ, that they need not harden their hearts against him when the law ought to be done away. . . .

"And, inasmuch as it shall be expedient, ye must keep the performances and ordinances of God until the law shall be fulfilled which was given unto Moses.

"And after Christ shall have risen from the dead he shall show himself unto you, my children, and my beloved brethren; and [then] *the words which he shall speak unto you shall be the law which ye shall do.*"[2]

There is neither time nor space in a study of Christ's influence, teachings, and presence in the Book of Mormon to make an exhaustive study of the law of Moses. Nevertheless, it is important to understand that for six hundred years the descendants of Lehi observed the law of Moses and recognized the purposes for which it had been given. In that sense one cannot fully understand the Nephite record or the majesty of Christ and the new covenant it celebrates without at least a passing acknowledgment of the earlier system of laws and observances that led to it.

The law of Moses was, for the rebellious children of Israel, an Elias, a forerunner, a "schoolmaster" to Christ.[3] And just as John the Baptist (a living Elias and forerunner of Christ) said, "He [Christ and the gospel] must increase, but I [John and the law of Moses] must decrease,"[4] so also is an increase of gospel understanding and a decrease in the significance of the law of Moses seen in the pages of the Book of Mormon.

The modern reader should not see the Mosaic code—

anciently or in modern times—as simply a tedious set of religious rituals slavishly (and sometimes militantly) followed by a stiffnecked people who did not accept the Christ and his gospel. This historic covenant, given by the hand of God himself and second only to the fulness of the gospel as an avenue to righteousness, should be seen rather as the unparalleled collection of types, shadows, symbols, and prefigurations of Christ that it is. For that reason it was once (and still is, in its essence and purity) a guide to spirituality, a gateway to Christ, a path of strict commandment-keeping that would, through laws of duty and decency, lead to higher laws of holiness on the way to immortality and eternal life.

OLD TESTAMENT SIMILITUDES

In teaching this way of statutes and commandments, Jehovah used an abundance of archetypes and symbols. Indeed, these have always been a conspicuous characteristic of the Lord's instruction to his children. Examples of those figures—especially prefigurations of Christ—are present throughout the pre-Messianic record. To Hosea the Lord declared what he had repeatedly done through his chosen oracles on earth: "I have . . . spoken by the prophets, and I have multiplied visions, and used similitudes, by the ministry of the prophets."[5]

In no ministry did he use similitudes more than in that of Moses, whose law was to serve as the ultimate "shadow of heavenly things" that the precious son of Mary would bring to earth.[6] Furthermore, Moses (like Isaac, Joseph, and so many others in the Old Testament) was himself a prophetic symbol of the Christ who was to come. As the Father said to him, speaking through Jehovah, "I have a work for thee, Moses, my son; and thou art in the similitude of mine Only Begotten; and mine Only Begotten is and shall be the Savior, for he is full of grace and truth."[7] We know from the opening pages of the Creation story that all people are created in the image of God.[8] But from other scriptural sources, especially the following passage from the book of Deuteronomy, we learn there was something special in the similarity between Moses and Christ. As the children of Israel were fleeing Egypt and making their way to the promised land (note the Messianic prefiguration of delivering, of saving, of rescuing a covenant people from the sins and evils of the unbelieving world), Moses told them:

"The Lord thy God will raise up unto thee a Prophet from the midst of thee, of thy brethren, like unto me; unto him ye shall hearken. . . .

"And the Lord said unto me, . . .

"I will raise them up a Prophet from among their brethren, like unto thee, and will put my words in his mouth; and he shall speak unto them all that I shall command him.

"And it shall come to pass, that whosoever will not hearken unto my words which he shall speak in my name, I will require it of him."[9]

This Prophet—note the upper case *P* in the text—who would be raised up like unto Moses is, of course, Jesus Christ. As the footnotes in the LDS edition of the scriptures indicate, this passage from Deuteronomy is quoted, with some variation, twice in the New Testament, twice in the Book of Mormon, and once in the Pearl of Great Price. In every instance, those references make it clear that Christ is the future prophet to whom they refer. The earliest of those declarations comes from Nephi, who said, "This prophet of whom Moses spake was the Holy One of Israel; wherefore, he shall execute judgment in righteousness."[10] Not surprisingly, the most authoritative declaration of this truth also comes in the Book of Mormon from the lips of the resurrected Savior himself. To the Nephites gathered at his feet, Christ said,

"Behold, I am he of whom Moses spake, saying: A prophet

shall the Lord your God raise up unto you of your brethren, like unto me; him shall ye hear in all things whatsoever he shall say unto you. And it shall come to pass that every soul who will not hear that prophet shall be cut off from among the people."[11]

Surely that is one of the reasons Jesus was so disappointed, not only that his Jewish audience did not recognize him, but also that they used their distorted interpretations of the law of Moses against him in denying his Messianic ministry. With great regret he said to them, "Search the scriptures [including and especially the writings of Moses]; . . . they are they which testify of me. . . . I am come in my Father's name, and ye receive me not. . . . Do not think that I will accuse you to the Father: there is one that accuseth you, even Moses, in whom ye trust. For had ye believed Moses, ye would have believed me: for he wrote of me. But if ye believe not his writings, how shall ye believe my words?"[12]

Nephi taught the same lesson to his own "stiffnecked people." Speaking so plainly "that [they could not] misunderstand," he said to these Israelites in the New World, "The right way is to believe in Christ and deny him not; for by denying him ye also deny the prophets and the law."[13]

That underscores yet another divine purpose served by the Book of Mormon. It is a second witness from the Old Testament period of the true worth and original intent of the law of Moses and the positive influence it can have on a people who obey it. Nephi and his fellow prophets knew that salvation was not in the law, but they also understood the importance of obeying it in order to realize the full benefit of Christ's earthly mission to fulfill it, wherein salvation *did* come. The first law of heaven is obedience, and every dispensation of truth has required such. Certainly the fulness of the gospel requires commandment-keeping every bit as much as the lesser law of Moses, so notwithstanding their greater understanding of the gospel, the Nephite prophets and parents were determined to "keep the law because of the commandments" if only out of sheer loyalty to the principles of obedience and integrity.[14]

In fact, the Book of Mormon does more to bridge dispensations and put the law of Moses in its true perspective—that is, to clarify and emphasize its relationship to the gospel of Jesus Christ—than any other book available, linking in one document a people who understood and loyally obeyed the many codes and covenants traditionally seen as "Old Testament" even as they taught and lived with great devotion those higher teachings of Christ usually identified as "New Testament" in their orientation.

ELEMENTS OF THE LAW

The law of Moses consists generally of the material contained in the first five books of the Old Testament, known to the Jews as the Torah and to the rest of the world as the Pentateuch, material that was available to the Nephite writers because they were included on the brass plates obtained from Laban before Lehi and his family left the Old World.[15] But this is not always a useful definition.

For one thing, the book of Genesis precedes the Mosaic period and therefore the Mosaic commandments. It documents several dispensations that lived by the light of the higher teachings of the gospel and that do not historically or theologically fit within the "very strict law . . . of performances and of ordinances" traditionally associated with the law of Moses.[16]

Second, the law of Moses as it is known today consists of a rather loose and sometimes seemingly unrelated collection of prescriptions, proscriptions, observations, and rituals that are not structured in the coherent and codified way that we think of "law" in the modern sense.

Finally, a great deal of material, primarily rabbinic refinement and commentary on the original Mosaic writings, has been added to the original law of Moses. In fact, so much was added in the first millennium of its existence, and so obscure became its original requirements even in that relatively brief period of time, that while living in mortality he who had given the law in its purity was repeatedly accused of breaking some minute aspect of it. This complexity in and occasional confusion about the development of the Mosaic code as presently taught poses challenges for the student of the testaments—Old, New, and Nephite—even today.

Elder Bruce R. McConkie outlined the dilemma this way:

"We cannot always tell . . . whether specific sacrificial rites performed in Israel were part of the Mosaic system or whether they were the same ordinances performed by Adam and Abraham as part of the gospel law itself. Further, it appears that some of the ritualistic performances varied from time to time, according to the special needs of the people and the changing circumstances in which they found themselves. Even the Book of Mormon does not help us in these respects. We know the Nephites offered sacrifices and kept the law of Moses. Since they held the Melchizedek Priesthood and there were no Levites among them, we suppose their sacrifices were those that antedated the ministry of Moses and that, since they had the fulness of the gospel itself, they kept the law of Moses in the sense that they conformed to its myriad moral principles and its endless ethical restrictions. We suppose this would be one of the reasons Nephi was able to say, 'The law hath become dead unto us.'[17] There is, at least, no intimation in the Book of Mormon that the Nephites offered the daily sacrifices required by the law or that they held the various feasts that were part of the religious life of their Old World kinsmen."[18]

In any case, the original writings of Moses are seen rabbinically to contain some 613 commandments—roughly falling into two broad categories of moral and ethical laws, plus ceremonial and regulatory statutes—covering topics ranging from the role of the priesthood to the specifications for the Tabernacle to the prohibition against certain foods to the management of agricultural endeavors, *ad infinitum*. These laws and directives provided the religious, civil, and criminal code for virtually all Jewish people at least until the Dispersion in the first century after Christ and for the orthodox portion of that people for two millennia since then. Furthermore, this ancient code and the Old Testament in which it is recorded has had a profound effect upon the social, cultural, and religious life of virtually all people living in the larger Western (Judeo-Christian) world for more than three thousand years. Its influence and significance can scarcely be overstated.

MELCHIZEDEK PRIESTHOOD

Latter-day revelation makes it clear that Moses and the prophets before him had Melchizedek Priesthood power and participated in the higher, gospel-related, temple-linked ordinances that attend it. Section 84 of the Doctrine and Covenants, one of the greatest declarations on priesthood ever given, records that "Abraham received the priesthood from Melchizedek," noting that such priesthood had come down to Melchizedek from Adam, Abel, Enoch, Noah, and the lineage of the "fathers":

"And this greater priesthood administereth the gospel and holdeth the key of the mysteries of the kingdom, even the key of the knowledge of God.

"Therefore, in the ordinances thereof, the power of godliness is manifest.

"And without the ordinances thereof, and the authority of the priesthood, the power of godliness is not manifest unto men in the flesh;

"For without this no man can see the face of God, even the Father, and live."[19]

Then the revelation notes that "this Moses plainly taught to the children of Israel in the wilderness, and sought diligently to sanctify his people that they might behold the face of God."[20] Clearly these people had access to the ordinances and authority of the Melchizedek Priesthood, with its gospel orientation, in order to pursue such sanctification.

"But they hardened their hearts and could not endure his presence; therefore, the Lord in his wrath, for his anger was kindled against them, swore that they should not enter into his rest while in the wilderness, which rest is the fulness of his glory.

"Therefore, he took Moses out of their midst, and the Holy Priesthood also;

"And the lesser priesthood continued, which priesthood holdeth the key of the ministering of angels and the preparatory gospel;

"Which gospel is the gospel of repentance and of baptism, and the remission of sins, and the law of carnal commandments, which the Lord in his wrath caused to continue with the house of Aaron among the children of Israel until John, whom God raised up, being filled with the Holy Ghost from his mother's womb."[21]

This marvelously revealing passage of scripture notes that something was taken from the children of Israel (the Melchizedek Priesthood with its higher, gospel-oriented, temple-linked principles and privileges), while the essential elements of what we often call the law of Moses continued with them under the keys and guidance of the Aaronic or "lesser" priesthood, which is basic to the "preparatory gospel." This preparation for the fulness of the gospel includes having faith, showing repentance, and submitting to baptism—principles and ordinances taught by and performed under the Aaronic Priesthood. Through their disobedience and hardheartedness the children of Israel lost the higher gospel and were left with a lesser portion of it that would prepare them to receive again the greater good and the higher law their forebears had enjoyed.

Regarding this loss, most readers are familiar with Moses' visit to the summit of Sinai, where he received the first set of stone tablets written by the very finger of God. It is important to realize, particularly in light of the passages above, that there was considerably more on those tablets than the Ten Commandments. When Moses descended the mountain and found some of his people in naked, riotous activity worshiping a golden calf, he was furious. The contrast between what he had just seen, heard, and felt in the presence of the Lord compared with the debauchery and idol worship he now witnessed must have been devastating in the extreme. Furthermore, such an extreme difference between what was and what could have been helps us understand the severity of the penalty the Israelites paid in losing for well over a thousand years the priesthood, gospel, and temple blessings they could have enjoyed in abundance.

Shattering the stone tablets at his feet, Moses disciplined the openly rebellious Israelites in some severity. Sometime later, he hewed out two new tables of stone "like unto the first" and returned to the summit of Sinai to receive new instructions of the Lord. There Jehovah gave Moses the same commandments recorded on the first tablets—but with a crucial element omitted. For the clearest delineation of this loss, we are indebted to Joseph Smith's translation of Exodus 34.[22] Note the comparison:

Joseph Smith Translation (JST)	*King James*
1. And the Lord said unto Moses, Hew thee two *other* tables of stone, like unto the first, and I will write upon	1. And the Lord said unto Moses, Hew thee two tables of stone like unto the first: and I will write upon these tables the

JST	*King James*
them also, the words *of the law, according as they were written at the first on the tables which thou brakest; but it shall not be according to the first, for I will take away the priesthood out of their midst; therefore my holy order, and the ordinances thereof, shall not go before them; for my presence shall not go up in their midst, lest I destroy them.*	words that were in the first tables, which thou brakest.
2. But I will give unto them the law as at the first, but it shall be after the law of a carnal commandment; for I have sworn in my wrath, that they shall not enter into my presence, into my rest, in the days of their pilgrimage. Therefore do as I have commanded thee, and be ready in the morning, and come up in the morning unto mount Sinai, and present thyself there to me, in the top of the mount.	2. And be ready in the morning, and come up in the morning unto mount Sinai, and present thyself there to me in the top of the mount.

Clearly some of what was originally contained on the first set of tablets was written again on the second (the Ten Commandments, for example). But it is much more important to note that vital doctrines upon the first set—specifically, the ordinances of the higher priesthood—were omitted from the second. Such a contribution from the Prophet Joseph Smith's translation of the Bible is further acknowledged in this passage from Deuteronomy 10:2:

JST	*King James*
2. And I will write on the tables the words that were on the first tables, which thou breakest, *save the words of the everlasting covenant of the holy priesthood,* and thou shalt put them in the ark.	2. And I will write on the tables the words that were in the first tables which thou brakest, and thou shalt put them in the ark.

Performances and Ordinances

Even with the loss of such vital information, it is important to see the remaining covenant, what survived the wrath of Sinai as the law of Moses (variously described as Mosaic, Aaronic, lesser, preparatory, carnal, or outward) in the true light it deserves and the strict obedience with which the Nephites observed it.

This "law of Moses" under which the Israelites continued from Moses' day onward included faith, repentance, and baptism, along with a host of other "performances and ordinances" such as sacrifices and offerings that were directly linked with the future atonement of Christ and were meant to be in every way "a similitude of him."

To get his sometimes disobedient children to understand the Atonement and the fundamental importance of first principles, Jehovah added to the standard gospel message (taught from the days of Adam down to Moses) what is now spoken of as "carnal commandments."[23] These were added as reminders, exercises, preparations stressing a return to first principles of the gospel. This basic code that remained with the children of Israel, this preparatory gospel built upon a law of carnal commandments, is what is now called the law of Moses. Principles of the truth that had been with the Israelites before the addition of the carnal commandments and that continued after these were added included the principles of faith in the Lord Jesus Christ, repentance, baptism for the remission of sins, the Ten Commandments, various offerings symbolic of Christ's atonement, and the law of the covenant. Elements added or amplified included other "performances and ordinances" such as dietary restrictions, purification rituals, and additional offerings. Other additions included the preparation of clothing, the planting of crops, and additional social obligations. These were all intended to reinforce self-control and create greater self-discipline (obedience) in the lives of the children of Israel so they could reclaim the higher promises, principles, and priesthood that had been enjoyed by their forebears.

Thus it is crucial to understand that the law of Moses was overlaid upon, and thereby included, many basic parts of the gospel of Jesus Christ, which had existed before it. It was never intended to be something apart or separated from, and certainly not something antagonistic to, the gospel of Jesus Christ. It was more elementary than the full gospel—thus its schoolmaster's role in bringing people to the gospel—but its purpose was never to have been different from the higher law. Both were to bring people to Christ.

In this spirit it is equally important to note what the law of Moses was *not*. We can be certain that Jesus was perfectly obedient to the spirit and the letter of the law of Moses. It was the law of the "church" and the law of his people during his lifetime. It was spiritually based, it had fundamental elements of the gospel, and in its purity it was to lead to the holier law and the higher priesthood. But he did not feel obliged to abide by the myriad additions, addendums, commentaries, and ultimately false insertions into the law that had been added in more than a thousand years of what was at best uninspired argument and at worst flagrant apostasy. The *Torah*, or five books of Moses, would have been perfectly known and accepted by Christ, at least in their pure and original form. What would give him grief would be the instructions and traditions added to the Torah. These instructions and traditions came, in time, to be known as the *Talmud* (authoritative traditions comprising the *Mishnah* and *Gemara*) and even what would become the haggadic *midrash* (rabbinic commentary) of later periods. When Jesus was in conflict with the scribes and Pharisees of his day—as he so frequently was—it was over these additions and embellishments of the law of Moses, not the law itself.

Perhaps one reason the Nephites kept the spirit and purpose of the law of Moses was that they had priesthood and prophets who safegaurded the doctrines. But in Book of Mormon times there were also those who misunderstood and distorted the law of Moses. We have noted earlier that in the first generation of Nephite experience, Sherem, the first of the anti-Christs in the Book of Mormon, used the law of Moses (as he erroneously viewed it) to strike out against Jacob and his prophetic teachings of Christ.

To Jacob, Sherem said, "Ye have led away much of this people that they pervert the right way of God, and keep not the law of Moses which is the right way; and convert the law of Moses into the worship of a being which ye say shall come many hundred years hence."[24]

Unfortunately, the dishonest Sherem knew that Moses and the other prophets had spoken of Christ and that their teachings were not only consistent with the gospel but also pointed people toward its future fulness. On his deathbed he "confessed the Christ" and lamented, "I fear lest I have committed the unpardonable sin, for I have lied unto God; for I denied the Christ, and said that I believed the scriptures; and they truly testify of him."[25]

And it was Jacob's grandson, Jarom, who noted that "the prophets, and the priests, and the teachers, did labor diligently, exhorting with all long-suffering the people to diligence; teaching the law of Moses, *and the intent for which it was given;* persuading them to look forward unto the Messiah, and believe in him to come as though he already was."[26]

Preceding chapters of this book note the degree to which the Nephite prophets knew and taught the life and mission of Christ. For Israelites in both the Old and New Worlds the law of Moses was given to overcome the stiffnecked obstinance of people like the anti-Christ Sherem.

"And many signs, and wonders, and types, and shadows showed he unto them, concerning his coming," King Benjamin said of Jehovah's use of the law of Moses and other divine declarations. "And yet they hardened their hearts, and understood not that the law of Moses availeth nothing except it were through the atonement of his blood."[27]

ABINADI AND THE LAW

It is in the brief but compelling ministry of Abinadi that the relationship between the law of Moses and the gospel of Christ is most thoroughly and tellingly explained. A prophet of unknown origin and background, Abinadi stepped forward in response to God's call and confronted the apostate, profligate King Noah. Abinadi was fearless and true, without artifice or concern for the personal danger his boldness might generate.

Standing captive before the king and his court, Abinadi defied their attempts to confuse and contradict him, thereby avoiding their effort to find grounds whereby they could condemn him: "He answered them boldly, and withstood all their questions, yea, to their astonishment; for he did withstand them in all their questions, and did confound them in all their words."[28] He confounded them by teaching the law of Moses as they *should* have understood it:

"Ye have not applied your hearts to understanding; therefore, ye have not been wise. Therefore, what teach ye this people?

"And they said: We teach the law of Moses.

"And again he said unto them: If ye teach the law of Moses why do ye not keep it? . . .

"And it shall come to pass that ye shall be smitten for your iniquities, for ye have said that ye teach the law of Moses. And what know ye concerning the law of Moses? Doth salvation come by the law of Moses? What say ye?

"And they answered and said that salvation did come by the law of Moses."[29]

Obviously that is an erroneous answer and could have drawn a sharp, immediate denial from Abinadi. But he did something much more fascinating and subtle. He appeared *almost* to agree with them, a tactic that both elevated the stature of the law *and* trapped them in their abominations. In answer to their reply that salvation did come by the law, Abinadi replied that they were partially correct—that ultimately salvation is in obedience to the laws and commandments God gives, inasmuch as only the obedient shall eat the fruit of salvation in the last days: "Abinadi said unto them: I know if ye keep the commandments of God ye shall be saved; yea, if ye keep the commandments which the Lord delivered unto Moses in the mount of Sinai."[30]

He then reviewed the Ten Commandments with genuine power and authority, including the manifestation of the Spirit of the Lord, which strengthened him physically and shone radiantly upon his face, just as it had the face of Moses when he received those same commandments.[31]

After rehearsing the decalogue in detail, Abinadi asked King Noah, "Have ye taught this people that they should observe to do all these things for to keep these commandments?" Then he answered his own question: "I say unto you, Nay; for if ye had,

the Lord would not have caused me to come forth and to prophesy evil concerning this people."[32]

It is as if to say that while the law of Moses (or the Ten
Commandments, which are central to it *and* the gospel) are not
sufficient to save, they can lead toward salvation and later recognition of the greater truths of which they are an essential part. If
King Noah or his people had sufficiently kept the law of Moses,
it would have been enough—or at least acceptable—for that day
and time, and probably no divine reprimand would have been
forthcoming. But they failed even in this lesser portion of the
divine decree and did not lay claim even to that preliminary path
to salvation for which the law of Moses was given.

To those holding him captive Abinadi said, "Ye have said
that salvation cometh by the law of Moses. I say unto you that it
is expedient that ye should keep the law of Moses *as yet;* but I say
unto you, that the time shall come when it shall no more be expedient to keep the law of Moses.

"And moreover, I say unto you, that salvation doth not come
by the law alone; and were it not for the atonement, which God
himself shall make for the sins and iniquities of his people, that
they must unavoidably perish, notwithstanding the law of
Moses.

"And now I say unto you that it was expedient that there
should be a law given to the children of Israel, yea, even a very
strict law; for they were a stiffnecked people, quick to do iniquity, and slow to remember the Lord their God;

"Therefore there was a law given them, yea, a law of performances and of ordinances, a law which they were to observe
strictly from day to day, to keep them in remembrance of God
and their duty towards him.

"But behold, I say unto you, that *all these things were types of
things to come.*"[33]

At that point Abinadi noted just how prescriptive—and

descriptive—the law of Moses had been, reminding them that "Moses . . . and . . . all the prophets who have prophesied ever since the world began—have they not spoken more or less concerning these things?"—specifically that "God should redeem his people," that "God himself" would come down from heaven, take upon himself by birth the form of a man, and "go forth in mighty power upon the face of the earth."[34]

To reinforce that declaration Abinadi quoted the 53rd chapter of Isaiah—surely the most powerful and extended passage regarding Christ in all the Old Testament—developing the symbolism of the Savior not so much as a shepherd but as a sheep.[35]

At that point Abinadi declared deep doctrine no longer found in the Old Testament or traditionally linked with the law of Moses in present times. He spoke of Christ's role as both Father and Son, of the Son's atoning intercession with the Father on behalf of the human family, of Christ's ability to insert mercy between the people and the demands of justice, of the "seed" of Christ as those for whom the Atonement is fully efficacious, and of the Resurrection, including those entitled to the first resurrection. With great power and authority he spoke of the need to declare these truths to "every nation, kindred, tongue, and people" by the watchmen of God who would sing the song of redeeming love and whose feet would be so beautiful upon the mountain of the Lord.[36]

At that crescendo of doctrine and testimony on the Atonement, Resurrection, and Final Judgment, Abinadi closed his remarkable theological discourse.

Noting that many in that final day would go according to their "own carnal wills and desires," repenting not and resisting the arms of divine mercy that were extended to them, he said:

"And now, ought ye not to tremble and repent of your sins, and remember that only in and through Christ ye can be saved?

"Therefore, if ye teach the law of Moses, also teach that it is a shadow of those things which are to come—

"Teach them that redemption cometh through Christ the Lord, who is the very Eternal Father. Amen."[37]

In the ultimate offering any prophet of God is capable of making, Abinadi then offered himself to his captors, becoming a type and shadow, a prophetic prefiguration of Christ's sacrifice, to which he had just testified.[38]

Later, when a large group of Lamanites were converted, they remembered the type and teachings of Abinadi, and immediately "they did keep the law of Moses; for it was expedient that they should keep the law of Moses as yet, for it was not all fulfilled. But notwithstanding the law of Moses, they did look forward to the coming of Christ, considering that the law of Moses was a type of his coming, and believing that they must keep those outward performances until the time that he should be revealed unto them.

"Now they did not suppose that salvation came by the law of Moses; but the law of Moses did serve to strengthen their faith in Christ."[39]

"IN ME IS THE LAW OF MOSES FULFILLED"

At approximately the same time these Lamanites were hearing the gospel, Alma and Amulek were teaching the Nephites of the Atonement. In doing so, Alma taught that "redemption cometh through the Son of God, and . . . [he] appealed unto Moses, to prove that these things are true."[40] Amulek immediately joined in to declare that the significance and symbolism of sacrifice, so central to the law of Moses, are centered in Christ. As a fulfillment of the ancient pattern of sacrifice, Amulek taught, there must be "a great and last sacrifice," following which there should be a "stop to the shedding of blood; *then shall the law of Moses be fulfilled;* yea, it shall be all fulfilled, every jot and tittle, and none shall have passed away.

"And behold, *this is the whole meaning of the law, every whit pointing to that great and last sacrifice.*"[41]

Of course, the adversary, ever anxious to confuse a principle of the gospel, encouraged the Nephites to believe that the law of Moses was fulfilled simply by the birth of Christ rather than by his consummate, fulfilling, atoning sacrifice at the end of his life.

After the day and night and day in which there was no darkness, the sign Samuel the Lamanite had promised, the record says "there were no contentions, save it were a few that began to preach, endeavoring to prove by the scriptures that it was no more expedient to observe the law of Moses. Now in this thing they did err, having not understood the scriptures.

"But it came to pass that they soon became converted, and were convinced of the error which they were in, for it was made known unto them that the law was not yet fulfilled, and that it must be fulfilled in every whit; yea, the word came unto them that it must be fulfilled; yea, that one jot or tittle should not pass away till it should all be fulfilled."[42]

When the crucifixion, death, resurrection, and ascension of Christ was completed in the Old World, his appearance to the Nephites in the New World was introduced with this declaration from his own lips:

"Behold, I am Jesus Christ the Son of God. I created the heavens and the earth, and all things that in them are. I was with the Father from the beginning. I am in the Father, and the Father in me; and in me hath the Father glorified his name.

"I came unto my own, and my own received me not. And the scriptures concerning my coming are fulfilled.

"And as many as have received me, to them have I given to become the sons of God; and even so will I to as many as shall believe on my name, for behold, by me redemption cometh, and in me is the law of Moses fulfilled.

"I am the light and the life of the world. I am Alpha and Omega, the beginning and the end.

"And ye shall offer up unto me no more the shedding of blood; yea, your sacrifices and your burnt offerings shall be done away, for I will accept none of your sacrifices and your burnt offerings.

"And ye shall offer for a sacrifice unto me a broken heart and a contrite spirit. And whoso cometh unto me with a broken heart and a contrite spirit, him will I baptize with fire and with the Holy Ghost."[43]

Unlike the Israelites in the Old World, the faithful Nephites of the New World found it easier to recognize the return of the higher gospel and thereby let go of the ancient law of Moses. For one thing, they seemed to grasp more readily that Christ had not destroyed the law but fulfilled it—given it breadth, dimension, meaning, and reality, just as a prophecy is spoken of as being "fulfilled." During his first day of teaching the Nephites in the New World, the resurrected Christ was able to teach this doctrine in more detail than he had taught (or at least than it was preserved) among the people of Jerusalem:

"Think not that I am come to destroy the law or the prophets," he said. "I am not come to destroy but to fulfil; for verily I say unto you, one jot nor one tittle hath not passed away from the law, but in me it hath all been fulfilled. And behold, I have given you the law and the commandments of my Father, that ye shall believe in me, and that ye shall repent of your sins, and come unto me with a broken heart and a contrite spirit. Behold, ye have the commandments before you, and the law is fulfilled. . . . Therefore those things which were of old time, which were under the law, in me are all fulfilled. Old things are done away, and all things have become new."[44]

Following this "sermon at the temple," the Savior gave even more commentary on this crucial transition from old covenant to new. Perceiving that some in the congregation "marveled, and wondered" about Christ's relationship to the law of Moses, "for they understood not the saying that old things had passed away, and that all things had become new," he said, making a distinction between "the law" and "the covenant":

"Behold, I say unto you that the law is fulfilled that was given unto Moses. Behold, I am he that gave the law, and I am he who covenanted with my people Israel; therefore, the law in me is fulfilled, for I have come to fulfil the law; therefore it hath an end. Behold, I do not destroy the prophets, for as many as have not been fulfilled in me, verily I say unto you, shall all be fulfilled. And because I said unto you that old things have passed away, I do not destroy that which hath been spoken concerning things which are to come. For behold, the covenant which I have made with my people is not all fulfilled; but the law which was given unto Moses hath an end in me. Behold, I am the law, and the light. Look unto me, and endure to the end, and ye shall live; for unto him that endureth to the end will I give eternal life. Behold, I have given unto you the commandments; therefore keep my commandments. And this is the law and the prophets, for they truly testified of me."[45]

Clearly the Nephite congregation understood this more readily than did the Jewish world, partly because the Nephite prophets had been so careful to teach the transitional nature of the law. Abinadi had said, "It is expedient that ye should keep the law of Moses *as yet*; but I say unto you, that the time shall come when *it shall no more be expedient to keep the law of Moses*."[46] In that same spirit Nephi emphasized, "We speak concerning the law that our children may know the deadness of the law; and they, by knowing the deadness of the law, may look forward unto that life which is in Christ, and know for what end the law was given. *And after the law is fulfilled in Christ, that they need not harden their hearts against him when the law ought to be done away.*"[47]

That kind of teaching—a caution against hardening one's heart against Christ in ignorant defense of the law of Moses—could have served (and saved) so many living in the Old World then and living throughout the world now. Or if, as is probable, this clear doctrine was taught emphatically in the Old World, then more is the pity that such "plain and precious things" were lost or taken from the pristine teachings of the Old Testament.

In light of the profound insight the Book of Mormon brings to an understanding of the law of Moses, it is significant that Paul's great statement that the law was to serve as a "schoolmaster to bring us unto Christ" is recorded in the Joseph Smith Translation of the Bible as "the law was our schoolmaster *until* Christ."[48] (And, of course, the Joseph Smith Translation was greatly influenced by the doctrinal education Joseph Smith received while translating the Book of Mormon.)

That this role for the law of Moses was clearly understood by the Nephite nation is best noted in the fourth book of Nephi, virtually the last reference to the law of Moses in the Book of Mormon. There the record says with finality as well as with a spirit of some success, "And they did not walk any more after the performances and ordinances of the law of Moses; but they did walk after the commandments which they had received from their Lord and their God. . . . And it came to pass that there was no contention among all the people, in all the land; but there were mighty miracles wrought among the disciples of Jesus."[49]

CHAPTER EIGHT

TYPES AND SHADOWS: ALL THINGS ARE THE TYPIFYING OF CHRIST

ephi testified that "all things which have been given of God from the beginning of the world, unto man, are the typifying of [Christ]."[1] The literary evidence of that is seen throughout the holy scriptures, with the Book of Mormon containing some of the most well-developed of those parables, metaphors, analogies, and allegories.

One image that has at least three variations in the Book of Mormon is the tree, a symbol through which Christ is seen as restoring and redeeming the human family by the fruitfulness of his love.

THE TREE OF LIFE

The reader finds the first manifestation of the symbolic Christ in the vision of the Tree of Life, which Lehi documented in 1 Nephi 8 and which was further explained in the vision that Nephi received shortly thereafter.[2] In Lehi's dream, "after many hours of darkness" (consider the darkness of an existence bereft of the Light of the World), he came upon a large and spacious field in which he saw "a tree, whose fruit was desirable to make one happy."

After partaking of the fruit, Lehi declared, "I beheld that it was most sweet, above all that I ever before tasted. Yea, and I beheld that the fruit thereof was white, to exceed all the whiteness that I had ever seen.

"And as I partook of the fruit thereof it filled my soul with exceedingly great joy."[3]

Shortly thereafter, as the Spirit revealed to Nephi the explanation of the vision his father had seen, the Spirit made explicit that the Tree of Life and its precious fruit are symbols of Christ's redemption: "This thing shall be given unto thee for a sign, that after thou hast beheld the tree which bore the fruit which thy father tasted, thou shalt also behold a man descending out of heaven. . . . Ye shall bear record that it is the Son of God."[4] Immediately following his vision of the Tree of Life, Nephi had revealed to him Christ's nativity in the Old World with the declaration that the infant in the virgin Mary's arms was "the Lamb of God, yea, even the Son of the Eternal Father!"[5]

Then, with the advent of the infant Jesus in visionary grandeur before this young prophet's eyes, the angel repeatedly took Nephi's mind back to the earlier elements of Lehi's dream, particularly the central image that commanded his father's attention from the beginning and by which his vision has come to be known. It was a tree that was so beautiful that "the beauty thereof [exceeded] . . . all beauty." And it was as desirable, precious, and pure as it was beautiful.

"Knowest thou the meaning of the tree which thy father saw?" the angel asked.

Nephi replied, "Yea, it is the love of God, which sheddeth itself abroad in the hearts of the children of men."[6]

As Nephi's vision continued, he saw the Son of God going forth among the children of men in love and power, and Nephi again declared, "I . . . beheld that the tree of life was a representation of the love of God,"[7] the images of Christ and the tree being inextricably linked.

The echo to the modern reader through all of this is, of course, John's apostolic declaration of the greatness of the Father's gift in offering the life of his Firstborn child to redeem the rest of the human family: "For God so loved the world, that he gave his only begotten Son. . . ."[8] The life, mission, and atonement of Christ are the ultimate manifestations of the Tree of Life, the fruit of the gospel, the love of God, which "sheddeth itself abroad in the hearts of the children of men."

The elements of this allegory are essentially the same as those in the Parable of the Sower—or more accurately the Parable of the Soils—in Matthew 13. Just as there were four different soils of varying receptivity to the gospel of Christ in this New Testament parable, so too were the same four types of people outlined in the vision of the Tree of Life. Least receptive, paralleling the seeds that fell by the wayside, were the multitudes who filled the great and spacious building, mocking, scoffing, and pointing the finger of scorn at those who sought the Tree of Life. Some of these, blindly seeking the building and the worldly values it represented, never reached their telestial goal but were drowned in the depths of the river or were lost from view, wandering in strange roads.

The next group, comparable to the seed that was sown upon stony places and scorched by the sun, were those who had started toward the Tree of Life but had done little more. These "did come forth, and commence in the path" that led to the tree Lehi saw, but when a mist of temptation and darkness arose, they lost their way and were lost.[9]

In some ways the third group is the most pitiable of all, the element of the vision corresponding to the seed that was sown among thorns, which choked off the ongoing possibility of Christ-centered living that had actually taken root and begun. In Lehi's vision this group not only started the journey well but by "clinging" to the rod of iron—the eternally reliable word of

God—and pressing forward through the mist of darkness, they actually came unto Christ and did "partake of the fruit of the tree." But after partaking of the joy of the gospel, "they did cast their eyes about as if they were ashamed." They were particularly embarrassed because of those who were pointing at them from the great and spacious building, mocking and scoffing at their faith. Because of this social scorn, "they fell away into forbidden paths and were lost."[10]

Fortunately there is a group, like the seed that fell onto good ground, that savored the fruit of the tree (Christ and his gospel) and remained faithful. These included Lehi and Sariah, their sons Sam and Nephi, and "other multitudes" that "caught hold of the end of the rod of iron; and . . . did press their way forward, continually holding fast to the rod of iron, until they came forth and fell down and partook of the fruit of the tree."[11]

Thus, at the very outset of the Book of Mormon, in its first fully developed allegory, Christ is portrayed as the source of eternal life and joy, the living evidence of divine love, and the means whereby God will fulfill his covenant with the house of Israel and indeed the entire family of man, returning them to all their eternal promises.

THE OLIVE TREE

At the conclusion of the vision, Lehi (and then Nephi) taught more of the love of God by continuing the allegory of the tree, shifting it from the Tree of Life to the even more extensively developed image of the olive tree. Throughout the Book of Mormon, the olive tree is the central figure for Israelite history, including the Lord's effort to redeem Israel, both individually and collectively. Here, very early in the Book of Mormon, it is noted that Israel's natural branches would be broken off and scattered, then later grafted back into their own true heritage. At its most important level of interpretation this meant, as Lehi taught, that all of the house of Israel would come "to the knowledge of the true Messiah, their Lord and their Redeemer,"[12] truly a foundational teaching of the Book of Mormon.

Nephi's less perceptive and less receptive brothers, however, could not understand this symbolic imagery. With waning patience, Nephi continued his father's teaching and sketched for his brothers the history of Israel as an olive tree from which branches are broken off, scattered, and eventually grafted back in, noting (as did his father) that the life and mission of the Messiah are the keys to the meaning of this tree. It would be the gospel of Jesus Christ, he explained, that would teach the house of Israel "they are the covenant people of the Lord," and they would return "to the knowledge of the gospel of their Redeemer . . . and the very points of his doctrine, that they may know how to come unto him and be saved."[13]

This same metaphor—Christ as the source of Israel's life and safety—is developed even more completely by Zenos, via Jacob, in the longest single allegory (and longest single chapter) in the Book of Mormon.

As one writer has said of this extended symbolic portrayal, "One Jewish legend identifies the tree of life as the olive tree, and with good reason. The olive tree is an evergreen, not a deciduous tree. Its leaves do not seasonally fade nor fall. Through scorching heat and winter cold they are continually rejuvenated. Without cultivation the olive is a wild, unruly, easily corrupted tree. Only after long, patient cultivating, usually eight to ten years, does it begin to yield fruit. Long after that, new shoots often come forth from apparently dead roots. [The appearance of gnarled trunks gives] the impression of travail—of ancient life and renewing life."[14]

As Lehi himself taught, no symbol could serve more powerfully and profoundly of God's expansive, constant, redeeming love—including especially the love represented in the gift of his Only Begotten Son—than does the olive tree. The oil from the olive vineyards was everywhere present in ancient Israel, even as it is today. It is a staple in every kitchen for cooking and on every table for seasoning. It serves medicinally as an antidote for poison and an ointment for pain. It is burned for light in the smallest of lamps and for fuel in the largest of homes. In more sacred purposes it is used in anointing the sick, in purification and sacrifice, and in the consecration of priests and kings. As it was for Noah, so today is the olive branch a symbol of peace—with its obvious typological source in the Prince of Peace.

Olive oil is still used in the careful preparation of the paschal lamb at the Feast of the Passover. Christ ascended from and will return to his beloved Mount of Olives. Gethsemane is literally the "garden of the oil press." Christ is ultimately the Anointed One. Surely the majesty of Christ is inextricably linked with the olive grove, and no teaching explores that symbolism more profoundly than the Book of Mormon.

In Zenos' allegory as retold by Jacob, the Lord of the vineyard works almost desperately (certainly with frequent frustration and tears) to cultivate, protect, preserve, reclaim, and restore the trees of his vineyard. As with most symbols, there are multiple levels of meaning in this parable, with the vineyard representing at least (1) the individual child of God, (2) the House of Israel, and (3) the entire family of man. But the essential element in this story is Christ and his redemptive atonement, just as it was in Lehi's dream of the Tree of Life and the discourse Nephi gave his brothers on the meaning of that dream.

In this context it is instructive to note that Jacob said he gave this teaching from Zenos to "unfold [a] mystery unto you," the mystery of how the great stone of Christ, over which the Jews repeatedly stumbled and which they decidedly rejected, would in the end be the last and only sure stone foundation upon which the Jews could and would eventually build. Whatever other applications it may have—and it has several—this allegory as recounted by Jacob is from the outset intended to be about Christ, the "head of their corner."[15]

Even as the Lord of the vineyard and his workers strive to bolster, prune, purify, and otherwise make productive their trees in what amounts to a one-chapter historical sketch of the scattering and gathering of Israel, the deeper meaning of the Atonement undergirds and overarches their labors. In spite of cuttings and graftings and nourishings that mix and mingle trees in virtually all parts of the vineyard, it is bringing them back to their source that is the principal theme of this allegory. Returning, repenting, reuniting—at-one-ment—this is the message throughout.

That this allegory is explicitly intended to be linked with and serve as an extension of Lehi's vision of Christ as Tree of Life is underscored in Jacob's phrases that the fruit of the olive tree is "most precious above all other fruit" and "most precious unto him from the beginning"—the very language used by Lehi and Nephi in their teachings.[16] At least fifteen times the Lord of the vineyard expresses a desire to bring the vineyard and its harvest to his "own self," and he laments no less than eight times, "It grieveth me that I should lose this tree."[17] One student of the allegory says it should take its place beside the parable of the prodigal son, inasmuch as both stories "make the Lord's mercy so movingly memorable."[18]

Clearly this at-one-ment is hard, demanding, and, at times, deeply painful work, as the work of redemption always is. There is digging and dunging. There is watering and nourishing and pruning. And there is always the endless approaches to grafting—all to one saving end, that the trees of the vineyard would "thrive exceedingly" and become "one body; . . . the fruits [being] equal," with the Lord of the vineyard having "preserved unto himself the . . . fruit."[19] From all the distant places of sin and alienation in which the children of the Father find themselves, it has always been the work of Christ (and his disciples) in every dispensation to gather them, heal them, and unite them with their Master.

In his concluding commentary on the allegory, Jacob made explicit what Zenos taught in parable, concluding the answer to the "mystery" of Christ's redemption of disobedient Israel (mankind) that prompted the telling of this tale:

"How merciful is our God unto us," he said, "for he remembereth the house of Israel, both roots and branches; and he stretches forth his hands unto them all the day long; . . . as many as will not harden their hearts shall be saved in the kingdom of God. . . .

"Cleave unto God as he cleaveth unto you. And while his arm of mercy is extended towards you in the light of the day, harden not your hearts."

Do not, Jacob pleaded with his people in a cry that rings down through time to the family of mankind, "reject all the words which have been spoken concerning Christ."[20]

THE SEED, THE STAFF, AND THE CROSS

The third image of the tree in the Book of Mormon is the recreated image of Moses raising a serpent upon a staff (tree) to which men should look to be healed, with the significant additional element of Alma's great discourse on the seed of faith and its developing into the mature Tree of Life. Nephi reintroduced[21] this well-known Old Testament account[22] written upon the brass plates with this reference:

"And now, my brethren, I have spoken plainly that ye cannot err. And as the Lord God liveth that brought Israel up out of the land of Egypt, and gave unto Moses power that he should

heal the nations after they had been bitten by the poisonous serpents, if they would cast their eyes unto the serpent which he did
raise up before them . . . ; yea, behold I say unto you, that as
these things are true, and as the Lord God liveth, there is none
other name given under heaven save it be this Jesus Christ, of
which I have spoken, whereby man can be saved."[23]

Later, Nephi, son of Helaman, would testify against the corrupt judges of his day:

"Behold, ye not only deny my words, but ye also deny all the
words which have been spoken by our fathers, and also the
words which were spoken by this man, Moses, who had such
great power given unto him, yea, the words which he hath spoken concerning the coming of the Messiah.

"Yea, did he not bear record that the Son of God should
come? And as he lifted up the brazen serpent in the wilderness,
even so shall he be lifted up who should come.

"And as many as should look upon that serpent should live,
even so as many as should look upon the Son of God with faith,
having a contrite spirit, might live, even unto that life which is
eternal."[24]

This doctrine of the tree as salvation, taught early and late in
the Book of Mormon, has its most distinct development by Alma
and Amulek in a remarkable example of doctrinal team-teaching
that starts out with faith in the word of God as a seed and ends
up with faith in the Word of God as a tree of life.

In Alma 32 that prophet says: "Now, we will compare the
word unto a seed. Now, if ye give place, that a seed may be
planted in your heart, behold, if it be a true seed, or a good seed,
if ye do not cast it out by your unbelief, that ye will resist the
Spirit of the Lord, behold, it will begin to swell within your
breasts; and when you feel these swelling motions, ye will begin
to say within yourselves . . . the word is good, for it beginneth to
enlarge my soul; yea, it beginneth to enlighten my understand-

ing, yea, it *beginneth to be delicious to me.* [Compare Lehi's response to the fruit of the tree of life.[25]] . . .

"But behold, as the seed swelleth, and sprouteth, and beginneth to grow . . . ye know that the word hath swelled your souls, and ye also know that it hath sprouted up, that your understanding doth begin to be enlightened, and your mind doth begin to expand."[26]

Here the seed—the word of God—is moving toward full stature as the Word of God. Notice at this stage of the "experiment" the seed has developed into a growing tree:

"And behold, as the tree beginneth to grow, ye will say: Let us nourish it with great care, that it may get root, that it may grow up, and bring forth fruit unto us. . . .

"But if ye neglect the tree, and take no thought for its nourishment, behold it will not get any root; and when the heat of the sun cometh and scorcheth it, because it hath no root it withers away, and you pluck it up and cast it out.

"Now, this is not because the seed was not good, neither is it because the fruit thereof would not be desirable; but it is because your ground is barren, and ye will not nourish the tree, therefore ye cannot have the fruit thereof. [Note the echoes from the Parable of the Soils.]

"And thus, if ye will not nourish the word, looking forward with an eye of faith to the fruit thereof, ye can never pluck of the fruit of the tree of life.

"But if ye will nourish the word, yea, nourish the tree as it beginneth to grow, by your faith with great diligence, and with patience, looking forward to the fruit thereof, it shall take root; and behold it shall be a tree springing up unto everlasting life."

At this point the key phrases of "precious," "sweet," "white," and "pure" fruit—phrases originating with Lehi's vision—are again introduced.

"And because of your diligence and your faith and your

patience with the word in nourishing it, that it may take root in you, behold, by and by ye shall pluck the fruit thereof, which is most precious, which is sweet above all that is sweet, and which is white above all that is white, yea, and pure above all that is pure; and ye shall feast upon this fruit even until ye are filled, that ye hunger not, neither shall ye thirst.

"Then, my brethren, ye shall reap the rewards of your faith, and your diligence, and patience, and long-suffering, waiting for the tree to bring forth fruit unto you."[27]

In this brilliant discourse, Alma moves the reader from a general commentary on faith in the seedlike word of God to a focused discourse on faith in Christ as the Word of God, grown to a fruit-bearing tree, a tree whose fruit is exactly that of Lehi's earlier perception of Christ's love, "which is most precious, which is sweet above all that is sweet, and which is white above all that is white, yea, and pure above all that is pure; and ye shall feast upon [the gospel of Christ] even until ye are filled, that ye hunger not, neither shall ye thirst."[28] Christ is the bread of life, the living water, the true vine. Christ is the seed, the tree, and the fruit of eternal life.

But the profound and central Tree of Life imagery in this discourse is lost, or at least greatly diminished, if the reader does not follow it on into the next two chapters of the Book of Mormon.

In Alma 33, Alma quoted Zenos (source for the allegory of the olive tree) and Zenock on the role of Christ in rewarding faith, then focused on the fully developed image of Christ as Tree of Life.

"Behold, he [Christ] was spoken of by Moses; yea, and behold a type was raised up in the wilderness, that whosoever would look upon it might live. And many did look and live. . . .

"O my brethren . . . cast about your eyes and begin to believe in the Son of God, that he will come to redeem his people, and that he shall suffer and die to atone for their sins; and that he shall rise again from the dead, which shall bring to pass the resurrection, that all men shall stand before him, to be judged at the last and judgment day, according to their works.

"And now, my brethren, I desire that ye shall plant this word in your hearts, and as it beginneth to swell even so nourish it by your faith. And behold, it will become a tree, springing up in you unto everlasting life. And then may God grant unto you that your burdens may be light, through the joy of his Son."[29]

At this point Amulek, the newly involved member and even newer missionary, picked up the theme begun by his companion, saying in prelude to a powerful discourse on the Atonement:

"My brethren, I think that it is impossible that ye should be ignorant of the things which have been spoken concerning the coming of Christ, who is taught by us to be the Son of God. . . .

"Have . . . faith . . . to plant the word in your hearts, that ye may try the experiment of its goodness."[30]

Thus ends a tripartite theme beginning with Lehi's dream of the Tree of Life, running through Jacob's (Zenos') allegory of the tame and wild olive trees, and concluding with Alma's imagery of the seed that grows to a tree bearing fruit most precious, sweet, white, and pure. Through it all reigns Christ, "whom ye slew and hanged on a tree," to whom if men will look, they will be saved.[31]

Of course, Christ himself would crown this uplifting doctrine with his own declaration:

"And my Father sent me that I might be lifted up upon the cross; and after that I had been lifted up upon the cross, that I might draw all men unto me, that as I have been lifted up by men even so should men be lifted up by the Father. . . .

"And for this cause have I been lifted up; therefore, according to the power of the Father I will draw all men unto me."[32]

Abinadi

The Book of Mormon prophet who probably thought about scriptural symbolism and taught it more effectively than any other is Abinadi. Very early he warned King Noah that whatever he would do to Abinadi would be "a type and a shadow of things which are to come"[33]—and indeed it was.

Abinadi also stressed that the performances and ordinances of the law of Moses "were types of things to come"[34] and shadows "of those things which are to come."[35] But the most striking symbolic statement Abinadi ever made was his own living prefiguration of Christ.

Consider these foreshadowing links and parallel possibilities between Abinadi, the first Book of Mormon martyr, and Christ, the great and last sacrifice.

Abinadi	*Type/Shadow*	*Christ*
Mosiah 11:20	Called to preach repentance to those sinning	Matthew 9:13
Mosiah 11:21–23; 12:1–8	To deny message was to be afflicted by the hand of enemies and brought into bondage	Matthew 23:37–38; 24:3–51
Mosiah 11:20–25	Denounced unbelievers in public discourse	Matthew 2:39
Mosiah 12:9	Stood alone against accusers	Matthew 26:56

Abinadi	Type/Shadow	Christ
Mosiah 12:17–18	Bound and taken before religious priests and political ruler	John 18:12–40
Mosiah 12:19	Cross-examined	Matthew 26:59–60
Mosiah 13:1	Dismissed as mad	John 10:20
Mosiah 13:6	Spoke with power and authority	Matthew 7:28–29
Mosiah 13:7	Could not be slain until message/mission was completed	John 10:17–18
Mosiah 17:6	Three-day imprisonment (entombment)	Luke 24:4–8, 46
Mosiah 17:8	Condemned for blasphemy	Matthew 26:63–66
Mosiah 17:9	Would not recall words	Matthew 27:12–14
Mosiah 17:10	Innocent blood	Matthew 27:24
Mosiah 17:11–12	Leader tempted to release him but yielded to detractors and delivered him to be slain	John 18:4–25

Abinadi is the most extensively developed prophetic prefiguration of Christ in the Book of Mormon and one of the most conspicuously developed types in any of the scriptures. And it is yet another conspicuous irony that he, like Christ, died lamenting that those who claimed a belief in the law of Moses could not recognize the Messianic teachings—to say nothing of the Messiah himself—toward which that law in its purity had always been directed.

THE HOLY PRIESTHOOD AFTER THE ORDER OF THE SON OF GOD

We know from modern revelation that the high priesthood is an extension of Jesus Christ himself, a type of his being and power. To the Prophet Joseph Smith it was revealed that the full and proper name of the priesthood is "the Holy Priesthood, after the Order of the Son of God."[36] *Order* is a rich, broad word with several meanings—all instructive in this usage—one of which is "after the fashion or example of; like; similar to."

One obvious way in which Christ is like the priesthood that bears his name is in his eternal nature. The priesthood is, we are told, "without beginning of days or end of years, being prepared from eternity to all eternity, according to [God's] foreknowledge of all things."[37] Christ, who was made a high priest at the hand of his Father,[38] was also described as "without beginning of days or end of years, who is full of grace, equity, and truth."[39]

Clearly there are many other parallels between Christ and the priesthood, but an equally provocative contribution to the typology of the Book of Mormon is the way in which this direct link between Christ and the priesthood is extended to all who follow Christ and are ordained to the priesthood. The reason for every man's ordination to the priesthood, with its inextricable connection to Christ, is spelled out by Alma in a discourse on the symbolic significance of the priesthood.

Preaching to Zeezrom and those at Ammonihah he said, "I would that ye should remember that the Lord God ordained priests, after his holy order, which was after the order of his Son, to teach these things unto the people.

"And those priests were ordained after the order of his Son, in a manner that thereby the people might know in what manner to look forward to his Son for redemption. . . .

"Now these ordinances were given after this manner, that thereby the people might look forward on the Son of God, *it being a type of his order* . . . and this that they might look forward to him for a remission of their sins."[40]

Then Alma gave this precise description of the "manner" in which the priests of old were ordained. These men (and certainly Jesus) were:

- called and prepared from the foundation of the world.[41]

- called according to the foreknowledge of God.[42]

- called on account of their exceeding faith, good works, and righteousness before God.[43]

- called because they had not hardened their hearts or blinded their minds.[44]

- free to choose good or evil, and they chose good.[45]

- called to teach God's commandments to the children of men.[46]

- ordained with a holy ordinance.[47]

- made high priests forever.[48]

- sanctified, with their garments washed white through the blood of the Lamb.[49]

- unable to look upon sin save it were with abhorrence.[50]

- made pure and ushered into the rest of God.[51]

Considering these analogous links between men and the divine, we can only imagine what the Christlike qualities of Melchizedek must have been for his to be the name substituted for "the Holy Priesthood, after the Order of the Son of God." He surely would have to reflect all the typological strengths expected of any priesthood bearer (see above) but undoubtedly would have additional Christlike qualities beyond that.

Alma pleaded with the men of Ammonihah, "Humble yourselves even as the people in the days of Melchizedek, who was also a high priest after this same order which I have spoken, who also took upon him the high priesthood forever."[52] Then he proceeded to tell more about Melchizedek than is known anywhere else in scripture. Note the explicit foreshadowing of Christ:

- He was king over the land of Salem (Jeru-salem).[53]

- His people had waxed strong in iniquity and abomination, had all gone astray, were full of all manner of wickedness.[54]

- He exercised faith in spite of such opposition.[55]

- He received the "office of the high priesthood according to the holy order of God."[56]

- He preached repentance unto his people.[57]

- He established peace and was therefore called the prince of peace.[58]

- He reigned under his father.[59]

Alma noted that there were many prominent figures before and after Melchizedek, "but none were greater; therefore, of him they have more particularly made mention."[60]

Surely no greater tribute or more generous adulation could be mentioned than to be so much like the Son of God that one's name could be substituted for his in the title of the most powerful force in the universe—the Holy Priesthood, after the Order of the Son of God.

The Liahona

A number of other references to types of Christ are found in the Book of Mormon, including Jacob's explicit comparison of

Abraham and Isaac to the Father and the Son.[61] Perhaps just one other extended discussion will suffice on this subject.

When Lehi and his family were fleeing the impending captivity and destruction of Jerusalem, the Lord provided a "ball of curious workmanship," a compasslike instrument made of brass in which were two spindles, one of which "pointed the way whither [they] should go into the wilderness,"[62] while the other was perhaps fixed on some known, permanent direction (North? Jerusalem?).

Clearly this instrument was much more than a compass, however, because it also carried written information. At one point Lehi "beheld the things which were written upon the ball," and "he did fear and tremble exceedingly."[63] That suggests a message of significance and—we would assume—some length. The words, like the pointers, "did work [and appear] according to the faith and diligence and heed which we did give unto them," Nephi recorded. The writing was "a new writing, which was plain to be read, which did give us understanding concerning the ways of the Lord; and it was written and changed from time to time, according to the faith and diligence which we gave unto it."[64]

Later, Alma saw a type and shadow of Christ in this director that marked the way, the truth, and ultimately the life for its followers. As he told his son Helaman, "It was prepared to show unto our fathers the course which they should travel in the wilderness.

"And it did work for them according to their faith in God; therefore, if they had faith to believe that God could cause that those spindles should point the way they should go, behold, it was done; therefore they had this miracle, and also many other miracles wrought by the power of God, day by day. . . .

"[But] they were slothful, and forgot to exercise their faith and diligence and then those marvelous works ceased, and they did not progress in their journey."[65]

"And now, my son," Alma concluded, "I would that ye should understand that *these things are not without a shadow;* for as our fathers were slothful to give heed to this compass (now these things were temporal) they did not prosper; even so it is with things which are spiritual.

"For behold, it is as easy to give heed to the word of Christ, which will point to you a straight course to eternal bliss, as it was for our fathers to give heed to this compass, which would point unto them a straight course to the promised land.

"And now I say, *is there not a type in this thing?* For just as surely as this director did bring our fathers, by following its course, to the promised land, shall the words of Christ, if we follow their course, carry us beyond this vale of sorrow into a far better land of promise.[66]

The call of the Book of Mormon is always "Look that ye might live." Whether that is to look up to a staff held aloft by a prophet of God or down upon a personal, sphere-like Liahona, it is the same. They mark the way of eternal life. Indeed, they are similitudes of the Way of Eternal Life. All things are the typifying of Christ.

CHAPTER NINE

THE FATHER AND THE SON

The first Article of Faith of The Church of Jesus Christ of Latter-day Saints reads, "We believe in God, the Eternal Father, and in His Son, Jesus Christ, and in the Holy Ghost." That doctrine is enhanced in section 130:22 of the Doctrine and Covenants: "The Father has a body of flesh and bones as tangible as man's; the Son also; but the Holy Ghost has not a body of flesh and bones, but is a personage of Spirit."

The Prophet Joseph Smith added, "I have always declared God to be a distinct personage, Jesus Christ a separate and distinct personage from God the Father, and that the Holy Ghost was a distinct personage and a Spirit: and these three constitute three distinct personages and three Gods."[1]

This doctrine reaffirms what is clearly taught in all of the biblical experience, both Old Testament and New, about the separate and distinct nature of these three divine beings. The account written by Matthew of the baptism of Jesus makes an unequivocal case for the separation in both place and performance of the Father, the Son, and the Holy Ghost. Of Christ's baptism at the hands of John, he recorded: "Jesus, when he was baptized, went up straightway out of the water: and, lo, the heavens were opened unto him, and he saw the Spirit of God descending like a dove, and lighting upon him: and lo a voice from heaven, saying, This is my beloved Son, in whom I am well pleased."[2]

Of course, the most compelling evidence in modern times comes from the Sacred Grove, wherein Joseph Smith, under the revelatory influence of the Holy Ghost, saw the Father and Son in celestial splendor. He later wrote, "When the light rested upon me I saw two Personages, whose brightness and glory defy all description, standing above me in the air. One of them spake unto me, calling me by name and said, pointing to the other—*This is My Beloved Son. Hear Him!*"[3]

The Book of Mormon makes an additional contribution to our understanding of the Father and Son as separate and distinct beings, the most pervasive of which are Christ's urgent and longing prayers to his Father recorded in 3 Nephi. These are moving supplications from a Son to his Father that establish firmly and forever that these two are separate and distinct individuals who communicate and converse with each other just as any other Father and Son would.

UNITY OF THE GODHEAD

Having stressed the distinctiveness of the members of the Godhead and affirmed the fundamental and essential doctrine behind it, we can now note a clear and consistent theme running through the Book of Mormon that indicates important ways in which the Father and the Son are united for their common purposes and virtually synonymous in their interchangeable roles and functions. Indeed, their unity is the primary fact of their relationship; their distinctiveness seems to exist only in their corporeal separateness.

This unity between the Father and the Son catches the eye of the reader even before entering the Book of Mormon text. The title page of the Book of Mormon describes one of the purposes of this scripture as "the convincing of the Jew and Gentile that JESUS is the CHRIST, the ETERNAL GOD." Following that, Oliver Cowdery, David Whitmer, and Martin Harris, the three latter-day witnesses of the coming forth of the Book of Mormon, conclude their marvelous testimony with this conspicuous phrase: "And the honor be to the Father, and to the Son, and to the Holy Ghost, which is one God. Amen."

Many such declarations then appear throughout the Book of Mormon. In Nephi's foundational sermon on the "doctrine of Christ," the sermon in which Nephi recorded the distinct utterances of the Father and the Son regarding Christ's baptism, he concluded with this declaration about the necessity of remaining "steadfast in Christ":

"And now, behold, my beloved brethren, this is the way; and there is none other way nor name given under heaven whereby man can be saved in the kingdom of God. And now, behold, this is the doctrine of Christ, and the only and true doctrine of the Father, and of the Son, and of the Holy Ghost, which is one God, without end. Amen."[4]

When Amulek testified to Zeezrom about the nature and role of Christ—including Christ's physical distinction from the Father—he concluded with this bold assertion about the universality of the Resurrection: "[All] shall be brought and be arraigned before the bar of Christ the Son, and God the Father, and the Holy Spirit, which is one Eternal God, to be judged according to their works, whether they be good or whether they be evil."[5]

In his introductory message to the Nephites upon his appearance in the New World, the Savior made an urgent appeal for unity among the members, particularly regarding the doctrine of baptism. To emphasize this need he noted the unity of the Godhood: "After this manner shall ye baptize in my name; for behold, verily I say unto you, that the Father, and the Son, and the Holy Ghost are one; and I am in the Father, and the Father in me, and the Father and I are one. . . . The Father, and I, and the Holy Ghost are one."[6]

For one final example we note Mormon's last words, in which he gave this testimony of the Savior to any who will hear his voice:

"Know ye that ye must come to the knowledge of your fathers, and repent of all your sins and iniquities, and believe in Jesus Christ, that he is the Son of God, and that he was slain by the Jews, and by the power of the Father he hath risen again, whereby he hath gained the victory over the grave; and also in him is the sting of death swallowed up.

"And he bringeth to pass the resurrection of the dead, whereby man must be raised to stand before his judgment-seat.

"And he hath brought to pass the redemption of the world, whereby he that is found guiltless before him at the judgment day hath it given unto him to dwell in the presence of God in his kingdom, to sing ceaseless praises with the choirs above, unto the Father, and unto the Son, and unto the Holy Ghost, which are one God, in a state of happiness which hath no end."[7]

The doctrine of Christ with roles as a Father as well as as a Son was the source of some confusion and contention in Book of Mormon times. One of the most skillful and cunning of adversaries in the Book of Mormon (until his conversion) was Zeezrom. He used the complexity of this doctrine to try to trap new missionary Amulek.

With a skillful line of reasoning indicative of his training in the law, Zeezrom asked a series of questions leading to his ultimate question and potentially troublesome snare: "Is the Son of God the very Eternal Father?"[8]

Amulek, fearless and forthright in his answer, responded with a boldness worthy of his interrogator: "Yea, he is the very

Eternal Father of heaven and of earth, and all things which in them are; he is the beginning and the end, the first and the last;

"And he shall come into the world to redeem his people; and he shall take upon him the transgressions of those who believe on his name; and these are they that shall have eternal life, and salvation cometh to none else."[9]

This relationship among members of the Godhead deserves some brief consideration.

CHRIST IN THE ROLE OF FATHER

There are obvious ways in which Jesus, as literal offspring of the Father, is one with Him. For one thing, he is the spiritual son of God, the firstborn of the Father's spirit children. Following that, he was to become the physical son of God, the Only Begotten of the Father in the Flesh. And as the Book of Mormon prophet Abinadi makes uniquely clear, Christ is the Son of God because he subjected his will to the will of his Father.[10] No extensive explanation of these roles for Christ-as-Son is required for those who have read the exhaustive scriptural references to such in the Standard Works.

But what may at first seem less obvious is also taught in the scriptures—that there are ways in which Christ is so united with his Father that in some assignments he rightfully plays a fatherly role and rightfully bears the title of Father in doing so.

This fundamental—and admittedly deep—doctrine of the Son-as-Father is illuminated more definitively in the Book of Mormon than in any other revelation ever given to man. Repeated references in this sacred record teach that, under the direction of and with authority given by the Father (Elohim), the Son (Jehovah/Jesus) may act as the Father in several ways.

First and foremost, as Abinadi taught, Christ was "conceived by the power of God"[11] and therefore has the powers of the

Father within him. In addition to that divine lineal relationship, Christ also acts as the Father in that he is the Creator of heaven and earth, is the father of our spiritual rebirth and salvation, and is faithful in honoring—and therefore claiming the power of— the will of his Father above that of his own will. Because of this inseparable relationship and uncompromised trust between them, Christ can at any time and in any place speak and act for the Father by virtue of the "divine investiture of authority" the Father has given him.[12]

Let us consider briefly the contribution the Book of Mormon makes toward our understanding of this divine unity.

CHRIST AS HEIR OF THE FATHER

The first of these relationships—the power and authority of Christ's literal inheritance from the Father, both physically and spiritually, as his firstborn and only begotten child in the flesh— was noted by Abinadi. To Christ more than any other in time or eternity it is said, "All that [the] Father hath shall be given unto him,"[13] including authority to act for the Father under the Father's direction.

CHRIST AS FATHER OF CREATION

Without attempting to be exhaustive, we should note at least several major Book of Mormon teachings on Christ-as-Creator.

King Benjamin said of the coming of Christ, "For behold, the time cometh, and is not far distant, that with power, the Lord Omnipotent who reigneth, who was, and is from all eternity to all eternity, shall come down from heaven among the children of men, and shall dwell in a tabernacle of clay. . . .

"And he shall be called Jesus Christ, the Son of God, the Father of heaven and earth, the Creator of all things from the beginning; and his mother shall be called Mary."[14]

He concluded with this exhortation:

"Therefore, I would that ye should be steadfast and immovable, always abounding in good works, that Christ, the Lord God Omnipotent, may seal you his, that you may be brought to heaven, that ye may have everlasting salvation and eternal life, through the wisdom, and power, and justice, and mercy of him who created all things, in heaven and in earth, who is God above all."[15]

The power of that message had such an impact on the people that they cried aloud with one voice,

"O have mercy, and apply the atoning blood of Christ that we may receive forgiveness of our sins, and our hearts may be purified; for we believe in Jesus Christ, the Son of God, who created heaven and earth, and all things; who shall come down among the children of men."[16]

Speaking by direct revelation to Alma, the premortal Christ indicated that he is at liberty to "freely forgive" those who believe in his name and enter his Church through the spirit of repentance and the waters of baptism:

"For it is I that taketh upon me the sins of the world; for it is I that hath created them; and it is I that granteth unto him that believeth unto the end a place at my right hand."[17]

When Alma the Younger experienced his great conversion, he found himself "born of the Spirit," and he said of that process,

"I rejected my Redeemer, and denied that which had been spoken of by our fathers; but now that they may foresee that he will come, and that he remembereth every creature of his creating, he will make himself manifest unto all.

"Yea, every knee shall bow, and every tongue confess before him. Yea, even at the last day, when all men shall stand to be judged of him, then shall they confess that he is God."[18]

Samuel the Lamanite prophesied "that ye might know of the coming of Jesus Christ, the Son of God, the Father of heaven and of earth, the Creator of all things from the beginning."[19] The Savior himself made this triumphant announcement as he appeared to the Nephites in the New World:

"Behold, I am Jesus Christ the Son of God. I created the heavens and the earth, and all things that in them are. I was with the Father from the beginning. I am in the Father, and the Father in me; and in me hath the Father glorified his name."[20]

Clearly, Christ—under the direction of his Father—is the Father of creation, the Creator of heaven and earth and all things that in them are.

CHRIST AS FATHER OF SALVATION

Another way Christ is designated as Father in the Book of Mormon is in his role as Father of the Redeemed and Father of the Resurrected.

In his pivotal and doctrinally deep revelation to the brother of Jared, Christ said, "Behold, I am he who was prepared from the foundation of the world to redeem my people. Behold, I am Jesus Christ. I am the Father and the Son. In me shall all mankind have life, and that eternally, even they who shall believe on my name; and they shall become my sons and my daughters."[21]

It is in this role of providing rebirth, of giving new life—eternal life—that Christ is literally the Father of our salvation.

King Benjamin understood that doctrine when he said to those who had received his sermon, expressed belief in Christ, and had covenanted to do the will of God and keep his commandments, "Because of the covenant which ye have made ye shall be called the children of Christ, his sons, and his daughters; for behold, this day he hath spiritually begotten you; for ye say that your hearts are changed through faith on his name; therefore, ye are born of him and have become his sons and his daughters."[22]

In his magnificent pre-advent sermon on Christ, Abinadi expanded this concept, speaking specifically of the "seed" of Christ:

"Who shall declare his generation? Behold, I say unto you, that when his soul has been made an offering for sin he shall see his seed. And now what say ye? And who shall be his seed?

"Behold I say unto you, that whosoever has heard the words of the prophets, yea, all the holy prophets who have prophesied concerning the coming of the Lord—I say unto you, that all those who have hearkened unto their words, and believed that the Lord would redeem his people, and have looked forward to that day for a remission of their sins, I say unto you, that these are his seed, or they are the heirs of the kingdom of God.

"For these are they whose sins he has borne; these are they for whom he has died, to redeem them from their transgressions. And now, are they not his seed?"[23]

Of course, Alma was one of the great examples of one who claimed the eternal life Christ extends to the penitent, including the rebirth that is involved. Following the three days of his unconsciousness, during which he went through the cleansing of repentance, he said to those who had fasted and prayed for him, "I have repented of my sins, and have been redeemed of the Lord; behold I am born of the Spirit.

"And the Lord said unto me: Marvel not that all mankind, yea, men and women, all nations, kindreds, tongues and people, must be born again; yea, born of God, changed from their carnal and fallen state, to a state of righteousness, being redeemed of God, becoming his sons and daughters;

"And thus they become new creatures; and unless they do this, they can in nowise inherit the kingdom of God. . . .

"Nevertheless, after wading through much tribulation, repenting nigh unto death, the Lord in mercy hath seen fit to snatch me out of an everlasting burning, and I am born of God."[24]

Later, in recounting that painful personal experience to his son Helaman, Alma said of his moment of greatest anguish, "I cried within my heart: O Jesus, thou Son of God, have mercy on me, who am in the gall of bitterness, and am encircled about by the everlasting chains of death.

"And now, behold, when I thought this, I could remember my pains no more; yea, I was harrowed up by the memory of my sins no more.

"And oh, what joy, and what marvelous light I did behold; yea, my soul was filled with joy as exceeding as was my pain! . . .

"My limbs did receive their strength again, and I stood upon my feet, and did manifest unto the people that *I had been born of God.*

"Yea, and from that time even until now, I have labored without ceasing, that I might bring souls unto repentance; that I might bring them to taste of the exceeding joy of which I did taste; *that they might also be born of God,* and be filled with the Holy Ghost.

"Yea, and now behold, O my son, the Lord doth give me exceedingly great joy in the fruit of my labors;

"For because of the word which he has imparted unto me, behold, *many have been born of God,* and have tasted as I have tasted, and have seen eye to eye as I have seen; therefore they do know of these things of which I have spoken, as I do know; and the knowledge which I have is of God."[25]

This profound personal experience of spiritual rebirth is, of course, what led Alma to plead for it among others. To his brethren at Zarahemla he asked, "Have ye spiritually been born of God? Have ye received his image in your countenances? Have ye experienced this mighty change in your hearts?"[26] Much of the Book of Mormon is directed toward provoking such a rebirth in its readers.

SUBMITTING THE WILL OF THE SON
TO THE WILL OF THE FATHER

One Book of Mormon prophet—Abinadi—was put to death for teaching, among other things, that Christ could appropriately be called both the Father and the Son.

Before the reader ever gets to the actual account of Abinadi's ministry, Limhi alludes to that experience in his teaching to his people.

Of Limhi's father Noah, and Noah's unholy court, Limhi said, "A prophet of the Lord have they slain; yea, a chosen man of God, who told them of their wickedness and abominations, and prophesied of many things which are to come, yea, even the coming of Christ.

"And because he said unto them that Christ was the God, the Father of all things, and said that he should take upon him the image of man, and it should be the image after which man was created in the beginning; or in other words, he said that man was created after the image of God, and that God should come down among the children of men, and take upon him flesh and blood, and go forth upon the face of the earth—

"And now, because he said this, they did put him to death."[27]

Limhi then introduced Ammon to the record of Zeniff, which contained an account of Abinadi's teachings to Noah. In those teachings Abinadi introduced a fundamental consideration about the relationship of Christ's Fatherhood and Sonship, stressing that "[A] *God himself* shall make [atonement] for the sins and iniquities of his people," that "[A] *God himself* should come down among the children of men, and take upon him the form of man, and go forth in mighty power upon the face of the earth," and that "[A] *God himself* shall come down among the children of men, and shall redeem his people."[28]

With that introduction Abinadi undertook a deep discussion

of Christ in the roles of both Father and Son. Its complexity requires that it be quoted completely.

"And because he dwelleth in flesh he shall be called the Son of God, and having subjected the flesh to the will of the Father, being the Father and the Son—

"The Father, because he was conceived by the power of God; and the Son, because of the flesh; thus becoming the Father and Son—

"And they are one God, yea, the very Eternal Father of heaven and of earth.

"And thus the flesh becoming subject to the Spirit, or the Son to the Father, being one God, suffereth temptation, and yieldeth not to the temptation, but suffereth himself to be mocked, and scourged, and cast out, and disowned by his people.

"And after all this, after working many mighty miracles among the children of men, he shall be led, yea, even as Isaiah said, as a sheep before the shearer is dumb, so he opened not his mouth.

"Yea, even so he shall be led, crucified, and slain, the flesh becoming subject even unto death, the will of the Son being swallowed up in the will of the Father.

"And thus God breaketh the bands of death, having gained the victory over death; giving the Son power to make intercession for the children of men—

"Having ascended into heaven, having the bowels of mercy; being filled with compassion towards the children of men; standing betwixt them and justice; having broken the bands of death, taken upon himself their iniquity and their transgressions, having redeemed them, and satisfied the demands of justice."[29]

While that is the most thorough and challenging statement of the Father-Son role played by Christ, particularly as it involves the issue of the flesh versus the spirit, it is not the only reference to it in the Book of Mormon. Lehi said, in his great discussion of the Fall and the Atonement, "How great the importance to make these things known unto the inhabitants of the earth, that they may know that there is no flesh that can dwell in the presence of God, save it be through the merits, and mercy, and grace of the Holy Messiah, who layeth down his life according to the flesh, and taketh it again by the power of the Spirit, that he may bring to pass the resurrection of the dead, being the first that should rise."[30]

Later in that same sermon, he spoke of "the will of the flesh and the evil which is therein, which giveth the spirit of the devil power to captivate, to bring you down to hell, that he may reign over you in his own kingdom"—this as opposed to "the will of [the] Holy Spirit," which directs us to choose eternal life and be faithful to the commandments.[31]

At the time of Christ's annunciation of his own birth in the Old World, he said to Nephi,

"Behold, I come unto my own, to fulfil all things which I have made known unto the children of men from the foundation of the world, and to do the will, both of the Father and of the Son—of the Father because of me, and of the Son because of my flesh. And behold, the time is at hand, and this night shall the sign be given."[32]

Intriguingly, the "me" in Christ's reference to himself—his spiritual self—is identified with the Fatherly role, while his flesh is linked with his role as the Son. That is the very doctrine Abinadi taught—that the Father (the spirit) in Christ gave direction and had to be obeyed, while the Son (the flesh) in Christ had to yield and obey.[33]

An overly simplified model of this doctrine as Abinadi gave it might look like this:

Christ in the Roles of

Son	and	Father
• Was born into mortality	and	• Was an heir of immortality
• Dwelt on the earth in the flesh	and	• Lived according to Heaven in the Spirit
• Subjected the flesh to the Spirit and was slain	and	• Saw the spirit triumph over the flesh and broke the bands of death
	—Ultimately—	
• The will of the Son	was swallowed up in	• The will of the Father

Christ, in addition to being both the spiritual and physical Son of God (which in and of itself gave him unarguable, rightful claim upon his Father's virtues), and in addition to acting with divine investiture of authority (both to speak and act in his Father's stead), claimed a major portion of this divine, fatherly power through the fundamental gospel principle of obedience. By his obedience Christ showed the way to godhood to those of us who, although spirit children of God, are not physically begotten of Him and are not invested with the totality of his divine power.

By this doctrine Christ teaches us as mortal men and women that we can be one with the Father in a crucial, fundamental, eternally significant way: We can obey him. We can subject the flesh to the spirit. We can yield our will as children to the will of our Heavenly Father.

It was such yielding and such obedience that brought the mastery of Gethsemane, the victory of Calvary, the triumph of redemption. Surely one of the crucial moments in those awe-filled hours—moments leading to Christ's perfection, fulfillment, and eternal majesty—was the moment the Son in flesh yielded to the Father in Spirit, saying, "Father, if thou be willing, remove this cup from me: nevertheless not my will, but thine, be done"—"The will of the Son being swallowed up in the will of the Father."[34]

So must we all bend "the will of the flesh" to the "will of the Holy Spirit," to use Lehi's language. Because that same issue faces each mortal being and is with everyone throughout mortality, it should not be surprising that it would be among Christ's most exemplary moments.

Christ's final triumph and ultimate assumption of godly powers on the right hand of his Father came *not* because he had a divine parent (although that was essential to the victory over death) and *not* because he was given heavenly authority from the beginning (although that was essential to his divine power) but ultimately because he was, in his own mortal probation, perfectly obedient, perfectly submissive, perfectly loyal to the principle that the spiritual in his life must rule over the physical. That was at the heart of his triumph, and that is a lesson for every accountable man, woman, and child who ever lives. It is a lesson for which Abinadi—and Christ—were willing to die. It is the lesson for which virtually every prophet has given his voice and his life: spirit over flesh; discipline over temptation; devotion over inclination; "the will of the Son being swallowed up in the will of the Father."

ATONEMENT

CHAPTER TEN

THE ATONEMENT

he central fact, the crucial foundation, the chief doctrine, and the greatest expression of divine love in the eternal plan of salvation—truly a "plan of happiness," as Alma called it[1]—is the atonement of the Lord Jesus Christ. Much goes before it and much comes after, but without that pivotal act, that moment of triumph whereby we are made free from the spiritual bondage of sin and the physical chains of the grave, both of which are undeniable deaths, there would be no meaning to the plan of life, and certainly no ultimate happiness in it or after it.

The atonement of Jesus Christ, with its many doctrinal ramifications, constitutes the principal theme of the Book of Mormon. Not surprisingly, the Prophet Joseph Smith, who translated the Book of Mormon and declared it the keystone of our religion, stated that "all other things which pertain to our religion are only appendages" to the atonement of Jesus Christ.[2]

The literal meaning of the word *atonement* is self-evident: at-one-ment, the act of unifying or bringing together what has been separated or estranged. The atonement of Christ was indispensable because of the separating transgression, or fall, of Adam, which brought death into the world. In the words of Moroni, "By

Adam came the fall of man. And because of the fall of man came Jesus Christ . . . ; and because of Jesus Christ came the redemption of man. And because of the redemption of man, . . . they are brought back into the presence of the Lord."[3]

Near the beginning of the Book of Mormon story, Lehi referred to his son Jacob's difficult life (he was the firstborn child during Lehi's "tribulation in the wilderness") as a metaphor for humankind's suffering and affliction (the Fall, the consequence of sin, mortality) prior to redemption and salvation (the Atonement, resurrection, immortality, and eternal life).[4] Such a journey is the basic theme that runs throughout this testament of Jesus Christ. For the temporal challenges of life and the spiritual significance that flows from them, Lehi reassured his son that "the way is prepared from the fall of man, and salvation is free."[5] This echoes the precious doctrine he had earlier communicated to Nephi following Lehi's great vision of Christ's future advent.[6] What follows here is "the way" that was prepared.

THE PREMORTAL PLAN

The scriptural reassurance that such a sequence of fall and atonement was known and prepared for from before the foundation of this world reinforces the inseparable doctrinal relationship between the role of Adam and that of the Lord Jesus Christ. In the great premortal council in heaven, God the Father presided and presented his plan for the mortality and eventual immortality of his children. In this his two principal associates were the premortal Jesus (then known as Jehovah) and the premortal Adam (then known as Michael). The roles of these two were related from the beginning, each having a crucial part to play in providing life to all other children of God—temporal life through Adam and eternal life through Christ.

The fact that their roles are so intertwined led the Apostle

Paul to see them as counterparts to one another, calling them both by the same name: "The first man Adam was made a living soul; the last Adam was made a quickening spirit,"[7] an echo of his teaching to the Romans that Adam was "the figure of [Christ] that was to come."[8]

That this understood and agreed-upon fall of man would lead to the equally understood and agreed-upon atonement of Christ is one of the major contributions the Book of Mormon makes to our understanding of the plan of salvation. Threads remaining in the Bible show how clearly this was understood in ancient times. Peter spoke of Christ as "foreordained before the foundation of the world,"[9] and John described him as "the Lamb slain from the foundation of the world."[10] Nevertheless, much of this doctrine has been lost or expunged from the biblical records. It is therefore of great consequence that the Book of Mormon prophets taught that doctrine in detail and with clarity.

For example, King Benjamin, in his majestic discourse on the Savior, noted that the benefits of the Atonement were "prepared from the foundation of the world for all mankind, which ever were since the fall of Adam, or who are, or who ever shall be, even unto the end of the world."[11]

Later Alma noted, "If it had not been for the plan of redemption, which was laid from the foundation of the world, there could have been no resurrection of the dead; but there was a plan of redemption laid."[12] Aaron, teaching King Lamoni's father, "did expound unto him the scriptures from the creation of Adam, laying the fall of man before him, . . . and also the plan of redemption, which was prepared from the foundation of the world, through Christ, for all whosoever would believe on his name."[13]

Of course, the ultimate declaration of the eternal beginnings of the redemptive plan was given by Christ himself, who, when appearing to the brother of Jared, said, "Behold, I am he who was prepared from the foundation of the world to redeem my people."[14]

All of that provides doctrinal background and context for what Lehi gave as one of the most important and oft-quoted lines of Book of Mormon doctrine, summarizing succinctly the relationship of Adam to Christ, of the Fall to the Atonement: "Adam fell that men might be; and men are, that they might have joy. And the Messiah cometh in the fulness of time, that he may redeem the children of men from the fall."[15]

MORAL AGENCY

Basic to the great eternal plan of how we might come into a mortal world marked by death and still come out of it "alive," so to speak, was the quest for godhood, the search for eternal possibility, promise, and peace. God's premortal children could not become like him and enjoy his breadth of blessings unless they obtained both a physical body and temporal experience in an arena where both good and evil were present. Lehi stressed that for this to be possible, such a temporal experience must be predicated upon moral agency, which includes the moral and intellectual ability to distinguish right from wrong and the attendant freedom to make choices based on that knowledge.

Crucial to a full and effective exercise of moral agency in such a complex world of good and evil is having basic knowledge of the plan of salvation and the truths of the gospel of Jesus Christ, which are fundamental and essential to it. Such knowledge provides at least two things: a standard—eternal verities, if you will—for determining what is right and what is wrong, and an understanding of the consequences, including the eternal consequences, of our actions when such choices are made. Thus Lehi said that for moral agency to be fully efficacious, accountable men, women, and children must be "instructed sufficiently that they know good from evil."[16] Because such knowledge of the way of godliness is so fundamental to the plan of salvation, he cried out for all who know the truth to answer the unending call to teach and bear witness of gospel principles, to receive the joy that comes from making wise choices consistent with them, and to avoid the sorrow that most assuredly awaits all who act in defiance of them:

"How great the importance to make these things known unto the inhabitants of the earth, that they may know that there is no flesh that can dwell in the presence of God, save it be through the merits, and mercy, and grace of the Holy Messiah, who layeth down his life according to the flesh, and taketh it again by the power of the Spirit, that he may bring to pass the resurrection of the dead, being the first that should rise.

"Wherefore, he is the firstfruits unto God, inasmuch as he shall make intercession for all the children of men; and they that believe in him shall be saved.

"And because of the intercession for all, all men come unto God; wherefore, they stand in the presence of him, to be judged of him according to the truth and holiness which is in him."[17]

This agency, which was preserved for humankind in the premortal war in heaven[18] provided that "man . . . should act for himself. . . . The children of men . . . have become free forever, knowing good from evil; to act for themselves and not to be acted upon. . . . They are free to choose liberty and eternal life . . . or to choose captivity and death."[19] Clearly this freedom cannot be fully exercised or made efficacious without sufficient instruction in the consequences of such choices and a knowledge of the redeeming, forgiving atonement of Christ. The Atonement ransoms all who, in making such choices, err and fall short of the glory of God but repent of those errors and cry for the mercy of the Holy Messiah to come upon them. How great the importance to make these things known unto the inhabitants of the earth, indeed.

OPPOSITION IN ALL THINGS

A related principle Lehi introduced as another backdrop to the eternal drama of the Fall and the Atonement is that of opposition, of contending enticements, a concept closely linked with choice and agency. If choice is to exist and agency is to have any meaning, alternatives must be presented. As Lehi phrased it, "It must needs be, that there is an opposition in all things."[20] His reasoning and his vocabulary are clear and to the point. Righteousness has no meaning without the possibility of wickedness. Holiness would hold no delight unless we realized the pain of misery. Good could have no moral meaning if nothing could be considered bad. Even life—the nature and eternal possibilities of which are the subject of the plan of salvation and Lehi's discourse about it—would have no meaning if we knew nothing of the nature and limitations of death.

In short, without opposites and alternatives, "there would have been no purpose in the . . . creation [of human life]."[21] All experiences in time and eternity would have been common, lifeless, indistinguishable—"a compound in one."[22] At the end of this sequence would be the worst realization of all. There could be no happiness because there was no sorrow, and there could be no righteousness because there was no sin. But fortunately, there are happiness, righteousness, eternal life, and God, even as Lehi stresses that those blessings come only at the risk of confronting misery, wickedness, death, and the devil.

THE FALL

These terrible risks of sorrow and death were facts Adam and Eve were willing to face in order that "men might be." But they—like us—were able and willing to venture these only with the knowledge that there would be safety at the end of the day for those who wanted it and lived for it. They were willing to transgress knowingly and consciously (the only way they could "fall" into the consequences of mortality, inasmuch as Elohim certainly could not force innocent parties out of the garden and still be a just God) only because they had a full knowledge of the plan of salvation, which would provide for them a way back from their struggle with death and hell. As Adam would later say, "Blessed be the name of God, for because of my transgression my eyes are opened, and in this life I shall have joy, and again in the flesh I shall see God."[23]

On that same occasion Eve said even more poignantly, "Were it not for our transgression we never should have . . . known good and evil, and the joy of our redemption, and the eternal life which God giveth unto all the obedient."[24]

So Adam and Eve willingly made a choice, choosing the path toward growth and godhood inherent in the fruit of the tree of knowledge of good and evil over the potentially meaningless (at least at that point in their development) tree of life. With the enticement of Lucifer, "that old serpent that did beguile our first parents, which was the cause of their fall," as Abinadi phrased it,[25] they consciously chose to step out of the garden of Eden—a magnificent, terrestrial-like, paradisiacal world—into a fallen, telestial one, a world filled with very unparadisiacal thistles and thorns, sorrow and sin, disease and death.

In doing so, Adam and Eve answered forever the plaintive question that is so often heard: "If there is a God, why is there so much suffering in the world?" The answer to that is we now live in a fallen world filled with opposites, a world in which God is the most powerful but decidedly not the only spiritual influence. As part of the doctrine of opposition, Satan is also at work in the world, and we knew before we came here that he would bring grief and anguish with him. Nevertheless, we (through Adam and Eve) made the conscious choice to live in and endure this mortal sphere of opposition in all things, for only through such an experience was godly progress possible. Adam and Eve—and we—knowingly and lovingly absolved God of the responsibility for the "thorns and thistles" of a fallen world that was personally chosen by us, not capriciously imposed by him. We wanted the chance to become like our heavenly parents, to face suffering and overcome it, to endure sorrow and still live rejoicingly, to confront good and evil and be strong enough to choose the good. In this telestial, mortal world filled with competing voices, enticements, and experiences, we get a lifetime of opportunity to refine and strengthen these virtues.

Understanding this doctrine, Lehi noted that for Adam and Eve to have remained in the garden of Eden would have kept all things "in the same state in which they were after they were created," a situation in which they would have "remained in a state of innocence, having no joy, for they knew no misery; doing no good, for they knew no sin."

But Adam and Eve made their choice for an even more generous reason than those of godly knowledge and personal progress. They did it for the one overriding and commanding reason basic to the entire plan of salvation and all the discussions ever held in all the councils of heaven. They did it "that men might be." Had Adam and Eve never left the garden, Lehi noted, "they would have had no children."[26]

There were, of course, these other benefits just mentioned stemming from the Fall, benefits that are essential and eternal. But they would have been shallow privileges indeed if they had come only to Adam and Eve. No, even the significant blessings of a physical body and the refinement of growth experiences leading to godhood would be pathetic promises if they were not also extended to all of God's spirit children. The privilege of mortality granted to the rest of us is the principal gift given by the fall of Adam and Eve.

Thus, and only with this knowledge, can a student of the

gospel of Jesus Christ grasp the full import of the magnificent line already cited: "Adam fell that men might be." That doctrine, fully understood and thoroughly taught only in the restored gospel, is as important as any taught in the entire Book of Mormon. Without it the world would be ignorant of the true nature of the fall of Adam and Eve, ignorant of their life-giving decision, and ignorant of the unspeakable love they demonstrated for all of God's sons and daughters.

In summation Lehi said, "After Adam and Eve had partaken of the forbidden fruit they were driven out of the garden of Eden, to till the earth.

"*And they have brought forth children; yea, even the family of all the earth.*"[27]

Natural Man

Many things happened in the process of the Fall, including changes that came to the physical bodies of Adam and Eve. For one thing, they fell into "nature," the word becoming something of a synonym for the Adamic process. King Benjamin would say of little children, "As in Adam, *or by nature*, they fall, even so the blood of Christ atoneth for their sins."[28]

Part of the natural world Adam and Eve entered included the addition to their bodies of blood—a corruptible ingredient—in what had been to that point an uncorrupted body of bloodless flesh and bone. But even more important than such physical changes were the temptations of and threats to the spirit. Spiritual as well as physical separation from God came with the Fall. Humankind was cut off from the immediate personal companionship with God that Adam and Eve had enjoyed in the garden of Eden. As a result, they were distanced from the Holy Spirit and became less responsive to many of the things of righteousness.

King Benjamin made that issue one of the central tasks for men and women to deal with in their fallen, or natural, state.

"The natural man is an enemy to God," he taught, "and has been from the fall of Adam, and will be, forever and ever, unless he yields to the enticings of the Holy Spirit, and putteth off the natural man and becometh a saint through the atonement of Christ the Lord, and becometh as a child, submissive, meek, humble, patient, full of love, willing to submit to all things which the Lord seeth fit to inflict upon him, even as a child doth submit to his father."[29]

More extreme language than that of "natural man" or even "enemy to God" is Abinadi's pronouncement that as a result of the Fall and the increased influence of Satan in the fallen world, "all mankind [became] carnal, sensual, devilish, knowing evil from good, subjecting themselves to the devil.

"Thus all mankind were lost; and behold, they would have been endlessly lost were it not that God redeemed his people from their lost and fallen state.

"But remember that he that persists in his own carnal nature, and goes on in the ways of sin and rebellion against God, remaineth in his fallen state and the devil hath all power over him. Therefore he is as though there was no redemption made, being an enemy to God; and also is the devil an enemy to God."[30]

The brother of Jared made reference to that mortal alienation between man and God when he plaintively cried to the Lord, "O Lord, . . . do not be angry with thy servant because of his weakness before thee; for we know that thou art holy and dwellest in the heavens, and that we are unworthy before thee; because of the fall our natures have become evil continually."[31]

Because this doctrine is so basic to the plan of salvation and also because it is so susceptible to misunderstanding, we must note that these references to "natural" evil emphatically do *not* mean that men and women are "inherently" evil. There is a crucial difference. As spiritual sons and daughters of God, all mortal men and women are divine in origin and divine in their potential destiny. As Doctrine and Covenants 93:38–39 teaches, the spirit of every man, woman, and child "was innocent in the beginning." But it is also true that as a result of the Fall they are now in a "natural" (fallen) world where the devil "taketh away light" and where some elements of nature—including temporal human nature—need discipline, restraint, and refinement. It is as if men and women are given, as part of their next step in development along the path to godhood, raw physical and spiritual ingredients—"natural" resources, if you will. Those resources are not to run rampant but are to be harnessed and focused so that their power and potential (as is sometimes done with a "natural" river or a "natural" waterfall) can be channeled and thereby made even more productive and beneficial.

Natural man, with all of his new and wonderful but as yet unbridled and unregenerated potential, must be made "submissive" to the Holy Spirit, a spirit that still entices and lifts us upward. The brother of Jared acknowledged the inherent goodness of the soul when he said that our mortal transgressions and temporal natures can be overcome when we call upon God and from him "receive according to our desires."[32] Our deepest desires, our premortal yearnings, are still divine in their origins, and they are still deep in our souls. The echoes of our earlier innocence still reverberate, and the light that forsakes the evil one still shines. Our hearts can—and in their purity, do—desire that which is spiritual and holy rather than that which is "carnal, sensual, and devilish.[33] If that were not so, we would be in a hopeless condition indeed, and the idea of real choice would be jeopardized forever. We praise God our Father that our true heritage is of him and that by yielding and submitting to his eternal influence we can overcome the enmity which separated us from him and turn those gifts from nature to our blessing rather than our cursing.

PROBATIONARY STATE

God's justice demanded that death accompany the violation of his command to Adam and Eve not to eat the fruit of the tree of knowledge of good and evil.[33] But his mercy (and certainly his knowledge of the plan, for all things were done "in the wisdom of him who knoweth all things"[34]) dictated that he delay the imposition of that penalty and that he put Adam and Eve on probation. In doing so, he allowed them time in mortality to hear the gospel of Jesus Christ, accept it, repent of their transgression, and make claim upon the promised atonement of Jesus for the remission of their sins before the hour of their mandated death. "The days of the children of men were prolonged, according to the will of God, that they might repent while in the flesh; wherefore, their state became a state of probation, and their time was lengthened, according to the commandments which the Lord God gave unto the children of men,"[35] Lehi taught.

As the word comes to us in English, *probation* is derived from the Latin *probare*, which means "to prove" or "to test." So the Eternal Judge was willing to provide a period of testing, a proving ground to allow for the demonstration of "good behavior" before imposing the final penalty against Adam, Eve, and each of their descendants. Of course, what ultimately saves all of us in this court scene is the good behavior—and determined advocacy in our behalf—of Christ, but our own good behavior is also important. Our desire, willingness, and effort to keep God's commandments, which are the terms of our probation, are essential to Christ's willingness to take our case and to the Father's merciful judgment in the end.

Alma gave a succinct summary of this probationary period granted to men and women in mortality: "We see that death comes upon mankind . . . which is the temporal death; nevertheless there was a space granted unto man in which he might repent; therefore this life became *a probationary state; a time to prepare to meet God; . . .*

"And after God had appointed that these things should come unto man, behold, then he saw that it was expedient that man should know concerning the things whereof he had appointed unto them;

"Therefore he sent angels to converse with them, who caused men to behold of his glory.

"And they began from that time forth to call on his name; therefore God conversed with men, and made known unto them the plan of redemption, which had been prepared from the foundation of the world; and this he made known unto them according to their faith and repentance and their holy works. . . .

"Therefore God gave unto them commandments, after having made known unto them the plan of redemption, that they should not do evil. . . .

"[Thus] God did call on men, in the name of his Son, (this being the plan of redemption which was laid) saying: If ye will repent, and harden not your hearts, then will I have mercy upon you, through mine Only Begotten Son."[36]

The word *probation* is found only ten times in the Standard Works, and nine of those references are in the Book of Mormon. What an essential doctrine in understanding the Fall and the Atonement, a doctrine of prolonged opportunity for mortal men and women in which the gospel can be taught to and accepted by them, a doctrine gleaned almost exclusively from the Book of Mormon!

With the choice offered through moral agency and sufficient instruction in the elements of the plan of redemption, Adam and Eve and all their children on this earth were free "to act for themselves and not to be acted upon . . . and all things [necessary for this exercise] are given them." In this term of mortal probation (whatever period that may be after eight years of age until the day of death), we have the teachings of the gospel and the commandments of God to guide our time of testing, a time in which we are "free to choose liberty and eternal life, through the great Mediator of all men, or to choose captivity and death, according to the captivity and power of the devil."[37]

In short, for each accountable person, transgression against eternal law has been committed, and the subsequent judgment has been passed. We, like our parents before us, have "sinned, and come short of the glory of God."[38] But we have a merciful judge and a compassionate, sacrificing Mediator. They have given us time to repent and thereby alter our sentence. Our judge and our advocate are doing everything possible, within the allowable limits of justice, to give us a way out of our plight. If we truly wish to sidestep the spiritual death penalty, we may. In this, his greatest sermon uttered just days before his death, Lehi pleaded with his own family—and all of us—to do just that: "I would that ye should look to the great Mediator, and hearken unto his great commandments; and be faithful unto his words, and choose eternal life, according to the will of his Holy Spirit;

"And not choose eternal death, according to the will of the flesh and the evil which is therein, which giveth the spirit of the devil power to captivate, to bring you down to hell, that he may reign over you in his own kingdom. . . .

"For he seeketh that all men might be miserable like unto himself."[39]

Then, with a poignancy that must be known only to those who realize they are about to die, Lehi brought forward to his own moment the link with Adam's sentence in the divine courtroom. "I have spoken these few words unto you all," he said, "in the last days of *my probation;* and I have chosen the good part, according to the words of the prophet. And I have none other object save it be the everlasting welfare of your souls."[40]

AN INFINITE ATONEMENT

That touching testimony—and indeed the entire sermon given us by Lehi—becomes more immediate when we realize that a general doctrine of probation for all mankind is reduced to a specific probationary period for each of us personally. Lehi skillfully brought what could be a rather abstract doctrine right down to the "three score and ten years" (or whatever we may be given) of a brief lifetime in which we must learn the gospel, exercise our agency in claiming its promises, and thereby take advantage of "the merits, and mercy, and grace of the Holy Messiah."[41]

What Lehi's "good part" consists of and what the "words of the prophet[s]" taught him is that Christ would be born "with healing in his wings" to overcome the effects of the Fall and to offer to every human soul the privilege of exaltation. That Lehi taught this so well to his children is perhaps best evidenced in the discourse his son Jacob gave to the Nephites at the request of his other son Nephi. Continuing these same doctrinal insights taught by his father on the relationship of the Fall to the Atonement, Jacob said of Christ's coming: "I know that ye know that in the body he shall show himself unto those at Jerusalem, from whence we came; for it is expedient that it should be among them; for it behooveth the great Creator that he suffereth himself to become subject unto man in the flesh, and die for all men, that all men might become subject unto him.

"For as death hath passed upon all men, to fulfil the merciful plan of the great Creator, there must needs be a power of resurrection, and the resurrection must needs come unto man by reason of the fall; and the fall came by reason of transgression;

and because man became fallen they were cut off from the presence of the Lord.

"Wherefore, it must needs be an infinite atonement—save it should be an infinite atonement this corruption could not put on incorruption. Wherefore, the first judgment which came upon man must needs have remained to an endless duration. And if so, this flesh must have laid down to rot and to crumble to its mother earth, to rise no more."[42]

Clearly teaching that Christ died for "all men," Jacob was the first in the Book of Mormon to use the phrase *infinite atonement*, one of the truly essential characteristics of the doctrine of the Atonement as taught in this volume of scripture. Amulek reinforced that doctrine later with his own witness of the scope and breadth of Christ's sacrifice. Because the sins, transgressions, and heartaches of mankind are so universal, he said, "I do know that Christ shall come among the children of men, to take upon him the transgressions of his people, and that he shall atone for the sins of the world; for the Lord God hath spoken it.

"For it is expedient that an atonement should be made; for according to the great plan of the Eternal God there must be an atonement made, or else all mankind must unavoidably perish; yea, all are hardened; yea, all are fallen and are lost, and must perish except it be through the atonement which it is expedient should be made.

"For it is expedient that there should be a great and last sacrifice; yea, not a sacrifice of man, neither of beast, neither of any manner of fowl; for it shall not be a human sacrifice; but *it must be an infinite and eternal sacrifice.* . . .

"*Therefore there can be nothing which is short of an infinite atonement which will suffice for the sins of the world.*"[43]

Because the Fall was universal, with spiritual and physical death coming to all of God's children, so too must the Atonement be universal. Jacob taught that its unconditional aspects would cover all mankind—non-Christians as well as Christians, the godless as well as the God-fearing, the untaught infant as well as the fully converted and knowledgeable adult: "He cometh into the world that he may save *all* men if they will hearken unto his voice; for behold, he suffereth the pains of *all* men, yea, the pains of *every living creature,* both men, women, and children, who belong to the family of Adam.

"And he suffereth this that the resurrection might pass upon *all* men, that *all* might stand before him at the great and judgment day."[44]

UNCONDITIONAL GIFTS

The universal, infinite, and unconditional aspects of the atonement of Jesus Christ are several. They include his ransom for Adam's original transgression so that no member of the human family is held responsible for it.[45] Another unconditional, universal gift is the resurrection from the dead of every man, woman, and child who lives, has ever lived, or will ever live on the earth. Thus, the Atonement is universal in that it saves the entire human family from the bondage of physical death. It is also infinite in its impact and efficacy in making redemption possible for all, reaching back to the beginning of time and forward throughout eternity.

In his great sermon on this subject Jacob gives telling commentary on what would have been some of the universal spiritual consequences linked to a universal physical death:

"O the wisdom of God, his mercy and grace! For behold, if the flesh should rise no more our spirits must become subject to that angel who fell from before the presence of the Eternal God, and became the devil, to rise no more.

"And our spirits must have become like unto him, and we become devils, angels to a devil, to be shut out from the presence of our God, and to remain with the father of lies, in misery, like unto himself; yea, to that being who beguiled our first parents, who transformeth himself nigh unto an angel of light, and stirreth up the children of men unto secret combinations of murder and all manner of secret works of darkness.

"O how great the goodness of our God, who prepareth a way for our escape from the grasp of this awful monster; yea, that monster, death and hell, which I call the death of the body, and also the death of the spirit."[46]

As Lucifer will suffer an unembodied, unhopeful, unhappy future, so too, without the Resurrection, would we be unembodied, unhopeful, and unhappy, thus bringing triumph to the devil, who seeks that all men and women "might be miserable like unto himself."[47] Further, there would have been some terrible form of subjection in addition to personal sorrow and pain, a subjection that would have made us "devils, angels to a devil."[48]

Jacob continued his characteristic exclamations (as an evidence of distinct literary style, note how often his declarations begin with "O") about the unconditional blessings of the Atonement:

"O how great the plan of our God . . . [for through the Atonement] all men become incorruptible, and immortal, and they are living souls, having a perfect knowledge like unto us in the flesh. . . .

"O the greatness of the mercy of our God, the Holy One of Israel! For he delivereth his saints from that awful monster the devil, and death, and hell, and that lake of fire and brimstone, which is endless torment.

"O how great the holiness of our God! For he knoweth all things, and there is not anything save he knows it.

"And he cometh into the world that he may save all men if they will hearken unto his voice; for behold, he suffereth the pains of all men, yea, the pains of every living creature, both men, women, and children, who belong to the family of Adam."[49]

In the broad reach of the Atonement, generous provision is made for those who die without a knowledge of the gospel or the opportunity to embrace it, including children under the age of accountability, the mentally impaired, those who never came in contact with the gospel, and so forth. Regarding such people Jacob declared:

"Where there is no law given there is no punishment; and where there is no punishment there is no condemnation; and where there is no condemnation the mercies of the Holy One of Israel have claim upon them, because of the atonement; for they are delivered by the power of him.

"For the atonement satisfieth the demands of his justice upon all those who have not the law given to them."[50]

One of the strongest teachings of the Book of Mormon is that children under that age of accountability, later revealed to be eight years of age, are included with those who are not susceptible of temptation and are universally and unconditionally redeemed by the atonement of Christ. [51] Indeed, when so much depraved behavior came among the Nephites by the book's end, Mormon was incensed that such depravity would also include the theological abuse of this doctrine of the Atonement. Upon hearing that little children were being baptized, Mormon veritably shouted this instruction to his son Moroni, that he in turn could decry the apostate behavior of those few remaining Nephites. The fervor and occasional flame with which Mormon spoke justifies quoting his declaration at some length.

Citing the revelation he received from the Savior on this subject, Mormon wrote,

"Listen to the words of Christ, your Redeemer, your Lord and your God. Behold, I came into the world not to call the righteous but sinners to repentance; the whole need no physician, but they that are sick; wherefore, *little children are whole, for they are not capable of committing sin; wherefore the curse of Adam is taken from them in me, that it hath no power over them;* and the law of circumcision is done away in me."[52]

Mormon then counseled his people through Moroni, "My beloved son, I know that it is solemn mockery before God, that ye should baptize little children.

"Behold I say unto you that this thing shall ye teach—repentance and baptism unto those who are accountable and capable of committing sin; yea, teach parents that they must repent and be baptized, and humble themselves as their little children, and they shall all be saved with their little children.

"*And their little children need no repentance, neither baptism.* Behold, baptism is unto repentance to the fulfilling the commandments unto the remission of sins.

"*But little children are alive in Christ, even from the foundation of the world;* if not so, God is a partial God, and also a changeable God, and a respecter to persons; for how many little children have died without baptism! . . .

"Behold I say unto you, that he that supposeth that little children need baptism is in the gall of bitterness and in the bonds of iniquity; for he hath neither faith, hope, nor charity. . . .

"*Little children cannot repent;* wherefore, it is awful wickedness to deny the pure mercies of God unto them, for they are all alive in him because of his mercy. . . .

"*For behold that all little children are alive in Christ, and also all they that are without the law. For the power of redemption cometh on all them that have no law; wherefore, he that is not condemned, or he that is under no condemnation, cannot repent; and unto such baptism availeth nothing—*

"But it is mockery before God, denying the mercies of Christ, and the power of his Holy Spirit, and putting trust in dead works."[53]

The doctrine of the salvation of little children being saved in Christ had been taught early in the Book of Mormon as well as at the end of it. King Benjamin taught in his great sermon, "Even if it were possible that little children could sin they could not be saved; but I say unto you they are blessed; for behold, as in Adam, or by nature, they fall, even so the blood of Christ atoneth for their sins. . . .

"And the infant perisheth not that dieth in his infancy; but men drink damnation to their own souls except they humble themselves and become as little children, and believe that salvation was, and is, and is to come, in and through the atoning blood of Christ, the Lord Omnipotent. . . .

"And behold, when that time cometh, none shall be found blameless before God, except it be little children, only through repentance and faith on the name of the Lord God Omnipotent."[54]

In the pattern set by the Savior's own teachings, it is telling that both of these declarations invite adults—Mormon said specifically "parents"—to become more like little children, not the other way around. An infant's purity and innocence, a baby's sense of wonder, a little one's willingness to believe, a toddler's inherent trust in a Father and Mother, a child's ability to almost instantly forgive and forget, to laugh again and see the very best in the world—these are just a few of the ways adults need to be more like children. Truly "of such is the kingdom of heaven."[55]

CONDITIONAL GIFTS

Even as there are these unrestricted blessings flowing from Christ's sacrifice, King Benjamin's concluding lines above indicate that other aspects of the Atonement are conditional, requiring such effort as "repentance and faith on the name of the Lord

God Omnipotent." The conditional blessings of the gospel, in both time and eternity, are predicated upon the moral agency and personal discipline of the individual before they can be fully efficacious. For example, while all members of the human family are freely and universally given reprieve from Adam's transgression through no effort of their own, they are not given reprieve from their own sins unless they follow the commandments of Christ. Indeed, the Book of Mormon prophets regularly give stern warning to those who, unlike little children, are accountable before the law and upon whom the full blessings of the Atonement are not so automatic. Jacob warned, "He commandeth all men that they must repent, and be baptized in his name, having perfect faith in the Holy One of Israel, or they cannot be saved in the kingdom of God.

"And if they will not repent and believe in his name, and be baptized in his name, and endure to the end, they must be damned; for the Lord God, the Holy One of Israel, has spoken it. . . .

"Wo unto him that has the law given, yea, that has all the commandments of God, like unto us, and that transgresseth them, and that wasteth the days of his probation, for awful is his state!"[56]

There are principles of the gospel that the accountable must follow and ordinances of the gospel that they must obtain. Mormon stresses this commitment to fundamental requirements: "The first fruits of repentance is baptism; and baptism cometh by faith unto the fulfilling the commandments; and the fulfilling the commandments bringeth remission of sins;

"And the remission of sins bringeth meekness, and lowliness of heart; and because of meekness and lowliness of heart cometh the visitation of the Holy Ghost, which Comforter filleth with hope and perfect love, which love endureth by diligence unto prayer, until the end shall come, when all the saints shall dwell with God."[57]

SPIRITUALLY BORN OF GOD

The significance of these symbolic steps, these first principles and ordinances of the gospel here emphasized, was developed by King Benjamin in his counsel that one must put "off the natural man and becometh a saint through the atonement of Christ the Lord."[58] As that fallen, dead, unregenerate man is "an enemy to God," so one overcomes that enmity by being reborn, a new birth that transcends spiritual death. This spiritual rebirth is symbolized by faith in the Lord Jesus Christ, repentance, baptism by immersion for the remission of sins, and the laying on of hands for the gift of the Holy Ghost, all followed by the faithful living of other gospel requirements thereafter. The elements of death, burial, and resurrection, symbolically represented by immersion in and emergence from the waters of baptism, signify the new birth by which we declare ourselves for Christ and lay claim to the gift of eternal life that comes through the Atonement.

As noted earlier in this book, when King Benjamin had concluded his masterful sermon on the life and mission of the Savior, his people were profoundly moved by that message and desired to claim the blessings of the gospel. They saw themselves as yet being "natural" and unregenerated, viewing themselves "in their own carnal state, even less than the dust of the earth."[59] With one voice these people cried, "O have mercy, and apply the atoning blood of Christ that we may receive forgiveness of our sins, and our hearts may be purified; for we believe in Jesus Christ, the Son of God, who created heaven and earth, and all things; who shall come down among the children of men."[60]

Inspired by their resolve, King Benjamin replied:

"I say unto you, if ye have come to a knowledge of the goodness of God, and his matchless power, and his wisdom, and his patience, and his long-suffering towards the children of men; and also, the atonement which has been prepared from the foundation of the world, that thereby salvation might come to him that should put his trust in the Lord, and should be diligent in keeping his commandments, and continue in the faith even unto the end of his life, I mean the life of the mortal body—

"I say, that this is the man who receiveth salvation, through the atonement which was prepared from the foundation of the world for all mankind, which ever were since the fall of Adam, or who are, or who ever shall be, even unto the end of the world.

"And this is the means whereby salvation cometh. And there is none other salvation save this which hath been spoken of; *neither are there any conditions whereby man can be saved except the conditions which I have told you.*"[61]

With a great shout from the people and their unanimous desire to enter into a covenant that would enable them to escape the effects of the physical and spiritual deaths awaiting them, King Benjamin taught the blessings of rebirth—birth into eternal life through Christ—including taking upon themselves his name as evidence of their new life, their new covenant, their new identity:

"And now, because of the covenant which ye have made ye shall be called the children of Christ, his sons, and his daughters; for behold, *this day he hath spiritually begotten you; for ye say that your hearts are changed through faith on his name; therefore, ye are born of him and have become his sons and his daughters.*

"And under this head ye are made free, and there is no other head whereby ye can be made free. There is no other name given whereby salvation cometh; therefore, I would that ye should take upon you the name of Christ, all you that have entered into the covenant with God that ye should be obedient unto the end of your lives.

"And it shall come to pass that whosoever doeth this shall be found at the right hand of God, for he shall know the name by which he is called; for he shall be called by the name of Christ."[62]

Later, when Alma was trying to stir up the hearts of the members of the Church in Zarahemla, he appealed to this same covenant and declaration of new birth that all were to have experienced. To those who were slacking, he recalled that they had been "encircled about by the bands of death, and the chains of hell" with "an everlasting destruction" awaiting them. But those bands of death were broken and the chains of hell were loosed through "the light of the everlasting word" of Christ.[63]

Noting the "mighty change" that had come to his father Alma, who in turn had brought a "mighty change" to the earlier generations in Zarahemla, Alma asked the question that must be asked of all: "Have ye spiritually been born of God? Have ye received his image in your countenances? Have ye experienced this mighty change in your hearts? . . .

"Could ye say, if ye were called to die at this time . . . [t]hat your garments have been cleansed and made white through the blood of Christ, who will come to redeem his people from their sins? . . .

"Behold, I say unto you, that the good shepherd doth call you; yea, and in his own name he doth call you, which is the name of Christ; and if ye will not hearken unto the voice of the good shepherd, to the name by which ye are called, behold, ye are not the sheep of the good shepherd. . . .

"I know that Jesus Christ shall come, yea, the Son, the Only Begotten of the Father, full of grace, and mercy, and truth. And behold, it is he that cometh to take away the sins of the world, yea, the sins of every man who steadfastly believeth on his name."[64]

We have already noted the most dramatic Book of Mormon example of such a person being reborn in Christ. After a youthful life devoted to destroying the Church, Alma the Younger was struck down by the power of a heavenly angel sent by God in response to the prayers of the Nephite faithful. In response to two days of fasting and prayer by his father and the other believers gathered around him, Alma stood and declared:

"I have repented of my sins, and have been redeemed of the Lord; behold *I am born of the Spirit.*

"And the Lord said unto me: Marvel not that *all mankind, yea, men and women, all nations, kindreds, tongues and people, must be born again; yea, born of God, changed from their carnal and fallen state, to a state of righteousness, being redeemed of God, becoming his sons and daughters;*

"And thus they become new creatures; and unless they do this, they can in nowise inherit the kingdom of God. . . .

"After wading through much tribulation, repenting nigh unto death, the Lord in mercy hath seen fit to snatch me out of an everlasting burning, and *I am born of God.*"[65]

That a whole new world of learning opened up to Alma (and to all who lay claim on the blessings of the Atonement and are born anew) is evidenced in his recounting of that experience to his son Helaman some twenty years after it happened. Teaching his son to trust in God through all manner of trials, troubles, and afflictions, Alma said,

"*If I had not been born of God I should not have known these things;* but God has, by the mouth of his holy angel, made these things known unto me, not of any worthiness of myself." And then, as so appropriately happens, the converted became the converter: "Yea, and from that time even until now, I have labored without ceasing, that I might bring souls unto repentance; that I might bring them to taste of the exceeding joy of which I did taste; *that they might also be born of God,* and be filled with the Holy Ghost. . . .

"For because of the word which he has imparted unto me, behold, *many have been born of God,* and have tasted as I have tasted, and have seen eye to eye as I have seen."[66]

As a result of such personal experience, Alma would be able

to stress, "The Son of God suffereth according to the flesh that he might take upon him the sins of his people, that he might blot out their transgressions according to the power of his deliverance. . . .

"Ye must repent, and be born again; for the Spirit saith if ye are not born again ye cannot inherit the kingdom of heaven; therefore come and be baptized unto repentance, that ye may be washed from your sins, that ye may have faith on the Lamb of God, who taketh away the sins of the world, who is mighty to save and to cleanse from all unrighteousness."[67]

RELIEF FOR THE REBORN

Virtually all Christian churches teach some kind of doctrine regarding the atonement of Christ and the expiation of our sins that comes through it. But the Book of Mormon teaches that and much more. It teaches that Christ also provides relief of a more temporal sort, taking upon himself our mortal sicknesses and infirmities, our earthly trials and tribulations, our personal heartaches and loneliness and sorrows—all done in addition to taking upon himself the burden of our sins.

Alma, who had experienced the joyous impact of Christ's redemption, taught that the Savior would "go forth, suffering pains and afflictions and temptations of every kind; and this that the word might be fulfilled which saith he will take upon him the pains and the sicknesses of his people.

"And he will take upon him death, that he may loose the bands of death which bind his people; and he will take upon him their infirmities, that his bowels may be filled with mercy, according to the flesh, that he may know according to the flesh how to succor his people according to their infirmities."[68]

Christ walked the path every mortal is called to walk so that he would know how to succor and strengthen us in our most difficult times. He knows the deepest and most personal burdens we carry. He knows the most public and poignant pains we bear. He descended below all such grief in order that he might lift us above it. There is no anguish or sorrow or sadness in life that he has not suffered in our behalf and borne away upon his own valiant and compassionate shoulders.[69] In so doing he "giveth power to the faint; and to them that have no might he increaseth strength. . . . [Thus] they that wait upon the Lord shall renew their strength; they shall mount up with wings as eagles; they shall run, and not be weary; and they shall walk, and not faint."[70]

That aspect of the Atonement brings an additional kind of rebirth, something of immediate renewal, help, and hope that allow us to rise above sorrows and sickness, misfortunes and mistakes of every kind. With his mighty arm around us and lifting us, we face life more joyfully even as we face death more triumphantly.

Only on the strong shoulders of the Master can we "fear not." Only in his embrace is there safety. Only in covenant with him is there freedom from death and "every sin, which easily doth beset you."[71] Only in him is there peace in this world and eternal life in the world to come. Some of the most reassuring counsel ever given to the children of men includes these words from the Master:

"He that ascended up on high . . . also descended below all things, in that he comprehended all things, that he might be in all and through all things, the light of truth . . . the light which is in all things which giveth life to all things."[72]

"In all their afflictions he was afflicted. And the angel of his presence saved them; and in his love, and in his pity, he redeemed them, and bore them, and carried them all the days of old."[73]

"Therefore, hold on thy way. . . . Thy days are known, and thy years shall not be numbered less; therefore, fear not what man can do, for God shall be with you forever and ever."[74]

JUSTICE AND MERCY

This loving, charitable, and merciful generosity of the Savior raises the inevitable question of the place of justice in his working out of the Atonement. The balance between seemingly contradictory principles is examined in the Book of Mormon most skillfully and—because it is a father speaking to his own transgressing son—most sensitively by Alma the Younger when instructing his son Corianton.

Obviously the demands of justice require that penalties must be paid for violation of the law. Adam transgressed and so have all of us; thus the judgment of death (physically) and the consequences of hell (spiritually) is pronounced as a just reward. Furthermore, once guilty, none of us could personally do anything to overcome that fate. We do not have in us the seeds of immortality allowing us to conquer death physically, and we have not been perfect in our behavior, thus forfeiting the purity that would let us return to the presence of God spiritually. Furthermore, God cannot simply turn a blind eye to the breaking of divine law, because in so doing he would dishonor justice and would "cease to be God,"[75] which thing he would never do. The sorry truth for mortal men and women was, then, that "there was no means to reclaim [them] from this fallen state which man had brought upon himself because of his own disobedience.

"Thus we see that all mankind were fallen, and they were in the grasp of justice; yea, the justice of God, which consigned them forever to be cut off from his presence."[76]

The claims of justice must be honored. The absence of law or the lack of any penalty for breaking it would leave the world in amoral chaos. Alma asked rhetorically, "If there was no law given—if a man murdered he should die—would he be afraid he would die if he should murder? And also, if there was no law given against sin men would not be afraid to sin."[77] Clearly one

of the purposes of law and the firm demands of justice behind it
is its preventive impact.

But what happens when *all* have sinned and come short of
the glory of God? How do we overcome the infinite impact of
Adam's transgression? How is the price to be paid for every sin
and sorrow and selfish thought that men and women have experienced from Adam to the end of the world? The number of
transgressors is as vast as the punishment is ominous. "Do ye
suppose that mercy can rob justice?" Alma asked. "I say unto
you, Nay; not one whit."[78]

King Benjamin had earlier reminded his people: "After ye
have known and have been taught all these things, if ye should
transgress and go contrary to that which has been spoken, that
ye do withdraw yourselves from the Spirit of the Lord, that it
may have no place in you to guide you in wisdom's paths that
ye may be blessed, prospered, and preserved—

"I say unto you, that the man that doeth this, the same
cometh out in open rebellion against God. . . . If that man repenteth not, and remaineth and dieth an enemy to God, the
demands of divine justice do awaken his immortal soul to a
lively sense of his own guilt, which doth cause him to shrink
from the presence of the Lord, and doth fill his breast with guilt,
and pain, and anguish, which is like an unquenchable fire,
whose flame ascendeth up forever and ever.

"And now I say unto you, that mercy hath no claim on that
man; therefore his final doom is to endure a never-ending torment."[79]

Usually when we speak of the atonement of Christ, we
emphasize (or find ourselves hoping for) the merciful aspects of
that gift. But we must always remember that the Atonement car-
ries with it the unfailing elements of justice as well. Justice *is* the
gulf separating the wicked from the righteous, and "justice cannot be denied."[80] Christ did all that he did so that "a righteous

judgment might come upon the children of men." It is a *righteous* judgment, but it *is* a judgment.

To the resistant congregation at Ammonihah, Amulek powerfully taught the justice of the Resurrection—that "the wicked remain as though there had been no redemption made, except it be the loosing of the bands of death," and they shall be "arraigned before the bar of Christ the Son, and God the Father, and the Holy Spirit, which is one Eternal God, to be judged according to their works, whether they be good or whether they be evil."[81] Upon hearing that doctrine, Zeezrom, the chief antagonist in that setting, "began to tremble under a consciousness of his guilt." When Alma stepped in to reinforce the words of Amulek on this doctrine, Zeezrom "began to tremble more exceedingly, for he was convinced more and more of the [justice] of God."[82]

An earlier prophet also thought someone in his audience should be alarmed at the justice of God. Abinadi asked King Noah (who displayed much the same spirit Zeezrom had initially shown), "Ought ye not to tremble? For salvation cometh to none such; for the Lord hath redeemed none such; yea, neither can the Lord redeem such; for he cannot deny himself; for he cannot deny justice when it has its claim."[83]

It is Book of Mormon doctrine that God must be just.[84] Furthermore, the guilty will, even in everlasting shame, acknowledge that "all his judgments are just; that he is just in all his works."[85] But God is a merciful God also, and so is the Son of God. Therefore, God devised a "plan of mercy"[86] that would satisfy the demands of justice and free those held hostage to sin. It would require that a God himself come to earth to atone for the sins of the world, a point that Abinadi made not once but three times in declaring the Atonement to King Noah and his wicked priests.[87]

No mere mortal could work such a miracle or bear such a

weighty load. As Amulek taught, "There is not any man that can sacrifice his own blood which will atone for the sins of another."[88] In such an earthly accounting, any mortals, however good they might wish to be, would have their own sins to account for, so they would hardly be in a position to take care of another's. And regarding death, no mortals, however strong they might be otherwise, carry in themselves the seeds of life whereby they can raise themselves—let alone others—from the tomb.

No, only a God (the Son) could meet these demands and thereby help another God (the Father) "be a perfect, just God, and a merciful God also."[89] Only a God himself would bear the seeds of divinity, the seeds of eternal life, that would allow a triumph over death. And only a person qualifying to be a God could live in a world of temptation and be subject to all the ills of the flesh but never yield to them.

So Christ came to earth, lived his thirty-three years, then fulfilled the ultimate purpose for his birth into mortality. In a spiritual agony that began in Gethsemane and a physical payment that was consummated on the cross of Calvary, he took upon himself every sin and sorrow, every heartache and infirmity, every sickness, sadness, trial, and tribulation experienced by the children of God from Adam to the end of the world. How he did that is a stunning mystery, but he did it. He broke the bands of physical death and gained victory over the grasp of spiritual hell. A God himself came down and made merciful intercession for all the children of men.[90]

Through his personal experience Alma came to appreciate that only with such mercy included could the great plan of redemption function. As he later taught his son Corianton, "According to justice, the plan of redemption could not be brought about, [except] on conditions of repentance of men in this probationary state, yea, this preparatory state; for except it were for these conditions, mercy could not take effect except it should destroy the work of justice. Now the work of justice could not be destroyed; if so, God would cease to be God. And thus we see that all mankind were fallen, and they were in the grasp of justice; yea, the justice of God, which consigned them forever to be cut off from his presence. . . .

"But there is a law given, and a punishment affixed, and a repentance granted; which repentance, mercy claimeth; otherwise, justice claimeth the creature and executeth the law, and the law inflicteth the punishment; if not so, the works of justice would be destroyed, and God would cease to be God.

"But God ceaseth not to be God, and mercy claimeth the penitent, and mercy cometh because of the atonement; and the atonement bringeth to pass the resurrection of the dead; and the resurrection of the dead bringeth back men into the presence of God; and thus they are restored into his presence, to be judged according to their works, according to the law and justice.

"For behold, justice exerciseth all his demands, and also mercy claimeth all which is her own; and thus, none but the truly penitent are saved."[91]

As he ascended into heaven, Christ did so "having the bowels of mercy; being filled with compassion towards the children of men; standing betwixt them and justice; having broken the bands of death, taken upon himself their iniquity and their transgressions, having redeemed them, and satisfied the demands of justice."[92] It is a matter of surpassing wonder that the voluntary and merciful sacrifice of a single being could satisfy the infinite and eternal demands of justice, atone for every human transgression and misdeed ever committed in the history of the world, and provide for the sweeping of all mankind into the encompassing arms of God's compassionate embrace—but that is what happened.

President John Taylor wrote, "In some mysterious, incomprehensible way, Jesus assumed the responsibility which naturally would have devolved upon Adam; but which could only be accomplished through the mediation of Himself, and by taking upon Himself their sorrows, assuming their responsibilities, and bearing their transgression or sins. In a manner to us incomprehensible and inexplicable, he bore the weight of the sins of the whole world; not only of Adam, but of his posterity; and in doing that, opened the kingdom of heaven, not only to all believers and all who obeyed the law of God, but to more than one-half of the human family who die before they come to years of maturity, as well as to the heathen, who, having died without law, will, through His mediation, be resurrected without law, and be judged without law, and thus participate . . . in the blessings of His atonement."[93]

Because Christ was willing to mediate for us in the courts of heaven, paying full price for every transgression and thereby meeting the legal demands of justice, he rightly became our new master and could mercifully offer freedom to all who would accept his terms. Thus by remaining just, "God ceaseth not to be God," but "mercy claimeth the penitent," which mercy "cometh because of the atonement." In a wonderful, preplanned way "justice exerciseth all his demands, and also mercy claimeth all which is her own; and thus, none but the truly penitent are saved."[94] Using a forceful image, Amulek explained that through Christ, mercy "overpowereth justice. . . . And thus mercy can satisfy the demands of justice, and encircles [the penitent] in the arms of safety, while he that exercises no faith unto repentance is exposed to the whole law of the demands of justice."[95]

Abinadi lamented over those who would not accept this generous act of mercy and freedom. These have, he said, "gone according to their own carnal wills and desires; having never called upon the Lord while the arms of mercy were extended towards them; for the arms of mercy were extended towards them, and they would not; they being warned of their iniquities and yet they would not depart from them; and they were commanded to repent and yet they would not repent."[96]

Those that "mercy claimeth" as "her own" are the followers of Christ. They understand, as Paul did, that they were "bought with a price"[97] and owe something in return for that freedom. As a consequence of the Atonement, we need not be in subjection to the devil, but we must be willing, as Jacob taught, to "become subject unto [Christ]."[98]

What that subjection means does not involve anything slavish or restrictive nor does it require any payment of money or worldly gifts. What that subjection means, what these people choosing redemption "owe" to Christ, their new master, is a life of discipleship, beginning with faith, repentance, and baptism and leading on to all the ordinances and covenants of the gospel and a life of loving kindness. Clearly all of humankind is still in debt even after the full effect of the Atonement has transpired. But fortunately he to whom we are indebted is Christ the Merciful rather than Lucifer the Miserable. We still have obligations, but they are of a much higher and happier sort. We are in debt, but we are not in bondage.

Jacob cried out, "O then, my beloved brethren, come unto the Lord, the Holy One. Remember that his paths are righteous. Behold, the way for man is narrow, but it lieth in a straight course before him, and the keeper of the gate is the Holy One of Israel; and he employeth no servant there; and there is none other way save it be by the gate; for he cannot be deceived, for the Lord God is his name."[99]

Christ is our master, our divine Lord (literally "keeper"), but he freely opens the door of salvation and joy to all who knock in faith and humility. Therefore Jacob's counsel: "Wherefore, do not spend money for that which is of no worth, nor your labor for that which cannot satisfy. Hearken diligently unto me, and remember the words which I have spoken; and come unto the

Holy One of Israel, and feast upon that which perisheth not, neither can be corrupted, and let your soul delight in fatness."[100]

Nephi drove home this same sense of an open, unlimited invitation for all to accept Christ as their Master. Declaring that the Savior's entire life, his entire existence, is devoted to the good and salvation of his Father's children, Nephi said,

"He doeth not anything save it be for the benefit of the world; for he loveth the world, even that he layeth down his own life that he may draw all men unto him. Wherefore, he commandeth none that they shall not partake of his salvation.

"Behold, doth he cry unto any, saying: Depart from me? Behold, I say unto you, Nay; but he saith: Come unto me all ye ends of the earth, buy milk and honey, without money and without price. . . .

"Hath he commanded any that they should not partake of his salvation? Behold I say unto you, Nay; but he hath given it free for all men; and he hath commanded his people that they should persuade all men to repentance.

"Behold, hath the Lord commanded any that they should not partake of his goodness? Behold I say unto you, Nay; but all men are privileged the one like unto the other, and none are forbidden. . . .

"For none of these iniquities come of the Lord; for he doeth that which is good among the children of men; and he doeth nothing save it be plain unto the children of men; and he inviteth them all to come unto him and partake of his goodness; and he denieth none that come unto him, black and white, bond and free, male and female; and he remembereth the heathen; and all are alike unto God, both Jew and Gentile."[101]

As just one group of many in the Book of Mormon who came back from the depths of transgression, the Anti-Nephi-Lehies thanked God that they had been forgiven their many sins and murders, and that their guilt had been taken away from their hearts "through the merits of [God's] Son."[102]

"Oh, how merciful is our God!" they said. "And now behold, since it has been as much as we could do to get our stains taken away from us, and our swords are made bright, let us hide them away that they may be kept bright, as a testimony to our God at the last day, or at the day that we shall be brought to stand before him to be judged, that we have not stained our swords in the blood of our brethren since he imparted his word unto us and has made us clean thereby."[103]

The story of the Book of Mormon is, at least in part, a story of the many men and women who cried out in laying claim upon the merciful redemption of Christ. King Lamoni cried out as he heard the gospel, "O Lord, have mercy; according to thy abundant mercy which thou hast had upon the people of Nephi, have upon me, and my people."[104]

Then, as Lamoni was redeemed in a miraculous fashion, his wife, the queen, arose from her converting experience to cry out with a loud voice, "O blessed Jesus, who has saved me from an awful hell! O blessed God, have mercy on this people!"[105]

A greater figure, but a less well-known one, is Zenos, whose gratitude for God's mercy was quoted at length by Alma. "Thou art merciful, O God, for thou hast heard my prayer," Zenos said, "even when I was in the wilderness; yea, thou wast merciful when I prayed concerning those who were mine enemies, and thou didst turn them to me.

"Yea, O God, and thou wast merciful unto me when I did cry unto thee in my field; when I did cry unto thee in my prayer, and thou didst hear me.

"And again, O God, when I did turn to my house thou didst hear me in my prayer.

"And when I did turn unto my closet, O Lord, and prayed unto thee, thou didst hear me.

"Yea, thou art merciful unto thy children when they cry unto thee, to be heard of thee and not of men, and thou wilt hear them.

"Yea, O God, thou hast been merciful unto me, and heard my cries in the midst of thy congregations.

"Yea, and thou hast also heard me when I have been cast out and have been despised by mine enemies; yea, thou didst hear my cries, and wast angry with mine enemies, and thou didst visit them in thine anger with speedy destruction.

"And thou didst hear me because of mine afflictions and my sincerity; and it is because of thy Son that thou hast been thus merciful unto me, therefore I will cry unto thee in all mine afflictions, for in thee is my joy; for thou hast turned thy judgments away from me, because of thy Son."[106]

One of the greatest appeals to the mercy of Christ recorded in the Book of Mormon is the already noted account Alma repeated to his son Helaman two decades after Alma's conversion. In teaching Helaman of his anguish and pain, he spoke of "a cry within [his] heart": "While I was harrowed up by the memory of my many sins, behold, I remembered also to have heard my father prophesy unto the people concerning the coming of one Jesus Christ, a Son of God, to atone for the sins of the world.

"Now, as my mind caught hold upon this thought, *I cried within my heart:* O Jesus, thou Son of God, have mercy on me, who am in the gall of bitterness, and am encircled about by the everlasting chains of death.

"And now, behold, when I thought this, I could remember my pains no more; yea, I was harrowed up by the memory of my sins no more.

"And oh, what joy, and what marvelous light I did behold; yea, my soul was filled with joy as exceeding as was my pain!

"Yea, I say unto you, my son, that there could be nothing so exquisite and so bitter as were my pains. Yea, and again I say unto you, my son, that on the other hand, there can be nothing so exquisite and sweet as was my joy."[107]

Later, teaching the same lesson to Shiblon, Alma said he never did have relief—and by implication never would have had relief—until he cried out to the Lord Jesus Christ for mercy: "I was three days and three nights in the most bitter pain and anguish of soul; and *never, until I did cry out unto the Lord Jesus Christ for mercy,* did I receive a remission of my sins. But behold, I did cry unto him and I did find peace to my soul."[108]

Such mercy granted by the Savior of the world is intended to prompt us to live as he lived, love as he loved, serve as he served, forgive as he forgave. The offer of eternal reward for such efforts was and is open to all.

"Whosoever will come may come and partake of the waters of life freely," Alma reassured Corianton, but adding that "whosoever will not come the same is not compelled to come."[109] Clearly Christ will not force the blessings of exaltation upon anyone. With everlasting agency before us, the ineluctable consequence of personal choice, Alma declared his wish for Corianton, which reflects our Father in Heaven's wish for all his children:

"O my son, I desire that ye should deny the justice of God no more. Do not endeavor to excuse yourself in the least point because of your sins, by denying the justice of God; but do you let the justice of God, and his mercy, and his long-suffering have full sway in your heart; and let it bring you down to the dust in humility. . . .

"And now, my son, go thy way, declare the word with truth and soberness, that thou mayest bring souls unto repentance, that the great plan of mercy may have claim upon them."[110]

GRACE

Even though there are some conditional aspects of the Atonement that require our adherence to gospel principles for the full realization of eternal blessings, the Book of Mormon makes clear that neither the conditional nor unconditional blessings of the Atonement would be available to mankind except through the grace and goodness of Christ. Obviously the unconditional blessings of the Atonement are unearned, but the conditional ones also are not fully merited. By living faithfully and keeping the commandments of God, we can receive a fuller measure of blessings from Christ, but even these greater blessings are freely given of him and are not technically "earned" by us. In short, good works are necessary for salvation, but they are not sufficient. And God is not obliged to make up the insufficiency. As Jacob taught, "Remember, after ye are reconciled unto God, that it is only in and through the grace of God that ye are saved."[111]

The Book of Mormon is unequivocal in its teaching that fallen man "could not merit anything of himself," as Aaron taught King Lamoni's father.[112] Lehi taught the same doctrine earlier when he declared, "There is no flesh that can dwell in the presence of God, save it be through the merits, and mercy, and grace of the Holy Messiah."[113]

Among the earliest Book of Mormon sermons on Christ—one establishing for future Nephite generations the "doctrine of Christ"—was Nephi's concluding testimony to his people shortly before his death. In that valedictory message, he taught that through baptism we enter the straight and narrow path that leads to eternal life. But even in such outward ordinances, even by such "works," if you will, do we earn our way to salvation? Emphatically not, said Nephi:

"Nay; for ye have not come thus far save it were by the word of Christ with unshaken faith in him, relying wholly upon the merits of him who is mighty to save."[114]

That is a variation on what Abinadi later taught about the relationship of the law of Moses to the gospel, a form of the works vs. grace controversy that was observed even in ancient days. Said he, "Salvation doth not come by the law alone; and were it not for the atonement, which God himself shall make for the sins and iniquities of his people . . . they must unavoidably perish, notwithstanding the law of Moses."[115]

As noted earlier, even the sometimes stern Jacob was brightened by the realization of God's grace. He taught, "Cheer up your hearts, and remember that ye are free to act for yourselves—to choose the way of everlasting death or the way of eternal life. Wherefore, my beloved brethren, reconcile yourselves to the will of God, and not to the will of the devil and the flesh; and remember, after ye are reconciled unto God, that it is only in and through the grace of God that ye are saved. Wherefore, may God raise you from death by the power of the resurrection, and also from everlasting death by the power of the atonement, that ye may be received into the eternal kingdom of God, that ye may praise him through grace divine."[116]

Moroni would close the Book of Mormon with his final reassurance of the grace of God, but noting it is a grace that requires our honest effort to claim and enjoy. To those of us who would live in the latter days, he wrote, "If ye shall deny yourselves of all ungodliness, and love God with all your might, mind and strength, then is his grace sufficient for you, that by his grace ye may be perfect in Christ; . . . then are ye sanctified in Christ by the grace of God, through the shedding of the blood of Christ."[117]

As summary, Nephi gave what surely must be the most succinct and satisfying resolution ever recorded in the history of the faith vs. works controversy. He said clearly and plainly for all who read the Book of Mormon to understand, "We know that it is by grace that we are saved, after all we can do."[118]

RESURRECTION

Inasmuch as the physical resurrection of Christ is the visible, outward manifestation of the more invisible and inward spiritual triumph of the Atonement, it remains the grand, central fact at the heart of the Christian message. It is the sublime reality that sets Christianity apart from all other religions. The message is that a man who was dead did, by his own power, infuse life back into his own body, never again to experience the separation of his spirit from that body in time or eternity. In so doing, he magnificently and magnanimously provided, by that same power, a similar experience for every other man, woman, and child who would ever live in this world. As "another testament of Jesus Christ," the Book of Mormon contains twice as many references to the Resurrection as does the New Testament. It is a strong and pervasive doctrine throughout the book, clear evidence of this latter-day testament's unvarying Christian message.

Lehi taught at the very outset of the record that the Holy Messiah, would lay "down his life according to the flesh, and [take] it again by the power of the Spirit, that he [might] bring to pass the resurrection of the dead, being the first that should rise."[119] Moroni, in his very final and fitting verse of the Book of Mormon, said, "I soon go to rest in the paradise of God, until my spirit and body shall again reunite, and I am brought forth triumphant through the air, to meet you before the pleasing bar of the great Jehovah, the Eternal Judge of both quick and dead."[120]

These observations from the first and last prophets in the book provide brackets to the Book of Mormon story, suggesting just how universally this crucial Christian doctrine was known to these people. And yet, as in our time so in theirs, there was a rising generation who "did not believe what had been said concerning the resurrection of the dead, neither did they believe concerning the coming of Christ."[121] To that audience as well as our modern one, the teachings of the Book of Mormon emphasize the resurrection of the Son of God.

One of the most powerful voices in the Book of Mormon on the doctrine of the Resurrection comes from Abinadi, who did so much to show that the law of Moses (and the Old Testament world generally) had no hope of salvation without the truths of the gospel, including the certainty of the Resurrection. Abinadi, "speaking of things to come as though they had already come," noted that "if Christ had not risen from the dead, or have broken the bands of death that the grave should have no victory, and that death should have no sting, there could have been no resurrection."[122]

Samuel the Lamanite was given to see some of the actual events of Christ's birth, life, ministry, and death, including the fact that at his crucifixion and subsequent resurrection, "many graves shall be opened, and shall yield up many of their dead; and many saints shall appear unto many."[123] That passage is particularly famous in Nephite literature because its fulfillment was not fully recorded by the Nephite record keepers at the time of Christ's crucifixion and resurrection, an omission caught by the Savior himself, who directed that the fulfillment of the prophecy be added to the record.[124]

The resurrection at the time of Christ—"a first resurrection," as Abinadi phrased it—did not apply to those who "wilfully rebelled against God, that have known the commandments of God, and would not keep them," who did not have claim upon that first resurrection experience.[125]

Clearly not all of the Nephite prophets knew the details of the Resurrection as we know them in our dispensation, though they knew a great deal for their time. For as much as was revealed about this first resurrection and whatever implications it had for later iterations of that event, at least Alma—for one—was not given to know many of the specifics of the Resurrection even though he had "inquired diligently of God" that he might know them. It was a question about the doctrine of the resurrection that the increasingly humble Zeezrom put to Alma which the prophet could refer to only as one of "the mysteries of God." Years later in teaching his son Corianton, Alma still called it a "mystery," the details of which only God himself knows.[126] That is, of course, a perfectly appropriate and accurate response to the complete doctrine of the Resurrection, even with the additional revelations we have received in the dispensation of the fulness of times. Only Deity knows the grand mystery of how everlasting life is actually restored to one who has died.

Alma knew there was a "time appointed that all shall come forth from the dead," though he confessed that he did not know just how many moments of such resurrection there would be. He was satisfied that God knew all such chronologies and that it was not necessary for him to know them.[127] Furthermore, he had to clarify for Corianton the erroneous teaching of some at the time who were teaching what was called a "resurrection" but clearly was not. These were speaking incorrectly of the Resurrection as a nonphysical, figurative event—"the raising of the spirit or the soul . . . to happiness or misery."[128]

Lastly, Alma could not say whether the wicked would be reunited in the same time frame as the righteous, but he gave it as his "opinion"—which would prove to be absolutely correct—that at least the soul and body of *the righteous* would be resurrected at the time of Christ's resurrection and ascension into heaven.[129] Understandably he was not so presumptuous as to say whether that would be precisely at the moment of Christ's resurrection or immediately thereafter,[130] a matter on which God had never spoken.

In spite of these few unknown details of the Resurrection, what Alma had inquired diligently of the Lord to know and had been told was that a time was granted between death and the Resurrection in which "the spirits of all men, as soon as they are departed from this mortal body, yea, the spirits of all men, whether they be good or evil, are taken home to that God who gave them life." He learned that there the spirits are divided into two broad categories. The righteous enter into a state of happiness, rest, and peace called paradise, "where they shall rest from all their troubles and from all care, and sorrow." The wicked, on the other hand, are cast into "outer darkness," a rather severe but accurate description of the spirit prison spoken of by Peter.[131] In fact, the spirit prison was a place of darkness until the redeeming light of the gospel came to those individuals. Furthermore, for those in the spirit prison who reject the offer of Christ's saving and enlightening doctrine, darkness will remain until the time of their resurrection.

RESTORATION

Alma also knew, as did other Book of Mormon prophets, that a doctrine of restoration accompanied the doctrine of the Resurrection. Physically this meant that "the soul shall be restored to the body, and the body to the soul; yea, and every limb and joint shall be restored to its body; yea, even a hair of the head shall not be lost; but all things shall be restored to their proper and perfect frame."[132] That declaration came with almost the same phrasing and certainly the same doctrinal insight that Amulek had earlier taught: "The spirit and the body shall be reunited again in its perfect form; both limb and joint shall be restored to its proper frame, even as we now are at this time; and we shall be brought to stand before God, knowing even as we know now, and have a bright recollection of all our guilt.

"Now, this restoration shall come to all, both old and young, both bond and free, both male and female, both the wicked and the righteous; and even there shall not so much as a hair of their heads be lost; but every thing shall be restored to its perfect frame, as it is now, or in the body, and shall be brought and be arraigned before the bar of Christ the Son, and God the Father, and the Holy Spirit, which is one Eternal God, to be judged according to their works, whether they be good or whether they be evil."[133]

The spiritual impact of that doctrine of restoration is sobering for those who may have believed that Christ's atonement and their resurrection would somehow bring something more than was deserved. Alma made it very clear that if our works are good in this life, and the desires of our hearts are good, then in the Resurrection we will be restored to that which is good. But, by the same token, if our works are evil, then our reward will be the restoration of evil in the Resurrection. To Corianton, who apparently was taking casually some of these "points of doctrine,"[134] Alma expressed strongly that no one should fallaciously assume that the restorative powers of the Resurrection could restore one "from sin to happiness." That can never be, for "wickedness never was happiness.

"And now, my son, all men that are in a state of nature, or I would say, in a carnal state, are in the gall of bitterness and in the bonds of iniquity; they are without God in the world, and they have gone contrary to the nature of God; therefore, they are in a state contrary to the nature of happiness.

"And now behold, is the meaning of the word restoration to take a thing of a natural state and place it in an unnatural state, or to place it in a state opposite to its nature?

"O, my son, this is not the case; but the meaning of the word restoration is to bring back again evil for evil, or carnal for carnal, or devilish for devilish—good for that which is good; righteous for that which is righteous; just for that which is just; merciful for that which is merciful."

On the strength of that doctrine Alma encouraged Corianton to do that which he would have done unto him. In his relationship with others he should act mercifully, deal justly, judge righteously, and "do good continually." On the divine principle of restoration, all such would then be returned to him in his eternal reward.

"Yea, ye shall have mercy restored unto you again; ye shall have justice restored unto you again; ye shall have a righteous judgment restored unto you again; and ye shall have good rewarded unto you again.

"For that which ye do send out shall return unto you again, and be restored; therefore, the word restoration more fully condemneth the sinner, and justifieth him not at all."[135]

Of course, the ultimate promise in the Resurrection is that we will "die no more." But it is important not to confuse the miracle of restored life in mortality, such as Christ gave to Lazarus (who would later die—again—like all other mortals), with the doctrine of resurrection into immortality, after which the spirit is never again separated from the body. Amulek made this point very clear: "Now, behold, I have spoken unto you concerning the death of the mortal body, and also concerning the resurrection of the mortal body. I say unto you that this mortal body is raised to an immortal body, that is from death, even from the first death unto life, that they can die no more; their spirits uniting with their bodies, never to be divided; thus the whole becoming spiritual and immortal, that they can no more see corruption."[136]

The limitations experienced by an unembodied spirit are well documented in the doctrine of the restored gospel, doctrine gleaned first from Book of Mormon passages.[137] Later, in 1833, the

Lord would say to the Prophet Joseph Smith, "Man is spirit. The elements are eternal, and spirit and element, inseparably connected [the definition of the Resurrection], receive a fulness of joy; and when separated, man cannot receive a fulness of joy."[138] The Lord also taught, "The spirit and the body are the soul of man. And the resurrection from the dead is the redemption of the soul."[139]

We should not be surprised at this definition of the soul, for it is contained in the very grammar of the Book of Mormon. For example, Jacob said, "The spirit and the body *is* [singular] restored to *itself* [singular] again, and all men become incorruptible, and immortal, and they are living souls."[140]

ROBED IN RIGHTEOUSNESS

In the imagery of the gospel of Jesus Christ, it is always better to be clothed than unclothed, to be robed rather than naked. Jacob taught that the wicked will have a knowledge of guilt and uncleanness that leads them to feel naked before God, whereas the righteous shall have a perfect knowledge of their enjoyment and their righteousness, "being clothed with purity, yea, even with the robe of righteousness."[141]

As a universal gift flowing from the atonement of Christ, the Resurrection will clothe with a permanent, perfected, restored body every spirit ever born into mortality. Furthermore, for every person who accepts the principles and ordinances of the gospel, that person's body will be something of a robe of righteousness. Therein is the redemption of the soul, and therein is a fulness of joy throughout all eternity, including, in its highest order, "a fulness and a continuation of the seeds forever and ever."[142]

The royal role and priestly power of celestial kings and queens, including the restored and perfected bodies commensurate with such a station, are among the highest and holiest gifts of the atonement of Jesus Christ. When we consider that the alternative was to see our bodies decayed and lifeless in the grave while our spirits became "devils, angels to a devil, to be shut out from the presence of our God, and to remain with the Father of lies, in misery, like unto himself,"[143] little wonder that we say of the Savior of the world, "O the greatness of the mercy of our God, the Holy One of Israel! For he delivereth his saints from that awful monster the devil, and death, and hell."[144] Little wonder that one stands "all amazed at the love Jesus offers me, confused at the grace that so fully he proffers me. . . . Oh, it is wonderful, wonderful to me!"[145]

APPEARANCE

CHAPTER ELEVEN

CHRIST IN
THE NEW WORLD:
THE FIRST DAY

alph Waldo Emerson once wrote, "If the stars should appear one night in a thousand years, how would men believe and adore; and preserve for many generations the remembrance of the city of God which has been shown them!"[1]

In the spirit of that thought, consider another startling—and much more important—scene that would evoke belief and adoration, a scene that, like the stars at night, we have undoubtedly taken too much for granted. Imagine the people of Nephi in the land of Bountiful in approximately A.D. 34. Tempests, earthquakes, whirlwinds, and storms, quickened and cut by thunder and sharp lightning, enveloped the entire face of the land. Entire cities burst into flame as if by spontaneous combustion. Others disappeared into the sea or were covered by mounds of soil. Some were carried away by the wind.[2]

All this was done in three hours—the final three hours Christ hung on the cross in the Old World—a time and destruction so severe, as prophesied by Zenos, that "the kings of the isles of the sea" would exclaim, "The God of nature suffers."[3] Then darkness settled upon the land for three days:

"And it came to pass that there was thick darkness upon all

the face of the land, insomuch that the inhabitants thereof who had not fallen could feel the vapor of darkness;

"And there could be no light, because of the darkness, neither candles, neither torches; neither could there be fire kindled with their fine and exceedingly dry wood, so that there could not be any light at all;

"And there was not any light seen, neither fire, nor glimmer, neither the sun, nor the moon, nor the stars, for so great were the mists of darkness which were upon the face of the land.

"And it came to pass that it did last for the space of three days that there was no light seen; and there was great mourning and howling and weeping among all the people continually; yea, great were the groanings of the people, because of the darkness and the great destruction which had come upon them."[4]

Later (after at least the Savior's forty-day post-resurrection ministry to his disciples in the Old World), people were milling about the temple grounds at Bountiful, still marveling at the changes that had come to the land. Suddenly, out of the heavens, a voice of sweet, piercing power said, "Behold my Beloved Son, in whom I am well pleased, in whom I have glorified my name— hear ye him."[5] As the people gazed into heaven, a man clothed in a white robe descended, emanating the very essence of light and life. His glory was a splendid and sharp contrast to the three days of death and darkness experienced earlier by these people.

Then the Son spoke, with a voice that penetrated to the marrow, saying simply, "I am Jesus Christ, whom the prophets testified shall come into the world."[6]

That appearance and that declaration constituted the focal point, the supreme moment, in the entire history of the Book of Mormon. It was the manifestation and the decree that had informed and inspired every Nephite prophet for the previous six hundred years, to say nothing of their Israelite and Jaredite forefathers for thousands of years before that.

Everyone had talked of him, sung of him, dreamed of him, and prayed for his appearance—but here he actually was. The day of days! The God who turns every dark night into morning light had arrived.

Of all the messages that could come from the scroll of eternity, what was the declaration he brought? The Nephite faithful listened as he spoke: "I am the light and the life of the world; and I have drunk out of that bitter cup which the Father hath given me, and have glorified the Father in taking upon me the sins of the world, in the which I have suffered the will of the Father in all things from the beginning."[7] Fifty-six words. The essence of his earthly mission. Obedience and loyalty to the will of the Father, however bitter the cup or painful the price. That is a lesson he would teach these Nephites again and again during the three days he would be with them. By obedience and sacrifice, by humility and purity, by unflagging determination to glorify the Father, Christ was himself glorified. In complete devotion to the Father's will, Christ had become the light and the life of the world. "And . . . when Jesus had spoken these words the whole multitude fell to the earth."[8]

Signs of Christ's Birth

Consider the events that led up to this New World advent. It was not mere coincidence that this appearance came following a severe test of Nephite faith, a test on the very subject with which Christ announced his arrival—obedience to the will of the Father.

Prior to the night of Christ's birth, the Nephites had been watching steadfastly for the sign of his mortal advent, "that day and that night and that day which should be as one day as if there were no night, that they might know that their faith had not been vain."[9] That sign was to be life-or-death evidence in more ways than one, for the unbelievers had declared that "all those who believed in those traditions should be put to death except the sign should come to pass."[10]

When Nephi, the son of Nephi, saw the wickedness of his people, his heart was "exceedingly sorrowful." With great concern for the safety of the faithful, he "went out and bowed himself down upon the earth, and cried mightily to his God in behalf of his people, yea, those who were about to be destroyed because of their faith in the tradition of their fathers."

After Nephi had prayed with such urgency throughout the entire day, the voice of the Lord came to him, saying, "Lift up your head and be of good cheer; for behold, the time is at hand, and on this night shall the sign be given, and on the morrow come I into the world, to show unto the world that I will fulfil all that which I have caused to be spoken by the mouth of my holy prophets.

"Behold, I come unto my own, to fulfil all things which I have made known unto the children of men from the foundation of the world, and to do the will, both of the Father and of the Son—of the Father because of me, and of the Son because of my flesh. And behold, the time is at hand, and this night shall the sign be given."[11]

In fulfillment of that promise, there was no darkness all that night. It was, rather, as light as midday. When morning came, the sun rose again, "according to its proper order," The Nephites knew it was the day the Lord would be born "because of the sign which had been given. . . . And it came to pass also that a new star did appear, according to the word."[12]

OPPOSITION FROM SATAN

It is revealing and ironic to note how the adversary will use any means possible to abuse the gospel plan, even to the point of encouraging its use—so long as that use is *not* what God desires, as in this instance where the law of Moses (not the gospel) was still the governing code. As with New Testament teachings, so too with Book of Mormon theology. It was not the birth of Christ that fulfilled the law of Moses but rather his death, his atoning sacrifice. Therefore the Nephites were still under obligation to observe that ancient Mosaic code even though the sign of Christ's birth had been received.

Even though this sequence of events would bring the triumph of the Savior and the ultimate defeat of Lucifer, the latter must have smiled just a little to see that "there were no contentions, save it were a few that began to preach, endeavoring to prove by the scriptures that it was no more expedient to observe the law of Moses. Now in this thing they did err, having not understood the scriptures."[13]

Something else must have given Lucifer foul delight as well. In spite of this miraculous moment of Christ's birth, in yet another manifestation of the natural man and the natural mind, "people began to forget those signs and wonders which they had heard, and began to be less and less astonished at a sign or a wonder from heaven, insomuch that they began to be hard in their hearts, and blind in their minds, and began to disbelieve all which they had heard and seen—

"Imagining up some vain thing in their hearts, that it was wrought by men and by the power of the devil, to lead away and deceive the hearts of the people; and thus did Satan get possession of the hearts of the people again, insomuch that he did blind their eyes and lead them away to believe that the doctrine of Christ was a foolish and a vain thing."[14]

Some things never seem to change.

PROPHETIC POWER

For the next thirty years, Nephite civilization proceeded according to their long-established pattern—moments of righteousness and consequent prosperity followed by transgression and alienation. But the transcendent moments were transcendent indeed. At one point "there was not a living soul among all the people of the Nephites who did doubt in the least the words of all the holy prophets who had spoken; for they knew that it must needs be that they must be fulfilled.

"And they knew that it must be expedient that Christ had come, because of the many signs which had been given, according to the words of the prophets. . . .

"Therefore they did forsake all their sins, and their abominations, and their whoredoms, and did serve God with all diligence day and night."[15]

That kind of faithfulness brought prosperity so great that "nothing in all the land [could] hinder the people from prospering continually, except they should fall into transgression." But fall into transgression they did, as a result of those two challenges that were forever the destruction of Nephite righteousness—pride and riches.[16] In a short time, great inequality developed in the Nephite church, insomuch that it "began to be broken up; yea, insomuch that in the thirtieth year the church was broken up in all the land save it were among a few of the Lamanites who were converted unto the truth faith; and they would not depart from it."[17]

It is interesting to note—again against the backdrop of Christ's appearance and the declaration that in all things he had obeyed the will of the Father—that the unfaithful "did not sin ignorantly, for they knew the will of God concerning them, for it had been taught unto them; therefore they did wilfully rebel against God."[18]

To counter such willful disobedience, many men, "inspired from heaven and sent forth," stood among the people and testified boldly of the redemption that the Lord would make for his people, "or in other words, the resurrection of Christ; and they did testify boldly of his death and sufferings."[19] The most powerful of these was Nephi, son of Nephi, who had been visited by angels, had heard the voice of the Lord, and was an eyewitness, "having had power given unto him that he might know concerning the ministry of Christ" and who testified boldly the principles of repentance, remission of sins, faith on the Lord Jesus Christ.

Although his opponents were often unresponsive, they could not gainsay such prophetic power. "And it came to pass that they were angry with him, even because he had greater power than they, for it were not possible that they could disbelieve his words, for so great was his faith on the Lord Jesus Christ that angels did minister unto him daily.

"And in the name of Jesus did he cast out devils and unclean spirits; and even his brother did he raise from the dead. . . . And he did also many more miracles, in the sight of the people, in the name of Jesus."[20]

THE VOICE OF CHRIST TO THE NEPHITES

In spite of these kinds of divine manifestations, unrighteousness largely prevailed. Recompense came with unprecedented force. On the fourth day of the first month in the thirty-fourth year of the new Nephite calendar (who now reckoned time from the night and the day that had indicated Christ's birth), there arose the great storm that has been mentioned, "such an one as never had been known in all the land."[21]

After noting the devastation among the people, over which "the devil laughe[d], and his angels rejoice[d], because of the slain of the fair sons and daughters" of the Lord's people, a voice from the darkness of destruction cried out, "O all ye that are spared because ye were more righteous than they, will ye not now return unto me, and repent of your sins, and be converted, that I may heal you?

"Yea, verily I say unto you, if ye will come unto me ye shall have eternal life. Behold, mine arm of mercy is extended towards you, and whosoever will come, him will I receive; and blessed are those who come unto me."[22]

Out of the darkness of destruction came the voice the Nephite nation had waited more than six hundred years to hear.

"Behold, I am Jesus Christ the Son of God," he said. "I created the heavens and the earth, and all things that in them are. I was with the Father from the beginning. I am in the Father, and the Father in me; and in me hath the Father glorified his name.

"I came unto my own, and my own received me not. And the scriptures concerning my coming are fulfilled. . . . By me redemption cometh, and in me is the law of Moses fulfilled.

"I am the light and the life of the world. I am Alpha and Omega, the beginning and the end.

"And ye shall offer up unto me no more the shedding of blood; yea, your sacrifices and your burnt offerings shall be done away, for I will accept none of your sacrifices and your burnt offerings.

"And ye shall offer for a sacrifice unto me a broken heart and a contrite spirit. And whoso cometh unto me with a broken heart and a contrite spirit, him will I baptize with fire and with the Holy Ghost. . . .

"Behold, I have come unto the world to bring redemption unto the world, to save the world from sin.

"Therefore, whoso repenteth and cometh unto me as a little child, him will I receive, for of such is the kingdom of God. Behold, for such I have laid down my life, and have taken it up again; therefore repent, and come unto me ye ends of the earth, and be saved."[23]

As should be expected, such an introductory pronouncement from the great Jehovah/Jesus himself is laden with doctrinal significance. Note the key doctrinal elements contained in these eight verses. Every line contains deep, divine meanings.

- The heavenly voice was that of Jesus Christ, who declared himself to be the Son of God.[24]

- He was the creator of the heavens, the earth, and "all things that in them are."[25]

- He was with the Father from the beginning.[26]

- He is in the Father, and the Father in him.[27]

- In him the Father has glorified his name.[28]

- He had come to his own people (his own tribe or family), and they had received him not.[29]

- All the scriptures concerning his coming were now fulfilled.[30]

- To those who had received him, including the ordinances and covenants involved, he provided a way to become the sons and daughters of God.[31]

- He would extend that same privilege to all who would yet believe on his name.[32]

- By him alone redemption comes.[33]

- In his completed mortal ministry the law of Moses was fulfilled.[34]

- He is the light and the life of the world.[35]

- He is Alpha and Omega, the hope of our victory in the beginning of the plan and the evidence of our triumph at the end of it.[36]

- All blood sacrifices and burnt offerings were to be done away. None such would be accepted by him in the future.[37]

- A "new" sacrifice, the spirit of which was always to have been the motivating force behind the earlier symbolic sacrifices, is that of "a broken heart and a contrite spirit." These are the ultimate symbols of Christ's death, a death that came as a result of the contrition he felt for the world's sins and the broken, sorrowing heart that ruptured as he hung upon the cross.[38]

· Whoever will come to Christ with a broken heart and a contrite spirit will be baptized with fire and with the Holy Ghost.[39]

· Christ came into the world to bring redemption and to save the world from sin.[40]

· All who so repent and come unto him "as a little child" will be received, "for of such is the kingdom of God." He said, "For such I have laid down my life, and have taken it up again."[41]

Concurrent with these and other such magnificent declarations,[42] the darkness lifted and the earth ceased to tremble. The light of the world had come. The more righteous part of the people had been saved, through their obedience, and were now prepared to receive the visitation of the Son of God himself.

CHRIST'S APPEARANCE AT THE TEMPLE

Following his appearance and declaration of obedience, Christ dramatically reinforced the price he had paid to suffer the will of the Father in all things. As evidence of his loyalty and as a reward to the congregation for theirs, Christ spoke to those gathered at the temple, saying, "Arise and come forth unto me, that ye may thrust your hands into my side, and also that ye may feel the prints of the nails in my hands and in my feet, that ye may know that I am the God of Israel, and the God of the whole earth, and have been slain for the sins of the world."[43]

At that invitation, the entire multitude went forth "one by one," thrusting their hands into his side and feeling the prints of the nails in his hands and feet. Even though the power of the Resurrection could have—and undoubtedly one day will have—

completely restored and made new the wounds from the crucifixion, nevertheless Christ chose to retain those wounds for a
purpose, including for his appearance in the last days when he
will show those marks and reveal that he was wounded "in the
house of [his] friends."[44]

The wounds in his hands, feet, and side are signs that in mortality painful things happen even to the pure and the perfect,
signs that tribulation is *not* evidence that God does not love us.
It is a significant and hopeful fact that it is the *wounded* Christ
who comes to our rescue. He who bears the scars of sacrifice, the
lesions of love, the emblems of humility and forgiveness is the
Captain of our Soul. That evidence of pain in mortality is
undoubtedly intended to give courage to others who are also
hurt and wounded by life, perhaps even in the house of their
friends.

In spite of the size of the great multitude, Christ nevertheless
took time for each one to have that personal experience. All "did
see with their eyes and did feel with their hands, and did know
of a surety and did bear record, that it was he, of whom it was
written by the prophets, that should come." They shouted their
exaltations and hosannahs and fell down at the feet of Jesus to
worship him.[45]

BAPTISM BY IMMERSION AT THE HANDS
OF ONE WHO HAS AUTHORITY

Before Christ taught these people the grand truths he was
about to deliver, he gave wonderful evidence for the importance
of ordinances in the gospel. Although these Nephites had
authority to baptize in the old Mosaic dispensation, Christ
invited Nephi forward to affirm his priesthood authority to baptize in the new gospel dispensation, and perhaps to ordain him
to the apostleship at the same time.[46] Then he called another
group forward, instructing them how to baptize and noting that

there would be "no disputations" among them on this crucial doctrine.

He instructed the Nephites to "go down and stand in the water" and to give a precise baptismal prayer; they were then to call the baptismal candidates by name and "immerse them in the water, and come forth again out of the water."

Stressing, "thus shall ye baptize," the Master in whose name and by whose authority baptisms are performed again said, "There shall be no disputations among you, as there have hitherto been; neither shall there be disputations among you concerning the points of *my doctrine*, as there have hitherto been."[47]

Perhaps anticipating the controversies that would creep into later Christendom over doctrines as fundamental as baptism by immersion, Christ made it clear from what source such confusion would come: "He that hath the spirit of contention is not of me, but is of the devil, who is the father of contention, and he stirreth up the hearts of men to contend with anger, one with another."

He continued, "Behold, this is not *my doctrine*, to stir up the hearts of men with anger, one against another; but *this is my doctrine*, that such things should be done away. . . .

"Behold . . . I will declare unto you *my doctrine*.

"And *this is my doctrine*, and it is the doctrine which the Father hath given unto me; . . . I bear record that the Father commandeth all men, everywhere, to repent and believe in me.

"And whoso believeth in me, and is baptized, the same shall be saved; and they are they who shall inherit the kingdom of God.

"And whoso believeth not in me, and is not baptized, shall be damned.

"Verily, verily I say unto you, that *this is my doctrine*. . . .

"Ye must repent, and become as a little child, and be baptized in my name, or ye can in nowise . . . inherit the kingdom of God.

"Verily, verily, I say unto you, that *this is my doctrine*, and whoso buildeth upon this buildeth upon my rock, and the gates of hell shall not prevail against them.

"And whoso shall declare more or less than this, and establish it for *my doctrine*, the same cometh of evil, and is not built upon my rock."[48]

The Savior stressed such strong, recurring themes as the unity of the Godhead and the need for all disciples to be as little children, but clearly the foundational doctrine of baptism is at the heart of Christ's saving ministry,[49] for he repeated the phrase "my doctrine"—particularly as applied to baptism—at least eight times in his unequivocal counsel to the Nephites.

SERMON AT THE TEMPLE

This clear, resonant call to baptism was important not only because of baptism's role as the first of the saving ordinances of the gospel but also because it provided the context for Christ's Sermon at the Temple, a sermon parallel to but more extensive than his Sermon on the Mount in the New Testament.[50] No attempt will be made in this volume to examine the verse-by-verse magnificence of this greatest of all Christian sermons. Entire books can—and have—been written doing just that. This present work will limit its review, as already begun in this chapter, to those elements in the Book of Mormon sermon that cast new or distinctive light on the New Testament account.

It is clear at the outset that the sermon in the Book of Mormon is built upon one overwhelmingly important premise that is not so obvious in the New Testament—that the doctrines taught and the blessings promised are predicated upon first principles, on saving ordinances and covenants of the gospel, including the baptismal covenant, which brings people through "the gate" to the strait and narrow path leading to eternal life. As Christ taught here, so Nephi taught earlier—that these first principles and ordinances constitute the "doctrine of Christ."[51]

That the full and complete promises of the sermon are intended for baptized members of his church is clear from the Savior's introductory admonition to those gathered. When he had concluded his message to Nephi and the eleven others who had joined him for that priesthood instruction, Christ turned to the congregation and said,

"Blessed are ye if ye shall give heed unto the words of these twelve whom I have chosen from among you to minister unto you, and to be your servants; and unto them I have given power that they may baptize you with water; and after that ye are baptized with water, behold, I will baptize you with fire and with the Holy Ghost; therefore blessed are ye if ye shall believe in me and be baptized, after that ye have seen me and know that I am.

"And again, more blessed are they who shall believe in your words because that ye shall testify that ye have seen me, and that ye know that I am. Yea, blessed are they who shall believe in your words, and come down into the depths of humility and be baptized, for they shall be visited with fire and with the Holy Ghost, and shall receive a remission of their sins."[52]

Clearly the last half of 3 Nephi 11 and the significant first two verses of 3 Nephi 12 indicate that the covenant and doctrine of baptism—over which there was to be *no* disputation—is fundamental to the full meaning and realization of what we then hear the Savior promise in the Sermon at the Temple or the Sermon on the Mount.

For example, Christ began, "Yea, blessed are the poor in spirit"; the Book of Mormon sermon added the phrase "who *come unto me*, for theirs is the kingdom of heaven."[53] Obviously in the 3 Nephi rendering, being poor in spirit is not in itself a virtue, but it will be so if such humility brings one to claim the blessings of the kingdom through the waters of baptism, making covenants, and moving toward all the promises given to covenant-making disciples. It is significant that the phrase "come unto me" is used at least four more times in the twenty or so verses that follow this one. So, too, with those who "hunger and thirst after righteousness." If they hunger and thirst enough to be baptized and keep the commandments, they will be filled *"with the Holy Ghost."*[54]

Latter-day Saints are not the only ones to see significance in the sermon, which goes well beyond standard Christian truths and noble Christian ethics. Some scholars have thought, for example, that the Sermon on the Mount was used by early Christians as a catechism for "baptismal candidates or newly baptized Christians." Others suggest it was produced for use in "a school for teachers and church leaders," a kind of general handbook of instructions for teaching and administration. Still others thought it was "the new law of God given at a mountain, replicating the giving of the law of Moses on Mount Sinai set in a five part structure that mirrors the five books of the Pentateuch."[55]

One example of the contribution made by the Book of Mormon to our understanding of the New Testament text is the explicit distinction made between the portion of the sermon that was for the multitude generally and the part that was for only the twelve disciples. The Book of Mormon text makes clear that all of 3 Nephi 12 and the first twenty-four verses of 3 Nephi 13 were given to the multitude at large.

Then (as recorded in 3 Nephi 13:25) Christ made a distinct shift in his audience. He ceased speaking to the multitude and turned to teach the twelve disciples, giving them specific apostolic promises. This distinction is not clear in the Sermon on the Mount.

"When Jesus had spoken these words he looked upon the

twelve whom he had chosen, and said unto them: Remember the words which I have spoken. For behold, ye are they whom I have chosen to minister unto this people. *Therefore I say unto you,* take no thought for your life, what ye shall eat, or what ye shall drink; nor yet for your body, what ye shall put on. Is not the life more than meat, and the body than raiment?

"Behold the fowls of the air, for they sow not, neither do they reap nor gather into barns; yet your heavenly Father feedeth them. Are ye not much better than they?

"Which of you by taking thought can add one cubit unto his stature?

"And why take ye thought for raiment? Consider the lilies of the field how they grow; they toil not, neither do they spin;

"And yet I say unto you, that even Solomon, in all his glory, was not arrayed like one of these.

"Wherefore, if God so clothe the grass of the field, which today is, and tomorrow is cast into the oven, even so will he clothe you, if ye are not of little faith.

"Therefore take no thought, saying, What shall we eat? or, What shall we drink? or, Wherewithal shall we be clothed?

"For your heavenly Father knoweth that ye have need of all these things.

"But seek ye first the kingdom of God and his righteousness, and all these things shall be added unto you.

"Take therefore no thought for the morrow, for the morrow shall take thought for the things of itself. Sufficient is the day unto the evil thereof."[56]

In a general sense these verses can apply to all believers, but at their most literal level they apply to those the Lord has called as his full-time witnesses. Most people must give some thought to what they will eat and what they will wear; the necessities of life require it. But the twelve disciples were not to do so, for they were chosen "to minister unto [the] people." Their call was to give complete devotion to their spiritual ministry and to trust in God's—and the people's—providence for their temporal needs.

Then, "when Jesus had spoken these words [to the twelve disciples] he turned again to the multitude, and did open his mouth unto them."[57]

THE LAW AND THE COVENANT

As Christ concluded, he perceived that some of his congregation were confused about the law of Moses, about old things passing away and all things becoming new, a theme running through the entire sermon.

To them he said, "The law is fulfilled that was given unto Moses. Behold, I am he that gave the law, and I am he who covenanted with my people Israel; therefore, the law in me is fulfilled, for I have come to fulfil the law; therefore it hath an end."[58]

Regarding the concluding of Moses' law, Christ made it clear what—or more properly who—was taking its place: "I am the law, and the light. Look unto me, and endure to the end, and ye shall live; for unto him that endureth to the end will I give eternal life. Behold, I have given unto you the commandments; therefore keep my commandments. And this is the law and the prophets, for they truly testified of me."[59]

Christ taught his twelve disciples that any knowledge of the existence of the Nephites, "who are a remnant of the house of Joseph," had been kept from those at Jerusalem, as had been any knowledge concerning "the other tribes of the house of Israel, whom the Father hath led away out of the land."[60] Except for the seemingly enigmatic comment in John 10:16 about his "other sheep," Christ was forbidden to say anything to the Jews about the location of these scattered groups.

Of this statement in the gospel of John, Christ said to the Nephites, "Because of stiffneckedness and unbelief they understood not my word; therefore I was commanded to say no more of the Father concerning this thing unto them."[61] It is undoubtedly of that restriction Christ spoke when he said to those in Jerusalem, "I have yet many things to say unto you, but ye cannot bear them now."[62] Guarding the knowledge of the location of "the other tribes [which] the Father [had] separated from them," Christ stated unequivocally of the Nephites, "Ye are they of whom I said: Other sheep I have which are not of this fold; them also I must bring, and they shall hear my voice; and there shall be one fold, and one shepherd.

"And they understood me not, for they supposed it had been the Gentiles; for they understood not that the Gentiles should be converted through their preaching.

"And they understood me not that I said they shall hear my voice; and they understood me not that the Gentiles should not at any time hear my voice—that I should not manifest myself unto them save it were by the Holy Ghost.

"But behold, ye have both heard my voice, and seen me; and ye are my sheep, and ye are numbered among those whom the Father hath given me."[63]

With that understanding about the children of Israel known and unknown, Christ returned to probe the interesting distinction between "the law," which had been fulfilled, and "the covenant," which had not. Regarding the larger covenant and the role of the Book of Mormon in gathering scattered Israel, he said to the Nephites: "I have other sheep, which are not of this land, neither of the land of Jerusalem, neither in any parts of that land round about whither I have been to minister.

"For they of whom I speak are they who have not as yet heard my voice; neither have I at any time manifested myself unto them.

"But I have received a commandment of the Father that I shall go unto them, and that they shall hear my voice, and shall be numbered among my sheep, that there may be one fold and one shepherd; therefore I go to show myself unto them."

The Savior then revealed the relationship between the gathering of the tribes of Israel and the fulfilling of the covenant. To the Nephites he continued, "I command you that ye shall write these sayings after I am gone, that if it so be that my people at Jerusalem, they who have seen me and been with me in my ministry, do not ask the Father in my name, that they may receive a knowledge of you by the Holy Ghost, and also of the other tribes whom they know not of, that these sayings which ye shall write shall be kept and shall be manifested unto the Gentiles, that through the fulness of the Gentiles, the remnant of their seed, who shall be scattered forth upon the face of the earth because of their unbelief, may be brought in, or may be brought to a knowledge of me, their Redeemer.

"And then will I gather them in from the four quarters of the earth; and *then will I fulfil the covenant which the Father hath made unto all the people of the house of Israel.*"[64]

That covenant will be remembered by Christ in those last days when people of the house of Israel are "to be smitten, and to be afflicted, and to be slain, and to be cast out from among them, and to become hated by them, and to become a hiss and a byword." At that time, if "the Gentiles shall sin against my gospel, and shall reject the fulness of my gospel," the Savior warned, they being lifted up in the pride of their hearts "above all nations, and above all the people of the whole earth," and being guilty of lyings, deceits, mischiefs, hypocrisy, murders, priestcrafts, whoredoms, and secret abominations, rejecting the fulness of Christ's gospel, "behold, saith the Father, I will bring the fulness of my gospel from among them. *And then will I remember my covenant which I have made unto my people, O house of Israel, and I will bring my gospel unto them.*"[65]

HEALING THE AFFLICTED

At the culmination of Christ's first day among the Nephites came one of the sweetest, most sacred moments recorded in the Book of Mormon. Realizing that after such a long and emotional day the people were physically weak and spiritually over-whelmed, the Lord invited them to go home and ponder the things he had taught. In a gesture that both underscores his own humility and emphasizes the importance of prayerful, spiritual confirmation of even the Savior's teachings, Jesus said to these Nephites, "Ask of the Father, in my name, that ye may under-stand, and prepare your minds for the morrow, and I come unto you again."[66]

His other duties that evening were not insignificant. "But now I go unto the Father," he said, "and also to show myself unto the lost tribes of Israel, for they are not lost unto the Father, for he knoweth whither he hath taken them."[67] Nevertheless, as he made that announcement, he looked into the faces of the multitude. The people were in tears. Out of respect for the Savior's obligations to these other Israelites, they said nothing to deter him. But the long-ing in their souls was as obvious as it was undeniable.

Looking "steadfastly upon him as if they would ask him to tarry a little longer with them," the Nephites touched the Savior's heart. Responding, he said, "Behold, my bowels are filled with compassion towards you." He seemed then to change his plans temporarily. In doing so, he provided these people with one of the spiritual highlights of his New World ministry, a testimony to the faith, devotion, and unspoken desire of these true disciples.

Calling for the sick and the blind, the halt and the maimed, the leprous and the withered, those that were "afflicted in any manner," Christ asked that they be brought forward that he might heal them. "For I have compassion upon you," he said, "my bowels are filled with mercy." Sensing with divine insight

that these people desired to behold the miracles he had performed for their brothers and sisters in Jerusalem, and recogniz-
ing instantly that their faith was sufficient for them to be healed,
Christ responded to each need within the multitude, "and he did
heal them every one as they were brought forth unto him." In
response to such an outpouring of compassion and mercy, all of
the congregation, the healed as well as the whole, did "bow
down at his feet, and did worship him; and as many as could
come . . . did kiss his feet, insomuch that they did bathe his feet
with their tears."[68]

CHILDREN AND ANGELS

In response to such great faith and the presence of such spiritual power, Christ then commanded that all the children should
be brought forward and gathered around him. The crowd immediately yielded space until every child had been brought to the
Master. With these sweet children gathered around him, something of their innocence, beauty and future brought to the Savior
a painful acknowledgment of what damage a sinful world could
bring to them. Standing with the children as a visual aid, as it
were, for the entire congregation of Nephites who looked on,
Christ "groaned within himself, and said: Father, I am troubled
because of the wickedness of the people of the house of Israel."[69]

Apparently thinking of the evil from which they must be
protected, Christ knelt and offered one of the most remarkable
prayers ever uttered—so remarkable that Mormon wrote, "The
things which he prayed cannot be written, and the multitude did
bear record who heard him.

"And after this manner do they bear record: The eye hath
never seen, neither hath the ear heard, before, so great and marvelous things as we saw and heard Jesus speak unto the Father;

"And no tongue can speak, neither can there be written by

any man, neither can the hearts of men conceive so great and marvelous things as we both saw and heard Jesus speak; and no one can conceive of the joy which filled our souls at the time we heard him pray for us unto the Father."[70]

One wonders what it might have been like to *hear* such a prayer, but it is impossible to grasp what might have been *seen* in such a prayer. What these people saw in addition to what they heard we are not told, but their experience had only begun.

Jesus concluded his supplication on behalf of the children and arose from his prayer. However, because of their overwhelming joy, the multitude did not—or could not—rise. Jesus bade them arise, saying that because of *their* faith *his joy* was full. What a remarkable gift to the Savior of the world to be so faithful and devoted, so humble and respectful, that he, the Man of Sorrows, who weeps so often for the sins of the world, could weep because his joy was full:

"And when he had said these words, he wept, . . . and he took their little children, one by one, and blessed them, and prayed unto the Father for them. And when he had done this he wept again; and he spake unto the multitude, and said unto them: Behold your little ones."[71]

Then the multitude saw the heavens open and angels descending "as it were in the midst of fire; and they came down and encircled those little ones about, and they were encircled about with fire; and the angels did minister unto them. And the multitude did see and hear and bear record; and they know that their record is true for they all of them did see and hear, every man for himself."[72]

That concluding testimony suggests something of the urgency Mormon must have felt in trying to convey that this really did happen. After this vivid description from his own words, he invoked witnesses—two thousand five hundred of them, "men, women, and children,"—stressing twice that the entire multitude "did see and hear and bear record" of this unprecedented experience.

INSTITUTION OF THE SACRAMENT

After focusing on the humility and purity of these children, Christ introduced the sacrament as an ordinance to deepen the humility and purity of the older, accountable, baptized members of the congregation. He commanded his disciples to "bring forth some bread and wine unto him," which he blessed and distributed in instituting the sacrament of the Lord's Supper among the Nephites.

He broke the bread and blessed it, giving it first to the twelve disciples. When they had eaten "and were filled" with the Holy Spirit, he commanded that they should give to the multitude. The purpose and permanence of the sacrament was explained when Christ said it was to be given to "the people of my church, unto all those who shall believe and be baptized in my name. And this shall ye always observe to do, even as I have done, even as I have broken bread and blessed it and given it unto you. And this shall ye do in remembrance of my body, which I have shown unto you. And it shall be a testimony unto the Father that ye do always remember me. And if ye do always remember me ye shall have my Spirit to be with you."[73]

Following that instruction regarding the bread, he took the cup of wine and commanded that the twelve disciples should drink, then give to the multitude that they might drink, each in turn being "filled" with the Spirit. When the disciples had done this, Jesus said to them, "Blessed are ye for this thing which ye have done, for this is fulfilling my commandments, and this doth witness unto the Father that ye are willing to do that which I have commanded you. And this shall ye always do to those who repent and are baptized in my name; and ye shall do it in remembrance of my blood, which I have shed for you, that ye may witness unto the Father that ye do always remember me. And if ye do always remember me ye shall have my Spirit to be with you."[74]

At the end of a most spiritually singular day, the sacrament recollected and reaffirmed the lesson at the beginning of the day when Christ had taught the importance of baptism. In 3 Nephi 18, he said virtually the same thing he had said in 3 Nephi 11:

Baptism	*Sacrament*
Verily, verily, I say unto you, that this is my doctrine, and whoso buildeth upon this buildeth upon my rock, and the gates of hell shall not prevail against them.	And I give unto you a commandment that ye shall do these things. And if ye shall always do these things blessed are ye, for ye are built upon my rock.
And whoso shall declare more or less than this, and establish it for my doctrine, the same cometh of evil, and is not built upon my rock; but he buildeth upon a sandy foundation, and the gates of hell stand open to receive such when the floods come and the winds beat upon them.[75]	But whoso among you shall do more or less than these are not built upon my rock, but are built upon a sandy foundation; and when the rain descends, and the floods come, and the winds blow, and beat upon them, they shall fall, and the gates of hell are ready open to receive them.[76]

"YE SEE THAT I HAVE PRAYED UNTO THE FATHER"

As a final protection against evil and to reinforce the principles of humility and purity he had been teaching, Christ enjoined the twelve disciples: "Watch and pray always, lest ye be tempted by the devil, and ye be led away captive by him," asking that these leaders pray in the Church as they had seen him pray among them. In this as in all things, Christ was the model: "Behold I am the light; I have set an example for you."[77]

Turning to the multitude, he said that they too "must watch and pray always." "For Satan desireth to have you," he said, "that he may sift you as wheat. Therefore ye must always pray unto the Father in my name; and whatsoever ye shall ask the Father in my name, which is right, believing that ye shall receive, behold it shall be given unto you. Pray in your families unto the Father, always in my name, that your wives and your children may be blessed."[78]

After the injunction to pray in families, Christ taught that we should meet in church "oft" and should pray for all who seek the Church, forbidding or casting out none. As this discourse concludes, it is clear and unequivocal that the "light" we are to hold up to the world is the fact that we pray—and pray always—as Christ prayed unto the Father: "Behold I am the light which ye shall hold up—that which ye have seen me do." And what had they seen him do? "Ye see that I have prayed unto the Father, and ye all have witnessed."[79]

Just as all of the Nephites were invited at the start of the day to see and feel the Savior's wounds,[80] all in this vast congregation were invited to experience the sacrament and the unity of prayer that they might "feel and see" in a spiritual way those same emblems of the Atonement, those reminders that Christ lived and died—and prayed—for others. The pleading of his lips and the very wounds in his flesh were in behalf of the children of God. Christ in prayer, Christ in sacrifice, Christ in supplication and suffering, the pure and humble Christ who always calls upon the Father and has sought the Father's will from the beginning—this is the light we are to hold up and, to the extent we can, the light we are to be. Our lives and our church meetings are to enable others to "feel and see" the atonement and merciful pleading of Christ in their behalf.

As with his initial counsel on baptism, so too with this concluding counsel on the sacrament and prayer: "I give you these commandments because of the disputations which have been among you. And blessed are ye if ye have no disputations among you."[81]

After touching each of his disciples personally, giving them power to bestow the Holy Ghost, Jesus ascended into heaven, concluding the first day of his ministry to the Nephites. In reviewing that day, it is impressive to note the cohesive, chiasmic nature of the messages that were delivered. Note the reinforcement and revealed unity of the manner in which this day's experience began and the way it concluded.

Christ descends (3 Nephi 11:8)

    He disperses the mists of darkness (10:9)

        He is the Light of the World (11:11)

            The people fall at the feet of Jesus,
                worship him, and kiss his feet (11:17, 19)

            Christ commands the people to arise (11:14, 20)

              He gives power to baptize (11:21–22)

                He is touched "one by one" (11:15)

                  The people see and feel the marks
                    of the Atonement (11:14–15)

                    There are to be no disputations
                      about baptism (11:22, 28)

                      Beware the temptations of the devil (11:29)

                      Repentance is the gate to baptism (11:23)

                      The significance of baptism (11:21–34)

                      Become as a little child (9:22; 11:38)

                        Build upon the Savior's rock (11:39)

                          Do no more or less than this (11:40)

                          Do no more or less than this (18:13)

                      Build upon the Savior's rock (18:12)

                      "Behold your little ones" (17:23)

                    Significance of the sacrament (18:1–32)

                    Repentance and baptism are the
                    gate to the sacrament (18:30)

                  Beware temptation of the devil (18:15, 18)

                There are to be no disputations
                about the sacrament (18:34)

                The people see and feel the spirit
                of the Atonement (18:25)

             Christ touches "one by one" (18:36)

           He gives power to bestow the Holy Ghost (18:37)

           He commands the people to arise (17:19)

        The people kiss Christ's feet and bathe
        them with their tears (17:10)

      Christ is the light unto the world (18:24)

    Overshadowing of a cloud (18:38)

Christ ascends (18:39)

CHAPTER TWELVE

CHRIST IN
THE NEW WORLD:
THE SECOND DAY

ollowing his first day's
discourse to the disciples in the New World, Jesus ascended into
heaven, and "the multitude did disperse, and every man did
take his wife and his children and did return to his own home."[1]

Inevitably, however, an event of this nature had an electrify-
ing impact on the participants, and "it was noised abroad among
the people immediately, before it was yet dark, that the multitude had seen Jesus, and that he had ministered unto them, and
that he would also show himself on the morrow unto the multitude."[2] Most of the night was spent in excited conversation and
exchange, insomuch that "an exceedingly great number, did
labor exceedingly all that night, that they might be on the morrow in the place where Jesus should show himself unto the multitude."[3]

The next morning the twelve Nephite disciples—identified
by name, including Timothy, who had been raised from the dead
by his brother Nephi—were joined by a multitude so large that
the group had to be divided into twelve segments, which the
newly called twelve disciples began to teach. It is interesting that
the twelve disciples did not have to be commanded to teach but
accepted that responsibility instinctively because of their com-

mission to be witnesses of Christ at all times and in all places. What they taught, not surprisingly, were the same lessons they had been taught the day before, "nothing varying from the words which Jesus had spoken." In the spirit of the counsel the Savior had left the night before, the twelve disciples commanded the multitude to kneel and pray to the Father in the name of Jesus, "and they did pray for that which they most desired; and they desired that the Holy Ghost should be given unto them."[4]

The limitations of this book do not allow for a definitive discussion of the role, gift, and divine influence of the Holy Ghost, but it is most significant that it was this for which the Nephite twelve prayed above all else. As Christ had not yet appeared to them for this second day (and because the Father and Son could not permanently be with them—or us—in a telestial world), the next best companionship came from that member of the Godhead who *can* be with mortals permanently—the Holy Ghost. In their ministry these newly called apostles could not always have the daily, physical presence of the Savior with them. Nevertheless, because they were to lead the Church of Jesus Christ in righteousness and be witnesses of his name throughout the Nephite world, they would surely need the prompting, the protection, the revelation, and the comfort of that One who is the spiritual extension and telestial representative of the Father and the Son.

In our own time the Prophet Joseph Smith was asked wherein The Church of Jesus Christ of Latter-day Saints differed from other religions of the day. He replied that the distinction lay in "the gift of the Holy Ghost" and that all other considerations "were contained in that gift."[5] In light of these experiences— ancient or modern, Old World or New—perhaps all disciples of Christ, all members of his true Church, should pray for the influence and guidance of the Holy Ghost as that heavenly gift "which they most desire."

When the Nephite twelve had offered up their prayer, they

went down to the water's edge, where, as part of the implementation of a new dispensation, Nephi was baptized (perhaps in the
same manner that Adam was baptized? or Alma? or Joseph
Smith?[6]). When he came up out of the water, he began to baptize
others, beginning with the other twelve Jesus had chosen.

When they were all baptized and had come up out of the
water, "the Holy Ghost did fall upon them, and they were filled
with the Holy Ghost and with fire."[7] Indeed, these who were
renewing their baptismal covenants in this newer, higher dispensation were encircled by fire, followed by angels who came
down from heaven and ministered to them. In the crowning
manifestation of this heavenly sequence, Jesus appeared, standing in the midst of the group. Reinforcing and encouraging his
teachings on humility and purity of the day before, and capital-
izing on the spiritual atmosphere established among the congregation by the twelve disciples, Jesus commanded the twelve
disciples and the multitude to kneel again and to pray.[8]

CHRIST'S INTERCESSORY PRAYER

Inviting the twelve disciples to lead out in prayer, Jesus himself "departed out of the midst of them, and went a little way off
from them and bowed himself to the earth" and prayed:

"Father, I thank thee that thou hast given the Holy Ghost
unto these whom I have chosen," he began, "and it is because of
their belief in me that I have chosen them out of the world.

"Father, I pray thee that thou wilt give the Holy Ghost unto
all them that shall believe in their words.

"Father, thou hast given them the Holy Ghost because they
believe in me; and thou seest that they believe in me because
thou hearest them, and they pray unto me; and they pray unto
me because I am with them.

"And now Father, I pray unto thee for them, and also for all those who shall believe on their words, that they may believe in me, that I may be in them as thou, Father, art in me, that we may be one."[9]

That is, of course, a variation on the great intercessory prayer Christ offered for his disciples on the eve of his crucifixion in the Old World, praying that his followers might be unified with the Father and the Son, as well as with each other, and be taken from the adverse temptations and evil influences of the world.[10]

From the Savior's language, we see clearly it is the Holy Ghost that provides such unity, a doctrinal point not so clearly communicated in the New Testament account. Furthermore, it is significant that one of the ultimate evidences God has of our belief in Deity is that we are seen and heard praying. Christ noted this evidence on behalf of the Nephites. To the Father he said, "Thou seest that they believe in me because thou hearest them."[11] Disciples of Christ should be seen and heard in prayer. It is the key to the miraculous manifestations of heaven and the personal companionship of the Holy Comforter(s).

After Jesus had prayed to the Father in this manner, he returned to the disciples, who continued to pray unceasingly, "and they did not multiply many words, for it was given unto them what they should pray, and they were filled with desire."[12] Many have wondered how one can pray without ceasing in a way that does not "multiply words." The key is that if our desire to communicate is great enough, we will be given what we should say. Furthermore, the Holy Ghost will intercede in our behalf, aiding in the communication of our hearts even if words seem to fail us. "The Spirit also helpeth our infirmities," Paul taught, "for we know not what we should pray for as we ought: but the Spirit itself maketh intercession for us with groanings which cannot be uttered."[13] Urgency and desire coupled with divine promptings preclude any shallow multiplication of words in prayer.

While the disciples were praying, "Jesus blessed them . . .

and his countenance did smile upon them, and the light of his countenance did shine upon them"[14] to the degree that the people became as white as Christ's countenance and clothing: "The whiteness thereof did exceed all the whiteness, yea, even there could be nothing upon earth so white as the whiteness thereof. And Jesus said unto them: Pray on; nevertheless they did not cease to pray."[15] What a wonderful image—Christ blessing the people in the very moment of their act of prayer!

Christ turned and walked away, bowed himself to the earth, and continued his New World intercessory prayer: "Father, I thank thee that thou hast purified those whom I have chosen, because of their faith, and I pray for them, and also for them who shall believe on their words, that they may be purified in me, through faith on their words, even as they are purified in me.

"Father, I pray not for the world, but for those whom thou hast given me out of the world, because of their faith, that they may be purified in me, that I may be in them as thou, Father, art in me, that we may be one, that I may be glorified in them."[16]

Here again was the plea for unity with the Father and the Son, referencing once more the influence of the Holy Ghost. In addition to this gift of the Spirit—or because of it—those who would be one with the Father and the Son had to be purified, a state that could come not only through faith in God but also through faith in the words of the twelve disciples, who acted in the purity given of God. Ultimately all believers will be safely "out of the world" because of their faith. All believers will ultimately be unified with the Father and the Son through purity.

Following the intercessory prayer, Christ returned again to his disciples, who were still praying "steadfastly, without ceasing." He smiled upon them again, and they were "white, even as Jesus." A third time he left them to go "a little way off"[17] and pray unto the Father.

This third segment of his intercessory prayer for these

Nephites was impossible to record. "Tongue cannot speak the words which he prayed, neither can be written by man the words which he prayed,"[18] Mormon said. But the multitude who were present did hear, and their hearts were opened, united by the Holy Ghost and personal purity, in a way that they could understand that which Christ prayed. "Nevertheless, so great and marvelous were the words which he prayed that they cannot be written, neither can they be uttered by man."[19]

Christ commended the prayerful attitude of his disciples, noting that it was evidence of faith more perfect than he had seen among all the Jews, and that none in the Old World had seen or heard the great things these Nephites had seen "because of their unbelief."[20] The image of the praying Christ was the light these Nephites were to hold up to the world, and they were already holding it up in a remarkably devoted way.

THE SACRAMENT

With the reminder that the multitude "should not cease to pray in their hearts,"[21] Christ commanded them that they should cease their vocal prayer and stand upon their feet. He again provided the sacrament, blessing the bread and giving it to the disciples to eat. Then, in a departure from the ordinance of the previous day, when it appears that the Savior alone blessed the bread and wine to be administered to all, he commanded that the twelve disciples should break and bless the bread, then give it to the multitude. We presume the same pattern was followed with the wine.

In this conscious act of involving the twelve disciples in the ordinance, Christ was obviously showing the multitude that these brethren had authority to administer it, and it was not a one-time occurrence to be administered by Christ alone. Partaking of the sacrament was, after all, a new experience for them, and without that visible expression of permission and authority for the twelve disciples to officiate, the multitude might have resisted any perpetuation of the ordinance once Christ had departed.

In a classic example of Hebraic understatement, a miracle associated with this sacramental ordinance is alluded to but given no explanation. The reference assumes—and requires—the reader's faith. Almost as an aside, Mormon said of the experience, "There had been no bread, neither wine, brought by the disciples, neither by the multitude; but he truly gave unto them bread to eat, and also wine to drink."[22]

We are left to ponder where the bread and wine came from. Was it a New World variation of the five barley loaves and two small fishes that expanded to feed five thousand in the Old World? Was there some kind of divine intervention, as when Jesus was seized in Nazareth to be thrown from the brow of a hill, "but he passing through the midst of them went his way"?[23] Whatever the answer, the writer presumed that future readers would understand that such things happen, and that how they happen probably cannot be written, but in every case these are manifestations of divine involvement and assistance in the work of the Lord's true church.

One of the invitations inherent in the sacramental ordinance is that it be a truly spiritual experience, a holy communion, a renewal for the soul. Jesus said to these Nephites, "He that eateth this bread eateth of my body *to his soul;* and he that drinketh of this wine drinketh of my blood *to his soul;* and *his soul shall never hunger nor thirst,* but shall be filled."[24]

In Mormon's account of the previous day's sacramental experience, he noted repeatedly that the disciples and the multitude were "filled" by the tiny emblems of a crust of bread and a sip of wine.[25] Obviously they were not "filled" physically. This invitation from Christ to take the meaning of the sacrament to our very souls provides the context for how one is filled by such tiny emblems, for when the multitude had eaten the bread and drunk the wine, they were "*filled with the Spirit;* and they did cry out with one voice, and gave glory to Jesus, whom they both saw and heard."[26]

THE COVENANT AND THE MESSENGER OF THE COVENANT

With the Savior's teachings, culminating in the implementation of the sacrament, a certain sense of completion came in his visit to the Nephites. At that juncture the Lord said to them, "Now I finish the commandment which the Father hath commanded me concerning this people, who are a remnant of the house of Israel."[27]

Keying off the personal covenant these people had just made, a covenant initiated at baptism and renewed by partaking of the sacrament, Christ gave a major discourse on the larger covenant that the Father has made with the house of Israel collectively.

After noting that the remnants of the house of Israel had been scattered over the face of the whole earth, Christ prophesied that they will "be gathered in from the east and from the west, and from the south and from the north; and they shall be brought to the knowledge of the Lord their God, who hath redeemed them." Whatever it takes will be done "that I will establish my people, O house of Israel."[28] To those whose inheritance is in these New World lands will come "a New Jerusalem," the Savior said. "And the powers of heaven shall be in the midst of this people; yea, even I will be in the midst of you."[29]

In this context Christ affirmed that it was he of whom Moses spoke when he said, "A prophet shall the Lord your God raise up unto you of your brethren, like unto me; him shall ye hear in all things whatsoever he shall say unto you. And it shall come to pass that every soul who will not hear that prophet shall be cut off from among the people."[30] Peter's declaration of this to the

Jews in the Old World is, of course, one of the verses quoted by the angel Moroni when he first visited the boy prophet Joseph Smith on the night of September 21, 1823.[31]

Christ acknowledged that these people of Lehi were emphatically of the house of Israel and that they were to be favored twice by God in a special way. In the meridian of time they were the first of scattered Israel to receive the resurrected Christ after his ascension into heaven, and in the last days they would be the first of the Israelites to receive Christ when he restored his gospel in the dispensation of the fulness of times.

Note this significant language: "Ye are the children of the prophets; and ye are of the house of Israel; and ye are of the covenant which the Father made with your fathers, saying unto Abraham: And in thy seed shall all the kindreds of the earth be blessed.

"*The Father having raised me up unto you first,* and sent me to bless you in turning away every one of you from his iniquities; and this because ye are the children of the covenant—

"*And after that ye were blessed then fulfilleth the Father the covenant which he made with Abraham,* saying: In thy seed shall all the kindreds of the earth be blessed—unto the pouring out of the Holy Ghost through me upon the Gentiles, which blessing upon the Gentiles shall make them mighty above all."[32]

It is most comforting to note that one of the principal benefits stemming from our promises made to God is that in a world of affliction, pain, and trouble, the Father sends the Son "to bless [us]," to turn every one of us and our posterity away from iniquity—and this simply, lovingly, because "[we] are the children of the covenant."

What then followed was a marvelous messianic prophecy, almost a messianic psalm, promising the return of scattered Israel to Jerusalem, where, the Lord said, "the fulness of my gospel shall be preached" unto them and "they shall believe in me, that I am Jesus Christ, the Son of God, and shall pray unto the Father in my name.

"Then shall their watchmen lift up their voice, and with the voice together shall they sing; for they shall see eye to eye.

"Then will the Father gather them together again, and give unto them Jerusalem for the land of their inheritance."[33]

With this redemption of Jerusalem and the comforting of his people there, the waste places will be reclaimed, Jerusalem will put on her beautiful garments, she will be protected from the unclean, and, the Savior continued, "all the ends of the earth shall see the salvation of the Father; and the Father and I are one."[34]

Christ's oneness with the Father and his role in saving Israel under the hand of his Father will bring great remorse to those who rejected Christ and sold themselves for naught. Christ said, "My people shall know my name; yea, in that day they shall know that I am he that doth speak. And then shall they say: How beautiful upon the mountains are the feet of him that bringeth good tidings unto them, that publisheth peace; that bringeth good tidings unto them of good, that publisheth salvation; that saith unto Zion: Thy God reigneth!"[35]

These familiar passages, written first by Isaiah but spoken of and inspired by Jehovah himself, are often applied to anyone—especially missionaries—who bring the good tidings of the gospel and publish peace to the souls of men. There is nothing inappropriate about such an application, but it is important to realize—as the prophet Abinadi did—that in its purest form and original sense, this psalm of appreciation applies specifically to Christ.[36] It is he and only he who ultimately brings the good tidings of salvation. Only through him is true, lasting peace published. To Zion, in both the old and new Jerusalems, it is Christ who declares, "Thy God reigneth!" It is his feet upon the mountain of redemption that are beautiful.[37]

At the time of recognition, all will be astonished that Christ's "visage [is] so marred, more than any man, and his form more than the sons of men,"[38] referring undoubtedly to the physical impact of the suffering and the scarring of the flesh that accompanied Christ's atoning sacrifice. "Then shall this covenant which the Father hath covenanted with his people be fulfilled; and then shall Jerusalem be inhabited again with my people, and it shall be the land of their inheritance."[39]

The sign as to when these final events would take place was that the gospel would be restored through the Gentiles, who would in turn take it to the remnant of the house of Jacob (the children of Lehi) remaining in their land of promise—"These things shall be made known unto them [the Gentiles] of the Father," Christ said to the Nephites, "and shall come forth of the Father, from them unto you."[40]

The restoration and teaching of the gospel of Jesus Christ—including the Book of Mormon as the divine distillation of "these things"—through the Prophet Joseph Smith and the "gentile church" to the children of Lehi, is the great declaration that the ancient covenant is being fulfilled: "When these works and the works which shall be wrought among you hereafter [the works recorded in the Book of Mormon] shall come forth from the Gentiles, unto your seed . . . it shall be a sign unto them, that they may know that the work of the Father hath already commenced unto the fulfilling of the covenant which he hath made unto the people who are of the house of Israel."[41]

In that day, Christ said, it would be for *his* sake—for the success of his mission and the full efficacy of his life—that the Father would restore the gospel and reestablish his church. "For my sake," Jesus taught, "shall the Father work a work, which shall be a great and a marvelous work among them; and there shall be among them those who will not believe it, although a man shall declare it unto them."[42]

Speaking of this "man," Joseph Smith, Christ prophesied of the danger he would face in that role: "The life of my servant shall be in my hand; therefore they shall not hurt him, although he shall be marred because of them. Yet I will heal him, for I will show unto them that my wisdom is greater than the cunning of the devil."[43]

If the Gentiles did not repent and receive the restored words of Christ, there would be a modern equivalent of those ancient destructions. In this warning Christ provided significant detail about the "tread[ing] down and tear[ing] in pieces" that could come to the Gentiles at the hands of the remnant of Jacob.[44]

In the midst of such destruction, the promise is extended that "if they [the unresponsive Gentiles] will repent and hearken unto my words, and harden not their hearts, I will establish my church among them, and they shall come in unto the covenant and be numbered among this the remnant of Jacob, unto whom I have given this land for their inheritance." These Gentiles will then assist the house of Israel in building "a city, which shall be called the New Jerusalem" and assist in the work of gathering all "who are scattered upon all the face of the land, in unto the New Jerusalem. And then shall the power of heaven come down among them," the Savior continued, "and I also will be in the midst." Again the ultimate sign of such latter-day work is the time "when this gospel shall be preached among the remnant of this people."[45]

It will be at this time—the threshold event, if you will—that the work of gathering will begin among all "the dispersed of my people," the Lord said, "yea, even the tribes which have been lost, which the Father hath led away out of Jerusalem. Yea, the work shall commence among all the dispersed of my people, with the Father to prepare the way whereby they may come unto me, that they may call on the Father in my name. Yea, and then shall the work commence, with the Father among all nations in preparing the way whereby his people may be gathered home to the land of their inheritance."[46]

Here Christ quoted in their entirety, with only slight varia-

CHRIST IN THE NEW WORLD: THE SECOND DAY   289

tions, three revelations that, as Jehovah, he had given to Isaiah and Malachi respectively in an earlier day. Except for the Sermon on the Mount and the Sermon at the Temple example discussed earlier (and those were sermons in which Jesus was speaking as Jesus, not as Jehovah), these three selections are the only such examples in the whole of the Savior's visit to the New World in which he repeated entire chapters of what he had spoken at another time and, as noted, in another role. That he would do so, and that he would select these particular chapters to quote, deserves some examination.

3 NEPHI 22 (COMPARE ISAIAH 54)

This chapter shows the Lord's promise and devotion to Zion in the last days. As such, it is a natural continuation of the prophetic, covenantal promises Christ was giving the Nephites, promises that would be fulfilled as a result of the restoration of the gospel and the gathering of Israel that would flow from that.

"Sing, O barren, thou that didst not bear; break forth into singing, and cry aloud, thou that didst not travail with child. . . . Enlarge the place of thy tent . . . lengthen thy cords, and strengthen thy stakes . . . thy seed shall . . . make the desolate cities to be inhabited."[47] Sometimes by choice and sometimes by circumstance, Israel has been a barren, childless woman who had not borne fruit or lived up to her promises, potential, and covenants. Nevertheless, desolate Israel can—and will—be fruitful, even in the times and places of her scattering and dispersion.

The large movement of Israel's conversion, gathering, and return to the lands of her inheritance will require strong, enlarged stakes in Zion. Growth will be "on the right hand and on the left," with Gentile cities (probably left desolate by the wrath "poured out without mixture upon the whole earth"[48]) inhabited by the children of the covenant. It is from this imagery of Israel's wilderness tent/tabernacle with its cords, curtains, borders, and stakes that The Church of Jesus Christ of Latter-day Saints draws its use of the word *stake* for the name of its basic ecclesiastical unit.

"*Fear not; for thou shalt not be ashamed . . . for thou shalt forget the shame of thy youth, and shalt not remember the reproach of thy widowhood any more. For thy Maker is thine husband; the Lord of hosts is his name; and thy Redeemer the Holy One of Israel; The God of the whole earth shall he be called. For the Lord hath called thee . . . when thou wast refused.*"[49] Even though there has been barrenness and sometimes unfaithfulness, yet will the husband (Christ) reclaim and redeem his bride (Israel). The imagery of Jehovah as bridegroom and Israel as bride is among the most commonly used metaphors in scripture, being used by the Lord and his prophets to describe the relationship between Deity and the children of the covenant.

"*For a small moment have I forsaken thee; but with great mercies will I gather thee. In a little wrath I hid my face from thee for a moment; but with everlasting kindness will I have mercy on thee, saith the Lord thy Redeemer. . . . I have sworn . . . that I would not be wroth with thee. . . . For the mountains shall depart, and the hills be removed; but my kindness shall not depart from thee, neither shall the covenant of my peace be removed, saith the Lord that hath mercy on thee.*"[50] Christ has, on occasion, been rightfully angry with backsliding Israel, but that has always been brief and temporary—"a small moment." Compassion and mercy always return and prevail in a most reassuring way. The mountains and the hills may disappear. The water of the great seas may dry up. The least likely things in the world may happen, but the Lord's kindness and peace will never be taken from his covenant people. He has sworn with a heavenly oath that he will not be wroth with them forever.

"*O thou afflicted, tossed with tempest, and not comforted, behold, I will lay thy stones with fair colours, and lay thy foundations with sapphires. And I will make thy windows of agates, and thy gates of car-*

buncles, and all thy borders of pleasant stones."[51] Even in the midst and aftermath of great affliction, the Lord will shower material and spiritual blessings on Israel, including those jewels and precious metals that will be used to build the New Jerusalem.[52]

"*And all thy children shall be taught of the Lord; and great shall be the peace of thy children. In righteousness shalt thou be established: thou shalt be far from oppression; for thou shalt not fear; and from terror; for it shall not come near thee.*"[53] This is a favorite and oft-quoted scripture noting the peace and freedom from fear that will come to those in Zion, including—and especially—to the children of those who have made and kept their covenants.

"*Whosoever shall gather together against thee shall fall for thy sake. Behold, I have created the smith that bloweth the coals in the fire. . . . No weapon that is formed against thee shall prosper. . . . This is the heritage of the servants of the Lord.*"[54] What is generally seen as a blessing for individuals and families in the preceding verses becomes a more collective blessing to Zion and the latter-day Church. Opposition has always existed whenever and wherever the gospel has been taught, but God has set bounds and limits to its influence, and everyone that shall revile against the truth will stand condemned and ultimately fall.[55]

By chapter's end, the relationship between the Lord and his children of covenant is seen fully and poetically. Consider this summary of God's promises and Israel's millennial hope:[56]

Verses	Husband Provides Wife	Jehovah Provides Israel
1–3	Children	Gathering and Great Growth
4–8	Love	Mercy and Redemption
9–10	Commitment	Unbreakable Covenant
11–12	Material Comfort	Splendor in a New Jerusalem
13–17	Protection for the Family	Peace, Freedom from Fear and Oppression for Zion

IMPORTANCE OF THE WRITTEN RECORD

Here Christ paused to stress the importance of the writings of Isaiah specifically and all of the scriptures generally. Again commanding the Nephites to "search these [writings] diligently; for great are the words of Isaiah," he observed the remarkable breadth of Isaiah's declarations with the acknowledgment that in his examination of Israel's history and covenants, Isaiah touched on "all things concerning [the Lord's] people," the fulfillment of which either had been or yet would be.[57] That message must also go to the Gentiles, Christ said, a mission accomplished at least in part by the publication and distribution of the Book of Mormon.

The importance of Nephite scripture for just such future purposes was stressed by the Savior at something of Nephi's embarrassment and expense. Saying that his disciples were to "give heed to [his] words," Christ emphasized that they should therefore always write the things he had told them in anticipation of their going forth to the Gentiles through the Book of Mormon in the last days. "Search the prophets," he said, because they teach the saving principles of the gospel.

Noting by his omniscient grasp of every circumstance that some elements of past manifestations might not have been fully or accurately recorded, Christ called for Nephi to bring forth the records that had been kept. With the records open before him, the Savior inquired why a significant fulfillment of the prophecy of Samuel the Lamanite had not been recorded. Samuel had prophesied that in the days of Christ's crucifixion and resurrection in the Old World, many Saints in the New World would arise from the dead, appearing and ministering unto many. The Savior asked if, in fact, Samuel did declare this. Nephi readily acknowledged that Samuel did so. However, when pressed on the matter by Jesus, Nephi remembered that the *fulfillment* of that prophecy had not been written. "How be it," the Savior asked, "that ye have not written this thing, that many saints *did* arise and appear unto many and *did* minister unto them? And . . . Nephi remembered that this thing had not been written."[58] At the Savior's direction, it was added to the record immediately, and he continued to expound "all the scriptures in one" from the records they had written, commanding them to teach the things he had given them.

3 NEPHI 24 AND 25 (COMPARE MALACHI 3 AND 4)

Having taught from the book of Isaiah and given encouragement to search all the prophets, Christ quoted in full Malachi 3 and 4 with their emphasis on the message and messenger "of the covenant." Of those passages from Malachi—obviously not available to Lehi at the time he left Jerusalem—Christ said, "These scriptures, which ye had not with you, the Father commanded that I should give unto you; for it was wisdom in him that they should be given unto future generations."[59]

Those chapters are particularly important to Latter-day Saints in light of the fact that when the angel Moroni first appeared to the Prophet Joseph Smith on September 21, 1823, "he commenced quoting the prophecies of the Old Testament. He first quoted part of the third chapter of Malachi; and he quoted also the fourth or last chapter of the same prophecy, though with a little variation from the way it reads in our Bibles."[60]

The Prophet did not identify all of the verses Moroni quoted from Malachi 3, but we may safely assume that those verses would have included the ones that deal with the second coming of the Savior.

"*Behold, I will send my messenger, and he shall prepare the way before me: and the Lord, whom ye seek, shall suddenly come to his temple, even the messenger of the covenant, whom ye delight in.*"[61] The

most obvious messenger to come preparing the way before the
Lord was John the Baptist. Not only did John serve as a forerunner to the Lord in New Testament times, but he has also played
that role in these latter days. On May 15, 1829, he appeared to
Joseph Smith and Oliver Cowdery and restored the Aaronic
Priesthood in preparation for greater priesthood powers to follow, including the keys and ordinances of the holy temple and
the Savior's appearance there. In a moment of great spiritual
manifestation when many keys and dispensational powers were
returned to the earth, Christ, who is the great "messenger of the
covenant," did come to the first temple in this dispensation, in
Kirtland, Ohio, on April 3, 1836.[62] He has, of course, come to
other temples and will yet do so—particularly in Jerusalem and
Jackson County, Missouri—as part of the culmination of his
majestic second coming.

"Who may abide the day of his coming? and who shall stand when
he appeareth? for he is like a refiner's fire, and like fullers' soap: And he
shall sit as a refiner and purifier of silver: and he shall purify the sons of
Levi, . . . that they may offer unto the Lord an offering in righteousness."[63] The Savior's return will be a cleansing, refining experience by fire. The righteous will endure and be purified by this
flame of truth, while the wicked will be burned as stubble,
unable to withstand its unquenchable demands. In that millennial moment, the sons of Levi (the tribe of Israel having a
birthright to the ministry of the Aaronic Priesthood) will be purified and restored to their ancient duties.

One of their "offerings," as taught by the Prophet Joseph
Smith, is a book of remembrance, to be presented to the Lord "in
his holy temple, . . . a book containing the records of our dead,
which shall be worthy of all acceptation."[64] The Prophet also
taught that these Levitical duties would include blood [animal]
sacrifice as "an offering in righteousness" to the Lord in the
temple of the New Jerusalem, perhaps as part of a final exercise

in which the various elements and ordinances of all earlier dispensations will be brought together, at least symbolically, in this triumphant, concluding moment of the dispensation of the fulness of times in which the completion of this world and its work is presented to its rightful Lord of lords and King of kings.[65]

The temple to which the Lord will come is to be a place for "your anointings, and your washings, and your baptisms for the dead, and your solemn assemblies, and your memorials for your sacrifices by the sons of Levi."[66] That such ordinances of the Levitical Priesthood and such bearers of that priesthood would be important in the restoration of the gospel is evident from John the Baptist's blessing given to Joseph Smith and Oliver Cowdery: "Upon you my fellow servants, in the name of Messiah I confer the Priesthood of Aaron, which holds the keys of the ministering of angels, and of the gospel of repentance, and of baptism by immersion for the remission of sins; and this shall never be taken again from the earth, until the sons of Levi do offer again an offering unto the Lord in righteousness."[67]

"I will come near to you to judgment; and I will be a swift witness. . . . Ye are gone away from mine ordinances, and have not kept them. Return unto me, and I will return unto you. . . . Will a man rob God? Yet ye have robbed me. But ye say, Wherein have we robbed thee? In tithes and offerings. Ye are cursed with a curse: for ye have robbed me, even this whole nation. Bring ye all the tithes into the storehouse, that there may be meat in mine house, and prove me now herewith, saith the Lord of hosts, if I will not open you the windows of heaven, and pour you out a blessing, that there shall not be room enough to receive it."[68] The Lord declares his anger not only against sorcerers, adulterers, and those who are untrue in any way, but also against those who are ungenerous to the hireling, the stranger, the widow, and the fatherless. In calling those to return who have strayed, he speaks of the good that could be done to such needy if there were "meat in my house." If such tithes and offerings are not

returned to the Lord, inasmuch as they are rightfully his, then the people and the land are "cursed with a curse"—the fruits of the vines are destroyed and the productivity of the fields are devoured. To those who reach out to the widow and the fatherless through freewill offering, the blessings are immeasurable— "a blessing, that there shall not be room enough to receive it."

"Your words have been stout against me, saith the Lord. . . . Ye have said, It is vain to serve God: and what profit is it that we have kept his ordinance, and that we have walked mournfully before the Lord of hosts? And now we call the proud happy; yea, they that work wickedness are set up; yea, they that tempt God are even delivered. . . . And a book of remembrance was written before him for them that feared the Lord, and that thought upon his name. And they shall be mine, saith the Lord of hosts, in that day when I make up my jewels; . . . then shall ye return, and discern between the righteous and the wicked, between him that serveth God and him that serveth him not."[69]

One of the challenges of the faithful is to realize that sometimes those who are not obedient and worthy seem to receive as many or more of the temporal blessings of life as do those who sacrifice and serve. It was to this issue that Christ had just spoken to the Nephites in his Sermon at the Temple when he reminded them that God "maketh his sun to rise on the evil and on the good."[70] The Saints are to be faithful to the end without too many sidelong glances at their neighbors. They are to keep the commandments because they are called to do so and because they need to be kept, regardless of the response of others. Undoubtedly the unfaithful will also have the sun shine upon them, perhaps at times even more abundantly than on the righteous. But the faith and devotion of the faithful is recorded in the Lamb's book of life, and the day will come when they will be included among God's jewels. In that day it will matter very much who was righteous and who was wicked, who served God and who did not. In the meantime, all must remember that God does not settle his end-of-year accounts in September.

"*The day cometh, that shall burn as an oven; and all the proud, yea, and all that do wickedly, shall be stubble.*"[71] This is a continuation of the theme with which chapter 3 began, reminding all that there will indeed be a refining fire to come. Those who will be destroyed will include those unrighteous ones who seemed to prosper in so many temporal ways, even faring better than their much more faithful neighbors, but who still gave not of their tithes and offerings to the needy and served not the Lord in righteousness. These are those whose names are not written in the book of remembrance, the Lamb's book of life, and who will not be spared "as a man spareth his own son that serveth him."

"*Behold, I will send you Elijah the prophet before the coming of the great and dreadful day of the Lord: And he shall turn the heart of the fathers to the children, and the heart of the children to their fathers, lest I come and smite the earth with a curse.*"[72] In quoting this passage to Joseph Smith, the angel Moroni modified it to speak of "promises made to the fathers," without the fulfillment of which "the whole earth would be utterly wasted at his coming."[73] God made those promises to the ancient patriarchs—Adam, Noah, Abraham, Isaac, Jacob, and so forth—and we undoubtedly made them to our own lineal fathers and mothers, those who came to earth before the gospel was restored but whom we promised to provide its saving ordinances.

The ability to fulfill both kinds of promises was made sure by the prophet Elijah's visit to the Prophet Joseph Smith and Oliver Cowdery in the Kirtland Temple on April 3, 1836. There Elijah restored the sealing powers whereby ordinances that were sealed on earth were also sealed in heaven. That would affect all priesthood ordinances but was particularly important for the sealing of families down through the generations of time, for without that link no family ties would exist in the eternities, and indeed the family of man would have been left in eternity with "neither root [ancestors] nor branch [descendants]."

Inasmuch as such a sealed, united, celestially saved family of God is the ultimate purpose of mortality, any failure here would have been a curse indeed, rendering the entire plan of salvation "utterly wasted." When Elijah made his appearance in the Kirtland Temple, he affirmed that this was in fulfillment of the prophecy "spoken . . . by the mouth of Malachi."[74]

THE LAST DAYS

When Christ had concluded this important, fundamental instruction on the highest matters of the priesthood and the work of the Saints in the days of his second coming, he noted that the Father had instructed him to give these particular scriptures because "it was wisdom in him that they should be given unto future generations." In that setting and frame of mind, Christ then expounded "all things, even from the beginning until the time that he should come in his glory."[75]

In a spirit of summary and culmination Christ prophesied of the last days wherein the elements will melt with fervent heat, the earth will be wrapped together as a scroll, and the heavens and the earth will pass away. All people, kindreds, nations, and tongues will then stand before God to be judged of their works.

Of this magnificent "last days" sermon, so directly linked with the three chapters from Isaiah and Malachi, Mormon wrote, "There cannot be written in this book even a hundredth part of the things which Jesus did truly teach unto the people." Nevertheless, he acknowledged that on the larger plates of Nephi (from which "this book" of abridged material was being taken), "the more part" of Christ's teachings were recorded.[76]

Mormon took some comfort that the "lesser part of the things which [Christ] taught the people"[77]—that Mormon *had* written—

would be of value when they came forward to the Gentiles. If they would receive Mormon's writings (the present Book of Mormon) to strengthen their faith, then they would have greater things made manifest to them—namely these more extensive lessons Christ taught to the Nephites. Mormon acknowledged that he was about to write all that had been taught, "but the Lord forbade it, saying: I will try the faith of my people."[78]

At the end of such powerful doctrinal teaching, Christ cast his gaze upon the crowd and, with a gentle touch, "did teach and minister unto the children of the multitude of whom hath been spoken, and he did loose their tongues, and they did speak unto their fathers great and marvelous things, even greater than he had revealed unto the people; and he loosed their tongues that they could utter."[79]

We are left to wonder at the marvelous messages given to these children that could in any way have been "greater than he had revealed unto the people." He had spoken of faith, repentance, baptism, the gift of the Holy Ghost, prayer, the sacrament, the law of Moses, the scattering and gathering of Israel, the Book of Mormon, the fulness of the covenant, the work of the priesthood, and his own second coming—to name just a few of the principal topics! What he told the children that was greater than these is a question of surpassing wonder. On that astonishing note Christ ascended into heaven, concluding the second day: "After having healed all their sick, and their lame, and opened the eyes of their blind and unstopped the ears of the deaf, and even had done all manner of cures among them, and raised a man from the dead, and had shown forth his power unto them, . . . [he] ascended unto the Father."[80]

CHAPTER THIRTEEN

CHRIST IN
THE NEW WORLD:
THE THIRD DAY AND BEYOND

he sequence and cir-
cumstance of Christ's third day of ministering to the Nephites
is not entirely clear in the text we have been given, but Mormon
did record that "the Lord truly did teach the people, for the
space of three days; and after that he did show himself unto
them oft, and did break bread oft, and bless it, and give it unto
them."[1]

Apparently after the close of the second day—a day in
which Christ raised a man from the dead, giving us a significant case in point of what Mormon was *not* able or allowed to
record—the people gathered "on the morrow" (the third day) to
be taught by the Master. As he had done the first and second
days, so too on the third he again ministered to the children,
loosing their tongues and filling their hearts with spiritual
truths. As a result, not only children but also babes in arms "did
open their mouths and utter marvelous things; and the things
which they did utter were forbidden that there should not any
man write them."[2]

It is significant that in each of the three days of his Nephite
ministry, Christ had a singular spiritual experience with children.
Those experiences, linking each of the days of his Nephite min-

istry, trumpet again the truth that Christ taught in the Old World as well as the New, that "of such is the kingdom of heaven."[3]

From that time forth, the disciples began to teach, baptize, and confer the Holy Ghost upon as many as sought the privilege. The new converts, as with the children whom they were like in many ways, "saw and heard unspeakable things, which [were] not lawful to be written." With such conversion and infusion of the Spirit, all self-centeredness and vanity were swept away, and they did "minister one to another; and they had all things common among them, every man dealing justly, one with another. And it came to pass that they did do all things even as Jesus had commanded them."[4]

THE NAME OF THE CHURCH

As the days unfolded, the disciples were out "journeying and . . . preaching the things which they had both heard and seen" Jesus teach. On one occasion when they were gathered together and united in "mighty prayer and fasting," Jesus again showed himself unto them, a dramatic manifestation of the power inherent in this ancient practice of turning one's entire being—physically and spiritually—to God.[5]

Obviously moved by their faith and prayerful supplication, the Lord immediately asked the question Deity always asks: "What will ye that I shall give unto you?"[6]

Of all the responses that could be given to that generous offer, we learn much about the purity of these Nephites' hearts when their request was not for temporal blessings but to resolve a controversy within the Church family: What should the name of the Church be?[7]

Christ seemed surprised there would be confusion on that subject in light of the fact that it was his name they had taken upon themselves and that only in his name were they to be called and to be saved.

"Whatsoever ye shall do, ye shall do it in my name," he replied, "therefore ye shall call the church in my name."[8] The logic was obvious. "How be it my church save it be called in my name?" the Savior asked. If the Lord's church is called after Moses—or any man—it must be the church of men. But if it is called after Christ, the Lord said, "it is my church, if it so be that they are built upon my gospel."[9] Then, "If it so be that the church is built upon my gospel then will the Father show forth his own works in it."[10] This principle was reaffirmed in latter-day revelation when the Lord said, "Thus shall my church be called in the last days, even The Church of Jesus Christ of Latter-day Saints."[11]

The Father's relationship to the Son and to the Son's church is further sketched in the Lord's suggestion to the Nephites about prayer: "Call upon the Father in my name that he will bless the church for my sake. . . . Call upon the Father, for the church, if it be in my name the Father will hear you."[12]

That emphasis on the gospel and the Father's primacy in blessing all that is done in the name of the Son sets the stage for what would be Christ's final declaration about his gospel. He closed his visit to the Nephites as he began it, with the fundamental declaration that he had come into the world to do the will of the Father.

"My Father sent me that I might be lifted up upon the cross," he said, "that I might draw all men unto me, that as I have been lifted up by men even so should men be lifted up by the Father, to stand before me. . . .

"And for this cause have I been lifted up; therefore, according to the power of the Father I will draw all men unto me, that they may be judged according to their works."[13]

Yielding to the divine will and obeying it through our own

moments of suffering, whatever the cost, is the key to our being "lifted up" in the last day:

"Whoso repenteth and is baptized in my name shall be filled [with the Holy Ghost[14]]; and if he endureth to the end, behold, him will I hold guiltless before my Father at that day when I shall stand to judge the world.

"And he that endureth not unto the end, the same is he that is also hewn down and cast into the fire. . . .

"Nothing entereth into his rest save it be those who have washed their garments in my blood, because of their faith, and the repentance of all their sins, and their faithfulness unto the end."[15]

As always, help is provided for the journey. Those who make this effort to endure faithfully shall be sanctified by the reception of the Holy Ghost—the principal gift for which these Nephites had been praying—a source of comfort, strength, and guidance freely given to children of the covenant. With its help we can "submit to all things which the Lord seeth fit to inflict upon [us]."[16]

Christ in Gethsemane and at Calvary is the great example of submission, obedience, faithfulness, and endurance—of seeing things through to the end. Those uncompromising moments from the Savior's life—and death—are to be our lodestar, our fundamental formula for living the gospel: "This is my gospel; and ye know the things that ye must do in my church; for the works which ye have seen me do that shall ye also do; for that which ye have seen me do even that shall ye do. . . .

"Therefore, what manner of men ought ye to be? Verily I say unto you, even as I am."[17]

Obedience and submission to the end, including whatever suffering physically or spiritually that may entail, are the key to our blessings and our salvation. In the suffering as well as in the serving, we must be willing to be like our Savior.

With that great call to obedience and endurance, Christ made a promise of the Father's answer to the Nephites' supplications and desires:

"And now I go unto the Father. And verily I say unto you, whatsoever things ye shall ask the Father in my name shall be given unto you.

"Therefore, ask, and ye shall receive; knock, and it shall be opened unto you; for he that asketh, receiveth; and unto him that knocketh, it shall be opened."[18]

THREE TRANSLATED NEPHITES

Sensing even as he gave that general promise that the twelve disciples might have specific desires of their own, Jesus asked them one by one, "What is it that ye desire of me, after that I am gone to the Father?"[19]

Nine of them asked for the privilege of a sure and swift return to the Savior's side after their earthly ministries were complete. This the Master granted at the close of their designated term of mortality—seventy-two years.

The other three disciples held back, reluctant to express their desires. After all, who would not wish to be in the Savior's presence as soon—and as long—as possible. To desire anything to the contrary could surely be misunderstood.

But Jesus perceived their thoughts and granted them their wish—to remain on the earth in a translated state to further the work of the ministry until the Savior's second coming. In granting their selfless request, Christ told them that had also been the request of the Apostle John, and that they would "never taste of death." Rather, they would "live to behold all the doings of the Father unto the children of men" until his return in glory.[20]

Mormon called this change upon the Three Nephites a "transfiguration,"[21] and they did have a transfiguring experience.

However, the more traditional understanding of the status of these three is that they were "translated" beings.

A person who is transfigured is one who is temporarily taken into a higher, heavenly experience, as were Peter, James, and John, and then returned to a normal telestial status.[22] As noted above, these three Nephites, as part of their translation experience, were also transfigured, caught up into heaven, where they "saw and heard unspeakable things.

"And it was forbidden them that they should utter; neither was it given unto them power that they could utter the things which they saw and heard."[23]

This circumstance and promise was so new to Mormon, who was reading and writing it nearly 400 years after it happened, that he did not initially know whether the three "were in the body or out of the body" during such a heavenly experience, or whether they had moved permanently beyond mortality into immortality.[24]

So moved was Mormon by this promise and the account of their deeds that he inquired of the Lord about their state. In reply, the Lord informed him that translated beings were still mortal but that a special change, more permanent than transfiguration, was "wrought upon their bodies, that they might not suffer pain nor sorrow save it were for the sins of the world . . . , insomuch that Satan could have no power over them, that he could not tempt them; and they were sanctified in the flesh, that they were holy, and that the powers of the earth could not hold them."[25]

This terrestrial condition, however, was not to be their final state, for when Christ came they would move from mortality to immortality in an instantaneous, deathlike transition, being "changed in the twinkling of an eye." That would be a "greater change" than that of their translation, a permanent change that would put them forever beyond the pale of death and anchor them in "the kingdom of the Father to go no more out, but to dwell with God eternally in the heavens."[26]

From the heavenly transformation granted to these Nephites, involving in their case both a translation and a transfiguration, the three returned to minister among their people, teaching, baptizing, conferring the Holy Ghost. Prisons could not be built strong enough to hold them. Pits could not be dug deep enough to bury them. Three times they were cast into a furnace, and three times they came out without harm. Twice they were cast into a den of wild beasts, only to play with them as a child would a suckling lamb, receiving no harm. Such is not surprising when we remember that they (and therefore these animals?) now existed in a terrestrial state. When the earth is returned to its paradisiacal glory, the lamb will lie down with the lion, and all will be able to so play.

These three Nephites continue in their translated state today, just as when they went throughout the lands of Nephi. At one point Mormon was about to reveal their names to his latter-day readers, but he was forbidden by the Lord from doing so.[27] Nevertheless, these three ministered to Mormon[28] and Moroni,[29] and they are yet ministering to Jew, Gentile, and the scattered tribes of Israel, even all nations, kindreds, tongues, and people.

Mormon commented, "They are as the angels of God, and if they shall pray unto the Father in the name of Jesus they can show themselves unto whatsoever man it seemeth them good.

"Therefore, great and marvelous works shall be wrought by them."[30]

THE CALL TO COVENANT

Christ concluded his visitation to the New World by touching the nine who did not have the same special privileges and protections of the other three. Then "he departed,"[31] leaving the promise and transformation of the Three Nephites as a symbolic statement of "the marvelous works of Christ"[32] and the words of salvation that would remain with and be sent to all people through his servants.

Mormon concluded his description of this majestic season with the "messenger of the covenant" by testifying that when a record of his visit would come to the Gentiles (in the form of the Book of Mormon), then all might know that the covenant and promises to Israel of the last days were "already beginning to be fulfilled."[33]

With five warnings Mormon cautioned against any temptation to minimize or negate God's covenant with the house of Israel, a covenant that had been declared by the Son of God himself. In the last days no one was to spurn at the doings of the Lord, deny Christ and his works, deny the revelations of the Lord and the gifts of the Holy Spirit, deny the miracles of Christ, or hiss, spurn, or make game of the Jews or any of the remnant of the house of Israel.

God's covenant will be kept with all of his covenant people. No one will be able to "turn the right hand of the Lord unto the left" on this matter. And the call to the Gentiles, for which Christ's visit to the Nephites published in the Book of Mormon is the ultimate latter-day declaration, is for them to claim the same covenant and promises.

As the curtain descended on the greatest three-day drama in New World history, Mormon recorded:

"Hearken, O ye Gentiles, and hear the words of Jesus Christ, the Son of the living God, which he hath commanded me that I should speak concerning you, for, behold he commandeth me that I should write, saying:

"Turn, all ye Gentiles, from your wicked ways; and repent of your evil doings, of your lyings and deceivings, and of your whoredoms, and of your secret abominations, and your idola-

tries, and of your murders, and your priestcrafts, and your envyings, and your strifes, and from all your wickedness and abominations, and come unto me, and be baptized in my name, that ye
may receive a remission of your sins, and be filled with the Holy
Ghost, that ye may be numbered with my people who are of the
house of Israel."[34]

AFTERWARD

CHAPTER FOURTEEN

THE HEAVENLY GIFT
AND THE SINS
OF THE WORLD

hat unfolded in the years following Christ's personal ministry to the Nephites included the best of times and the worst of times in a way Charles Dickens could never have dreamed. To our knowledge there has never been a historical sequence like it, before or since.

Immediately after Christ's ascension into heaven, the disciples he had commissioned to minister to the people "formed a church of Christ in all the lands round about."[1] In these branches of the kingdom they taught the first principles and ordinances of the gospel, seeing the people repent of their sins, enter the waters of baptism, and receive the gift of the Holy Ghost.

So remarkable was their success that in two short years all the people throughout the land were converted, Nephites and Lamanites alike. It was a heavenly time, with "no contentions and disputations among them," and with every man dealing justly with his neighbor. "And they had all things common among them; therefore there were not rich and poor, bond and free, but they were all made free, and partakers of the heavenly gift."[2]

So great were the works performed by the disciples of Christ that "they did heal the sick, and raise the dead, and cause the lame to walk, and the blind to receive their sight, and the deaf to hear." All manner of miracles were performed by these faithful followers, "and in nothing did they work miracles save it were in the name of Jesus."[3]

Inevitably, prosperity came. Zarahemla was rebuilt. Other cities burned or otherwise destroyed during the destruction at the Crucifixion were rebuilt, renewed, or reestablished. The people married and multiplied and were blessed "according to the multitude of the promises which the Lord had made unto them."[4] Having left the law of Moses behind, they "did walk after the commandments which they had received from their Lord and their God, continuing in fasting and prayer, and in meeting together oft both to pray and to hear the word of the Lord."[5] With no contention among any of the people, there were mighty miracles at every turn. Even after the hundredth year of the new calendar (since the sign of Christ's birth), there was no contention in the land "because of the love of God which did dwell in the hearts of the people."[6]

"There were no envyings, nor strifes, nor tumults, nor whoredoms, nor lyings, nor murders, nor any manner of lasciviousness" among them. Such righteous lives brought blessed peace and the greatest characterization of it all: "Surely there could not be a happier people among all the people who had been created by the hand of God." There were no robbers or murderers, neither were there Lamanites or "any manner of -ites," but they were "in one, the children of Christ, and heirs to the kingdom of God." Mormon wrote longingly (for he lived to see the years beyond these), "How blessed were they! For the Lord did bless them in all their doings."[7]

But then, in the 184th year after Christ's birth, exactly 150 years after his ministry in the New World, "a small part of the people . . . revolted from the church."[8] That was the beginning of the end of Nephite society. It took several years to happen, and several pages of Book of Mormon history to record it, but those words marked the end of the great Christian epoch in the New World of which so many prophets had dreamed and prophesied and for which so many had died. With that phrase, the saga we know as the Book of Mormon began drawing to a close.

After two hundred years, the movement away from the Zionlike principles of Christ's teachings was inexorable: "There began to be among them those who were lifted up in pride, such as the wearing of costly apparel, and all manner of fine pearls, and of the fine things of the world. And from that time forth they did have their goods and their substance no more common among them. And they began to be divided into classes; and they began to build up churches unto themselves to get gain, and began to deny the true church of Christ."[9]

Although they "professed to know the Christ," these false churches denied essential elements of the gospel, entertained wickedness within their ranks, "and did administer that which was sacred unto him to whom it had been forbidden because of unworthiness."[10] These churches multiplied because of their iniquity and the power of Satan, "who did get hold upon their hearts."[11]

The apostate churches persecuted the true church of Christ and viciously turned against the Three Nephites, who tried to work among them. Regardless of God's deliverance of these disciples, the enemies of righteousness hardened their hearts and with "many priests and false prophets" did all manner of iniquity.[12]

By the 234th year after Christ's birth, the unbelievers were more numerous than the people of God. These wicked ones, now again called Lamanites, began to build up the secret combinations of Gadianton. But even more tragically, the righteous, those who had been called Nephites, "began to be proud in their hearts, because of their exceeding riches, and become vain like unto their brethren, the Lamanites."[13] Thus both the people of Nephi and the new Lamanites became exceedingly wicked, one like unto another. In such a circumstance, it is a painful understatement to say that the Three Nephites "began to sorrow for the sins of the world."[14]

Steadily Gadiantonism spread until finally no righteous remained but the three disciples of Jesus. And the others? "Gold and silver did they lay up in store in abundance, and did traffic in all manner of traffic."[15]

The concluding record keeper of the period, Ammaron, being constrained by the Holy Ghost, finally hid the sacred writings of his forefathers that had been handed down so faithfully from generation to generation. With no broad audience remaining who would heed what had been taught and passed down to them, how that phrase "from generation to generation" echoes painfully Nephi's early use of that same language. [16] Only one faithful father and son remained to read these plates, protect and abridge them, and pass on their message to those of a later day. Mormon and Moroni could now only write for a generation yet unborn, those of the dispensation of the fulness of times, who, if they would, might hear these records speak "as one crying from the dead, yea, even as one speaking out of the dust."[17]

CHAPTER FIFTEEN

A HEART FILLED
WITH SORROW

In one of the loneliest scenes in scriptural history, a silent, war-weary soldier looked out across time and the unspeakable tragedy his family and followers faced. Mormon, the man destined before the world was formed to abridge and summarize the Nephite story—and in so doing to have his name forever immortalized with this additional testament of Jesus Christ—surveyed the casualties of a nation that had turned from the Lord. As sobering as the account is, it does not give a full account of all the sin and sadness Mormon had seen. Indeed, such an account probably would have been impossible to record, for as the prophet-general recorded, "a continual scene of wickedness and abominations has been before mine eyes ever since I have been sufficient to behold the ways of man.

"And wo is me because of their wickedness; for my heart has been filled with sorrow because of their wickedness, all my days."[1]

In fact, "all [his] days" had included a significant portion of Nephite history, a period in which the young Mormon had been called to service in his earliest youth. Because he was "a sober child" and "quick to observe," he had been called to prepare himself at the tender age of ten years. God had a work for him to do.[2]

It would be in this short, significant lifetime that the destruction of an entire nation would be seen. At age eleven, Mormon remembered the Nephite center of Zarahemla as having been "covered with buildings, and the people . . . as numerous almost, as it were the sand of the sea."[3]

But wickedness began to prevail in the land, so much so that "the Lord did take away his beloved [three translated Nephite] disciples, and the work of miracles and of healing did cease because of the iniquity of the people.

"And there were no gifts from the Lord, and the Holy Ghost did not come upon any, because of their wickedness and unbelief."[4]

The maturing Mormon, by then fifteen years of age, stood beyond the sinfulness around him and rose above the despair of his time. Consequently, he "was visited of the Lord, and tasted and knew of the goodness of Jesus,"[5] trying valiantly to preach to his people. But as God occasionally does when those with so much light reject it, Mormon literally had his mouth shut. He was forbidden to preach to a nation that had wilfully rebelled against their God. These people had rejected the miracles and messages delivered them by the three translated Nephite disciples, who had now also been silenced in their ministry and been taken from the nation to whom they had been sent.

Remaining among those people but silenced in his testimony, Mormon had such physical and exemplary stature with the people that he was appointed to lead the Nephite army at sixteen years of age! But his task was hopeless. The ever-present Lamanite armies took their toll on the Nephite nation.

Almost as destructive as the bloodletting on the field of battle was the rending of the social fabric at home. Here, too, the faithlessness of a people made community life chaotic. "For behold," Mormon wrote, "no man could keep that which was his own, for the thieves, and the robbers, and the murderers, and the magic art, and the witchcraft which was in the land."[6] In such circumstances there was "mourning and lamentation and sorrow" among the people. But to Mormon's dismay, this sorrow was not unto repentance, nor was it a recognition of the right ways of God. It was rather "the sorrowing of the damned, because the Lord would not always suffer them to take happiness in sin.

"And they did not come unto Jesus with broken hearts and contrite spirits, but they did curse God, and wish to die."[7]

It is at this moment in Nephite history—just under 950 years since it had begun and just over 300 years since they had been visited by the Son of God himself—that Mormon realized the story was finished. In perhaps the most chilling line he ever wrote, Mormon asserted simply, "I saw that the day of grace was passed with them, both temporally and spiritually." His people had learned that most fateful of all lessons—that the Spirit of God will not always strive with man; that it is possible, collectively as well as individually, to have time run out. The day of repentance can pass, and it had passed for the Nephites. Their numbers were being "hewn down in open rebellion against their God," and in a metaphor almost too vivid in its moral commentary, they were being "heaped up as dung upon the face of the land."[8]

Even in brief moments of temporary Nephite triumph, Mormon lamented, "The strength of the Lord was not with us; yea, we were left to ourselves, that the Spirit of the Lord did not abide in us; therefore we had become weak like unto our brethren."[9]

The Lord commanded Mormon, "Cry unto this people—Repent ye, and come unto me, and be ye baptized, and build up again my church, and ye shall be spared." And Mormon did cry, "but it was in vain; and they did not realize that it was the Lord that had spared them, and granted unto them a chance for repentance. And behold they did harden their hearts against the Lord their God."[10]

At one point Mormon "utterly refuse[d]" to be the comman-
der and leader of a people so wicked, so ignorant, so bent on
self-destruction. It was a wrenching time for him because these
were his people, and he loved them. Indeed, he loved them "with
all [his] heart." Furthermore, he had poured out his soul in
prayer "all the day long for them." But alas, such earnest
prayer—and we can scarcely imagine a more loving and faithful
effort on behalf of a people—was by Mormon's own admission
uttered "without faith" because of the hardness of the hearts of
the people.[11]

In such frustration and sorrow, Mormon stepped back from
leading an army that would not repent, and he refused to go up
against their enemies. At the Lord's command, he stood as "an
idle witness" to his own generation while writing to a future
generation the lessons his people had failed to learn.

To the descendants of the twelve tribes of Israel, including
those in "the land of Jerusalem" and those "in this land,"
Mormon wrote that "every soul who belongs to the whole
human family of Adam" must "stand before the judgment-seat
of Christ . . . to be judged of [their] works, whether they be good
or evil." He also wrote that all in those last days may "believe the
gospel of Jesus Christ." That gospel would be among the people
in part because of Mormon's writings, a witness not only to the
Gentiles and the descendants of Lehi in the New World but also
among the Jews, "the covenant people of the Lord." The Book of
Mormon would be to all these another witness that Jesus "was
the very Christ and the very God."[12]

As Mormon increasingly looked beyond the tragedy before
him to a generation he hoped would profit from their mistakes,
the destruction continued unabated. Mormon was torn not only
by what he saw but also by what he must—and must not—write:

"I, Mormon, do not desire to harrow up the souls of men in
casting before them such an awful scene of blood and carnage as

was laid before mine eyes; but I . . . write a small abridgment, daring not to give a full account of the things which I have seen, because of the commandment which I have received, and also that ye might not have too great sorrow because of the wickedness of this people. . . .

"For I know that such will sorrow for the calamity of the house of Israel; yea, they will sorrow for the destruction of this people; they will sorrow that this people had not repented that they might have been clasped in the arms of Jesus."[13]

These, his people, were now hopeless before Mormon's gaze, and the fate of the destructive Lamanites was equally tragic. In a prophecy of the future that is even more dark and loathsome than the present "description of that which ever hath been amongst us," Mormon foresaw that "the Spirit of the Lord hath ceased to strive with [them]; and they are without Christ and God in the world. . . . They were once a delightsome people, and they had Christ for their shepherd; yea, they were led even by God the Father."[14]

Following the tremendous battle at Cumorah, Mormon looked out over the catastrophic carnage—the destruction of a thousand years of dreams—and cried to ears that could no longer hear:

"O ye fair ones, how could ye have departed from the ways of the Lord! O ye fair ones, how could ye have rejected that Jesus, who stood with open arms to receive you!

"Behold, if ye had not done this, ye would not have fallen. But behold, ye are fallen, and I mourn your loss.

"O ye fair sons and daughters, ye fathers and mothers, ye husbands and wives, ye fair ones, how is it that ye could have fallen!

"But behold, ye are gone, and my sorrows cannot bring your return."[15]

In a soliloquy of death, Mormon reached across time and

space to all, especially to that "remnant of the house of Israel" who would one day read his majestic record. Those of another time and place must learn what those lying before him had forgotten—that all must "believe in Jesus Christ, that he is the Son of God," that following his crucifixion in Jerusalem he had, "by the power of the Father . . . risen again, whereby he hath gained the victory over the grave; and also in him is the sting of death swallowed up.

"And he bringeth to pass the resurrection of the dead . . . [and] the redemption of the world." Those who are redeemed may then, because of Christ, enjoy "a state of happiness which hath no end."[16]

To this future and unseen audience—because it was everlastingly too late for his people now silent before him—Mormon pleaded:

"Repent, and be baptized in the name of Jesus, and lay hold upon the gospel of Christ, which shall be set before you, not only in *this* record but also in [*that*] record which shall come unto the Gentiles from the Jews, which record shall come from the Gentiles unto you.

"For behold, *this* [the Book of Mormon] is written for the intent that ye may believe *that* [the Bible]; and if ye believe *that* [the Bible] ye will believe *this* [the Book of Mormon] also. . . .

"And ye will also know that ye . . . are numbered among the people of the first covenant. . . .

"Believe in Christ," he said "[and be baptized] first with water, then with fire and with the Holy Ghost, following the example of our Savior . . . [and] it shall be well with you in the day of judgment."[17]

To "believe in Christ," especially when measured against such tragic but avoidable consequences, was Mormon's last plea and his only hope. It is the ultimate purpose of the entire book that would come to the latter-day world bearing his name.

CHAPTER SIXTEEN

MORONI'S THREE WITNESSES: A CRY FOR FAITH, HOPE, AND CHARITY

ollowing this dismaying decline of Nephite civilization documented by his father, Moroni picked up the recorder's task, but he did not write to any living audience. Rather, he directed his final testimony—in fact, three final testimonies—to those who would receive the record in the last days. A book that began with three witnesses of Christ ends the same way but with a difference—with three final declarations of the Savior from the writings of one man. Moroni's experience was painful, for he observed in life, in history, and in vision the pollution and destruction of three glorious civilizations—his own Nephite world, the Jaredite nation, and our latter-day dispensation.

THE CONCLUSION OF MORMON'S RECORD

The first of Moroni's testimonies came as he concluded the book named for his father.[1] At the time of Mormon's death, four hundred years had passed away "since the coming of [the] Lord and Savior," Moroni noted. How he must have longed for those magnificent days compared to the ones he now faced. "I . . . remain alone to write the sad tale of the destruction of my people," he lamented. "But behold, they are gone, and I fulfil the commandment of my father. And whether they will slay me, I know not. Therefore I will write and hide up the records in the earth; and whither I go it mattereth not."[2]

Apostasy and destruction were so rampant among the Nephites that none of them knew "the true God save it be the [three translated] disciples of Jesus, who did tarry in the land until the wickedness of the people was so great that the Lord would not suffer them to remain with the people; and whether they be upon the face of the land no man knoweth," Moroni wrote. "But behold, my father and I have seen them, and they have ministered unto us."[3]

In this state of lonely witnessing, Moroni was shown the last days of another civilization—our own. And Moroni saw they would be very much like his own. In these days it would be said that miracles were done away, and secret combinations would delight in works of darkness. Fires and tempests and vapors of smoke would singe the earth, while wars, rumors of wars, and earthquakes would rage in divers places. Pollutions would come upon the face of the earth, including the moral pollution of murders, robbery, lying, whoredoms, and "all manner of abominations."[4] Even churches would be defiled, lifted up in the pride of their hearts. They would be built up to get gain and to offer forgiveness of sins through the payment of money, becoming as polluted as the physical and moral environment around them.

Calling out to those in the latter days who would receive the Book of Mormon "even as if one [were speaking] from the dead,"[5] Moroni focused inexorably upon the future reader. "Behold, I speak unto you as if ye were present," he wrote, "and yet ye are not. But behold, Jesus Christ hath shown you unto me, and I know your doing."[6] His despair, which was tinged with both disappointment and anger, is evident in his words.

"O ye pollutions, ye hypocrites, ye teachers, who sell yourselves for that which will canker, why have ye polluted the holy church of God? Why are ye ashamed to take upon you the name of Christ? Why do ye not think that greater is the value of an endless happiness than that misery which never dies—because of the praise of the world?

"Why do ye adorn yourselves with that which hath no life, and yet suffer the hungry, and the needy, and the naked, and the sick and the afflicted to pass by you, and notice them not?

"Yea, why do ye build up your secret abominations to get gain, and cause that widows should mourn before the Lord, and also orphans to mourn before the Lord, and also the blood of their fathers and their husbands to cry unto the Lord from the ground, for vengeance upon your heads?

"Behold, the sword of vengeance hangeth over you; and the time soon cometh that he avengeth the blood of the saints upon you, for he will not suffer their cries any longer."[7]

That, of course, is a lecture born of his own tragic times but directed to those in the last days who would ostensibly believe in Christ. An even bolder message is directed toward those who would *not* believe in Christ.

Promising that one day the Lord would return to assume the leadership of his kingdom, with the earth rolling together as a scroll and the elements melting with fervent heat, Moroni asked how the unbelievers would feel standing before the Lamb of God in that fateful day. Stressing the guilt they would surely feel, the inevitable nakedness, and their wish to dwell in hell rather than stand before "the holiness of Jesus Christ," Moroni exhorted,

"O then ye unbelieving, turn ye unto the Lord; cry mightily unto the Father in the name of Jesus, that perhaps ye may be found spotless, pure, fair, and white, having been cleansed by the blood of the Lamb, at that great and last day.

"And again I speak unto you who deny the revelations of God, and say that they are done away, that there are no revelations, nor prophecies, nor gifts, nor healing, nor speaking with tongues, and the interpretation of tongues;

"Behold I say unto you, he that denieth these things knoweth not the gospel of Christ; yea, he has not read the scriptures; if so, he does not understand them."[8]

Turning to the ageless message of those scriptures, Moroni reminded his future readers that the gospel is a gospel of life and redemption. In a remarkable three-verse summary of the great plan of happiness, he wrote:

"Behold, [God] created Adam, and by Adam came the fall of man. And because of the fall of man came Jesus Christ, even the Father and the Son; and because of Jesus Christ came the redemption of man.

"And because of the redemption of man, which came by Jesus Christ, they are brought back into the presence of the Lord; yea, this is wherein all men are redeemed, because the death of Christ bringeth to pass the resurrection, which bringeth to pass a redemption from an endless sleep, from which sleep all men shall be awakened by the power of God when the trump shall sound; and they shall come forth, both small and great, and all shall stand before his bar, being redeemed and loosed from this eternal band of death, which death is a temporal death.

"And then cometh the judgment of the Holy One upon them; and then cometh the time that he that is filthy shall be filthy still; and he that is righteous shall be righteous still; he that is happy shall be happy still; and he that is unhappy shall be unhappy still."[9]

Moroni then wrote a moving "final" testimony, one that he undoubtedly assumed would be his last. His father was dead, the record was (for all intents and purposes) complete, and Moroni's life was virtually over. "I speak unto you as though I spake from the dead,"[10] he said. And his testimony stands as a powerful concluding declaration of the divinity of Christ and of Moroni's undying faith in him. It is a marvelous expression by one who now had so little but who knew that God would always grant "what things soever ye shall stand in need."

"Behold, I say unto you that whoso believeth in Christ, doubting nothing, whatsoever he shall ask the Father in the name of Christ it shall be granted him; and this promise is unto all, even unto the ends of the earth. . . .

"And now, behold, who can stand against the works of the Lord? Who can deny his sayings? Who will rise up against the almighty power of the Lord? Who will despise the works of the Lord? Who will despise the children of Christ? Behold, all ye who are despisers of the works of the Lord, for ye shall wonder and perish.

"O then despise not, and wonder not, but hearken unto the words of the Lord, and ask the Father in the name of Jesus for what things soever ye shall stand in need. Doubt not, but be believing, and begin as in times of old, and come unto the Lord with all your heart, and work out your own salvation with fear and trembling before him. . . .

"See that ye are not baptized unworthily; see that ye partake not of the sacrament of Christ unworthily; but see that ye do all things in worthiness, and do it in the name of Jesus Christ, the Son of the living God; and if ye do this, and endure to the end, ye will in nowise be cast out. . . .

"And may the Lord Jesus Christ grant that their prayers may be answered according to their faith; and may God the Father remember the covenant which he hath made with the house of Israel; and may he bless them forever, through faith on the name of Jesus Christ. Amen."[11]

THE CONCLUSION OF THE BOOK OF ETHER

Determined to preserve an account of the Jaredite nation, Moroni had an opportunity to bear his second "final" witness in his abridgment of the book of Ether. After recounting the remarkable vision of Christ beheld by the brother of Jared, Moroni traced the painful—and parallel—story of another Book of Mormon civilization that destroyed itself. The final prophet to speak in that era, a counterpart to Moroni, was Ether, who "did cry from the morning, even until the going down of the sun, exhorting the people to believe in God unto repentance lest they should be destroyed, saying unto them that by faith all things are fulfilled."[12] Then this reassuring verse:

"Wherefore, whoso believeth in God might with surety hope for a better world, yea, even a place at the right hand of God, which hope cometh of faith, maketh an anchor to the souls of men, which would make them sure and steadfast, always abounding in good works, being led to glorify God."[13]

This verse, full of hope and promise but now seen from the vantage point of a historian who knew that the Jaredites did *not* seize their opportunity, did *not* establish a better world here or earn a better one, did *not* ultimately live with faith or hope—all of that elicited a seminal sermon on faith. Keying off of Ether's testimony of faith, which would be "an anchor to the souls of men," Moroni wished to speak to his future audience "somewhat concerning these things."[14]

"I would show unto the world," he said, "that faith is things which are hoped for and not seen; wherefore, dispute not because ye see not," he cautioned, "for ye receive no witness until after the trial of your faith."[15]

He then outlined the "trial of faith" experienced and expressed by the descendants of Lehi. He reminded his readers that it was by faith that Christ showed himself in the New World after his crucifixion and resurrection. "He showed not himself unto them," Moroni wrote, "*until after they had faith in him*"—evidence that those allowed to behold the risen Christ were already believers. This may be among the greatest scriptural examples of a witness (in this case, the actual appearance of the Savior) coming after the trial of faith.[16]

It was by faith—that of his disciples—that Christ showed himself unto the world, glorifying the name of the Father and preparing a way for "others" (those who had not seen him in the flesh) to be partakers of his salvation, "that they might hope for those things which they have not seen."[17] It was by faith that:

- The ancients were called to the priesthood, "the holy order of God."[18]

- The law of Moses was given, and it was by faith in God's gift of his son—"a more excellent way"—that it was fulfilled.[19]

- God performed miracles among the children of men.[20]

- Alma and Amulek caused the prison to tumble to the earth.[21]

- Nephi and Lehi wrought the change upon their Lamanite audience, that the Lamanites were "baptized with fire and with the Holy Ghost."[22]

- Ammon and his brethren wrought such a great miracle among the Lamanites.[23]

- All who wrought any miracle did so before or after Christ.[24]

- The Three Nephites obtained their promise that they should not taste of death, and they did not obtain that promise "until after their faith."[25]

- *Many* could not be kept from within the veil, "even before Christ came," coming to see with their actual eyes what they had initially seen only with "an eye of faith."[26]

- The brother of Jared was *one* of these, his faith being so great that God "could not hide [his finger] from the sight of the brother of Jared." Ultimately the Lord "could not withhold anything from his sight; wherefore he showed him all things, for he could no longer be kept without the veil."[27]

- The Nephite prophets obtained the promise that the Book of Mormon record would come to the Lamanites "through the Gentiles."[28]

- All may have hope and be partakers of Christ's divine gift of redemption.[29]

Under commandment from Christ to express his own faith and prepare the sacred record, Moroni lamented his inability to convey these things powerfully in writing. He felt that his mortal weakness would limit the impact of such a faith-filled message upon those who read it. But Christ reassured him, saying,

"Fools mock, but they shall mourn; and my grace is sufficient for the meek, that they shall take no advantage of your weakness;

"And if men come unto me I will show unto them their weakness. I give unto men weakness that they may be humble; and my grace is sufficient for all men that humble themselves before me; for if they humble themselves before me, and have faith in me, then will I make weak things become strong unto them.

"Behold, I will show unto the Gentiles their weakness, and I will show unto them that faith, hope and charity bringeth unto me—the fountain of all righteousness."[30]

This introduction of faith, hope, and charity launched Moroni into a moving discourse on the subject, a subject that would carry through the conclusion of the Book of Mormon:

"And I, Moroni, having heard these words, was comforted, and said: O Lord, thy righteous will be done, for I know that thou workest unto the children of men according to their *faith*;

"For the brother of Jared said unto the mountain Zerin, Remove—and it was removed. And if he had not had faith it would not have moved; wherefore thou workest after men have faith.

"For thus didst thou manifest thyself unto thy disciples; for after they had faith, and did speak in thy name, thou didst show thyself unto them in great power.

"And I also remember that thou hast said that thou hast prepared a house for man, yea, even among the mansions of thy Father, in which man might have a more excellent *hope;* wherefore man must hope, or he cannot receive an inheritance in the place which thou hast prepared.

"And again, I remember that thou hast said that thou hast loved the world, even unto the laying down of thy life for the world, that thou mightest take it again to prepare a place for the children of men.

"And now I know that this love which thou hast had for the children of men is *charity;* wherefore, except men shall have charity they cannot inherit that place which thou hast prepared in the mansions of thy Father."[31]

As something of a concluding, corresponding witness to Nephi, Jacob, and Isaiah's introductory testimonies of the Savior, Moroni closed his second "final" testimony with an account of his own face-to-face experience with the Lord:

"And now I, Moroni, bid farewell unto the Gentiles, yea, and also unto my brethren whom I love, until we shall meet before the judgment-seat of Christ, where all men shall know that my garments are not spotted with your blood.

"And then shall *ye know that I have seen Jesus, and that he hath talked with me face to face, and that he told me in plain humility, even as a man telleth another in mine own language, concerning these things;* . . .

"And now, I would commend you to seek this Jesus of whom the prophets and apostles have written, that the grace of God the Father, and also the Lord Jesus Christ, and the Holy Ghost, which beareth record of them, may be and abide in you forever. Amen."[32]

THE CONCLUSION OF THE BOOK OF MORONI

In what was by then a desperate and virtually day-by-day existence, Moroni recorded the third witness of his faith. He had "supposed not to have written more," but inasmuch as he had not yet perished, he continued his witness to the end. Even though the Lamanites were putting to death every Nephite that would not deny the Christ, Moroni would not deny him. "Wherefore," he wrote, "I wander whithersoever I can for the safety of mine own life."[33]

What Moroni first recorded in the book carrying his own name were vignettes—a brief catalog, if you will—of things he felt needed to be recorded before he died and the Book of Mormon saga ended. These included the words of Christ to his twelve disciples when they were commissioned to bestow the Holy Ghost by the laying on of hands, the prayer by which priests and teachers were ordained, the sacramental prayers, and instructions as to how those who were baptized were to be received into the "church of Christ" and numbered among the "people of Christ."

But the classic contribution in Moroni's supplementary material is his recording of his father's masterful teaching on the theme Moroni had already developed in his own writing—that of faith, hope, and charity. Mormon's sermon was directed unto those "that are of the church, that are the peaceable followers of Christ," to be so recognized because of their "peaceable walk with the children of men."[34] Teaching that "all things which are good cometh of God; and that which is evil cometh of the devil," Mormon taught that everyone can make this assessment—a variation on Lehi's teaching about opposition in all things—because "the Spirit of Christ is given to every man, that he may know good from evil; . . . for every thing which inviteth to do good, and to persuade to believe in Christ, is sent forth by the power and gift of Christ; wherefore ye may know with a perfect knowledge it is of God."[35]

The ability to *see* these choices clearly and accurately is provided by "the light of Christ," a free gift to all even if it is not always received or cultivated. By this divine illumination we are to "search diligently in the light of Christ" that we "may know good from evil." And if we "will lay hold upon every good thing, and condemn it not," he said, we "certainly will be [children] of Christ."[36]

But as for the ability to *do* these things, to actually "lay hold" on what has been recognized as good, is a matter of motivating faith in Christ which takes genuine effort.

Even from the beginning, long before Christ had actually come to earth, such faith was available to the children of promise. Mormon wrote, "God knowing all things, being from everlasting to everlasting, he sent angels to minister unto the children of men, to make manifest concerning the coming of Christ; and in Christ there should come every good thing. . . . And all things which are good cometh of Christ."[37]

Thus, by the ministering of angels and by the Lord's word through his prophets, "men began to exercise faith in Christ; and thus by faith, they did lay hold upon every good thing; and thus it was until the coming of Christ."[38]

The same principle obtained after Christ came. Then, too, "men [are] saved by faith in his name; and by faith, they become the sons of God." But neither faith nor the miracles it brings were to cease "because Christ ascended into heaven." Rather, those who have faith in him will continue to cleave unto every good thing and thus be worthy to receive every good thing. The most dramatic of these gifts will be the power to witness and perform miracles as may be necessary for the well-being and salvation of the "children of Christ." True to the end, Christ lovingly claims these who have faith in him, and he advocates their cause before the great bar of justice.[39]

Through the continuing work of angels and the testimony of the chosen vessels of the Lord to whom they minister, we may also have faith in Christ in our day if we desire it. The believer's obligation is as it has always been. As the Master explained it, "If ye will have faith in me ye shall have power to do whatsoever thing is expedient in me. . . . Repent all ye ends of the earth, and come unto me, and be baptized in my name, and have faith in me, that ye may be saved."[40]

The miracles that accompany believers will be one of the genuine evidences that faith continues in the present day, "for no man can be saved, according to the words of Christ, save they shall have faith in his name; wherefore, if [miracles] have ceased, then has faith ceased also; and awful is the state of man, for they are as though there had been no redemption made" and "all is vain."[41]

That kind of redeeming faith, Mormon taught, leads to hope, a special, theological kind of hope. The word is often used to express the most general of aspirations—wishes, if you will. But as used in the Book of Mormon it is very specific and flows naturally from one's faith in Christ. "How is it that ye can attain unto faith, save ye shall [as a consequence] have hope?" Mormon asked.[42] This is the same faith-leads-to-hope sequence that Moroni used, saying, "Ye may also have hope . . . if ye will but have faith."[43]

What is the nature of this hope? It is certainly much more than wishful thinking. It is to have "hope through the atonement of Christ and the power of his resurrection, to be raised unto life eternal, and this because of your faith in him according to the promise."[44] *That* is the theological meaning of hope in the faith-hope-charity sequence. With an eye to that meaning, Moroni 7:42 then clearly reads, "If a man have faith [in Christ and his atonement] he must needs [as a consequence] have hope [in the promise of the Resurrection, because the two are inextricably linked]; for without faith [in Christ's atonement] there cannot be any hope [in the Resurrection]."[45]

Faith in Christ and hope in his promises of resurrected, eternal life can come only to the meek and lowly in heart. Such promises, in turn, reinforce meekness and lowliness of heart in that believer. Only thorough disciples of Christ, living as meekly as he lived and humbling themselves as he humbled himself, can declare uncompromised faith in Christ and have genuine hope in the Resurrection. These then, and only these, come to understand true charity—the pure love of Christ.

And what are the characteristics of such a love born of faith and hope? "Charity suffereth long, and is kind, and envieth not, and is not puffed up, seeketh not her own, is not easily provoked, thinketh no evil, and rejoiceth not in iniquity but rejoiceth in the truth, beareth all things, believeth all things, hopeth all things, endureth all things."[46]

The essential nature of this transcendent virtue of charity is clear in Mormon's declaration that without it we "are nothing," that of the many Christian virtues, charity "is the greatest of all."[47] This is consistent with what Paul would later teach in slightly different language but to the same end—that it matters not how many other virtues we possess or how many good things we have done if true charity is lacking. Without true charity in the heart of the servant, these good works would be as "sounding brass, or a tinkling cymbal," and in the end they would be "nothing." The means—or in this case the motive—is essential to the meaning of the end, the action. In just the sequence that Mormon taught it, Paul affirmed that faith, hope, and charity are the three great virtues that, as Christians, we must cling to and try to demonstrate, "but the greatest of these is charity."[48]

It is instructive to note that the charity, or "the pure love of Christ," we are to cherish can be interpreted two ways. One of its meanings is the kind of merciful, forgiving love Christ's disciples should have one for another. That is, all Christians should try to love as the Savior loved, showing pure, redeeming compassion for all. Unfortunately, few, if any, mortals have been entirely successful in this endeavor, but it is an invitation that all should try to meet.

The greater definition of "the pure love of Christ," however, is not what we as Christians try but largely fail to demonstrate toward others but rather what Christ totally succeeded in demonstrating toward us. *True* charity has been known only once. It is shown perfectly and purely in Christ's unfailing, ultimate, and atoning love for us. It is Christ's love for us that "suffereth long, and is kind, and envieth not." It is his love for us that is not "puffed up . . . , not easily provoked, thinketh no evil." It is Christ's love for us that "beareth all things, believeth all things, hopeth all things, endureth all things." It is as demonstrated in Christ that "charity never faileth." It is that charity—his pure love for us—without which we would be nothing, hopeless, of all men and women most miserable. Truly, those found possessed of the blessings of his love at the last day—the Atonement, the Resurrection, eternal life, eternal promise—surely it shall be well with them.

This does not in any way minimize the commandment that we are to try to acquire this kind of love for one another. We should "pray unto the Father with all the energy of heart, that [we] may be filled with this love."[49] We should try to be more constant and unfailing, more longsuffering and kind, less envious and puffed up in our relationships with others. As Christ lived so should we live, and as Christ loved so should we love. But the "*pure* love of Christ" Mormon spoke of is precisely that— Christ's love. With that divine gift, that redeeming bestowal, we have everything; without it we have nothing and ultimately are nothing, except in the end "devils [and] angels to a devil."[50]

Life has its share of fears and failures. Sometimes things fall short. Sometimes people fail us, or economies or businesses or governments fail us. But one thing in time or eternity does *not* fail us—the pure love of Christ.

"I remember," Moroni had said earlier, speaking directly to the Savior, "that thou hast said that thou hast loved the world, even unto the laying down of thy life for the world, that thou mightest take it again to prepare a place for the children of men. And now I know that this love which thou hast had for the children of men is charity; wherefore, except men shall have charity [trying to demonstrate it in their own lives but, even more important, being the worthy, willing recipient of it as given by Christ] they cannot inherit that place which thou hast prepared in the mansions of thy Father."[51]

Thus, the miracle of Christ's charity both saves and changes us. His atoning love saves us from death and hell as well as from carnal, sensual, and devilish behavior. That redeeming love also transforms the soul, lifting it above fallen standards to something far more noble, far more holy. Wherefore, we must "cleave unto charity"—Christ's pure love of us and our determined effort toward pure love of him and all others—for without it we are nothing, and our plan for eternal happiness is utterly wasted. Without the redeeming love of Christ in our lives, all other qualities—even virtuous qualities and exemplary good works—fall short of salvation and joy.

This idea of "pure" love, personified by Purity Himself, moved Moroni to his loftiest expression in this third "final" testimony of Christ. Note how Mormon ended his magnificent sermon on faith, hope, and charity, and set the stage for Moroni's concluding witness:

"Wherefore, my beloved brethren, pray unto the Father with

all the energy of heart, that ye may be filled with this love, which he hath bestowed upon all who are true followers of his Son, Jesus Christ; that ye may become the sons of God; that when he shall appear we shall be like him, for we shall see him as he is; that we may have this hope; that we may be purified even as he is pure."[52]

To his unseen latter-day audience, that is Moroni's ultimate appeal—for purity, a purity that is represented in Christ and is possible for us only through the cleansing grace of Christ. Bridging from his father's magnificent sermon to his own concluding lines, Moroni wrote,

"Wherefore, there must be faith; and if there must be faith there must also be hope; and if there must be hope there must also be charity.

"And except ye have charity ye can in nowise be saved in the kingdom of God; neither can ye be saved in the kingdom of God if ye have not faith; neither can ye if ye have no hope."[53]

Pleading "unto all the ends of the earth" for the demonstration of such virtues, Moroni made his appeal for that purity to which faith, hope, and charity lead. "Come unto Christ," Moroni pleaded, "and lay hold upon every good gift, and touch not the evil gift, nor the unclean thing . . . that the covenants of the Eternal Father . . . may be fulfilled."[54]

Moroni's last appeal, expressed on behalf of every prophet who ever wrote in this other testament of Jesus Christ, is for us to be cleansed from the blood and sin of our generation.[55] "Come unto Christ," he says, "and be perfected in him, and deny yourselves of all ungodliness; and if ye shall deny yourselves of all ungodliness, and love God with all your might, mind and strength, then is his grace sufficient for you, that by his grace ye may be perfect in Christ. . . .

"And again, if ye by the grace of God are perfect in Christ, and deny not his power, then are ye sanctified in Christ by the grace of God, through the shedding of the blood of Christ, which is in the covenant of the Father unto the remission of your sins, that ye become holy, without spot."[56]

The covenant of the Father unto the remission of our sins. Purity. Holiness. Character and conscience without blemish. All these through the grace of Christ, which cleanses our garments, sanctifies our souls, saves us from death, and restores us to our divine origins.

With his last recorded breath Moroni bore witness of his own firm faith in such divine redemption. To his fallen Nephites, to the warring Lamanites, to those tragic Jaredites, and to us, Moroni wrote:

"And now I bid unto all, farewell. I soon go to rest in the paradise of God, until my spirit and body shall again reunite, and I am brought forth triumphant through the air, to meet you before the pleasing bar of the great Jehovah, the Eternal Judge of both quick and dead. Amen."[57]

Thus the Book of Mormon ends, flying as it were with Moroni, on the promise of the Holy Resurrection.[58] That is most fitting, for this sacred testament—written by prophets, delivered by angels, protected by God—speaks as one "crying from the dead," exhorting all to come unto Christ and be perfected in him, a process culminating in the perfection of celestial glory. In anticipation of that triumphant hour, God has set his hand for the last time to gather Jew, Gentile, Lamanite, and all the house of Israel.

The Book of Mormon is his New Covenant memorializing that grand latter-day endeavor. All who receive it and embrace the principles and ordinances it declares will one day see the Savior as he is, and they will be like him. They will be sanctified and redeemed through the grace of his innocent blood. They will be purified even as he is pure. They will be holy and without spot. They will be called the children of Christ.

AFFIRMATION

CHAPTER SEVENTEEN

WITNESS

n my lifetime I have had a thousand spiritual witnesses—ten thousand of them?—that Jesus is the Christ, the Everlasting Son of the Everlasting God. In that lifetime I have also learned that the gospel of Jesus Christ, once lost to mankind through apostasy, has been restored to the earth and is found in its fulness in The Church of Jesus Christ of Latter-day Saints. This is the one church on the face of the earth that Christ himself has restored, authorized, and empowered to act in his name. With a commission that could not have been imagined in the days of my youth, I myself am now called as a witness of these facts, a special witness "of the name of Christ in all the world."[1]

In that role as witness I wish to declare that the spiritual experiences and holy affirmations I have had regarding the Savior and his restored church *first* came to me as a young man when I read the Book of Mormon. It was while reading this sacred record that I felt—again and again—the undeniable whispering of the Holy Ghost declaring to my soul the truthfulness of its message. To those first convictions have been added, one way or another, all of the other quickening moments and sanctifying manifestations that now give meaning to my days and purpose to my life.

I know with undeniable, unshakable certainty that the Book of Mormon is a record of ancient origin, written by Israelites called of God to do so, protected and delivered by the angels of heaven and translated in our time by a modern prophet, seer, and revelator, Joseph Smith, Jr. I know that he translated it as he said he did—"by the gift and power of God"—for such a book could not have been translated any other way.[2]

No other book has so affected my view of God and man, my view of mortality and eternity. No other book has stirred within me so many emotions. No other book has had such an impact upon my personal, family, educational, professional, and now apostolic life. Because I know that the Book of Mormon is a true witness—another testament and a new covenant—that Jesus is the Christ, I know that Joseph Smith was and is a prophet of God. As my great-great-great grandfather said of his own conversion in the earliest days of the Restoration, "No wicked man could write such a book as this; and no good man would write it, unless it were true and he were commanded of God to do so."[3] That is emphatically my own assertion more than a century and a half later. And this magnificent book was translated when Joseph Smith was barely a boy, a lad still coming of age. To paraphrase Winston Churchill, "Some boy. Some book."

Because Joseph Smith is a prophet of God as evidenced not least by his role in bringing forth the Book of Mormon, the Church he was instrumental in restoring is indeed the Church of Jesus Christ in these latter days. To this Church the keys of the priesthood were given, including (but not limited to) the keys of revelation, gathering, baptism, ordination, and sealing. The Church continues to bless the world with such keys and covenants to this day.

The Prophet Joseph's expression that the Book of Mormon is "the keystone of our religion" is a profound and crucial observation. A keystone is positioned at the uppermost center of an arch in such a way as to hold all the other stones in place. That key piece, if removed, will bring all of the other blocks crashing down with it. The truthfulness of the Book of Mormon—its origins, its doctrines, and the circumstances of its coming forth—is central to the truthfulness of The Church of Jesus Christ of Latter-day Saints. The integrity of this church and more than 165 years of its restoration experience stand or fall with the veracity or falsity of the Book of Mormon.

To consider that everything of saving significance in the Church stands or falls on the truthfulness of the Book of Mormon and, by implication, the Prophet Joseph Smith's account of how it came forth is as sobering as it is true. It is a "sudden death" proposition. Either the Book of Mormon is what the Prophet Joseph said it is, or this church and its founder are false, a deception from the first instance onward.

Not everything in life is so black and white, but the authenticity of the Book of Mormon and its keystone role in our religion seem to be exactly that. Either Joseph Smith was the prophet he said he was, a prophet who, after seeing the Father and the Son, later beheld the angel Moroni, repeatedly heard counsel from Moroni's lips, and eventually received at his hands a set of ancient gold plates that he then translated by the gift and power of God, or else he did not. And if he did not, he would not be entitled to the reputation of New England folk hero or well-meaning young man or writer of remarkable fiction. No, nor would he be entitled to be considered a great teacher, a quintessential American religious leader, or the creator of great devotional literature. If he had lied about the coming forth of the Book of Mormon, he would certainly be none of these.

I am suggesting that one has to take something of a do-or-die stand regarding the restoration of the gospel of Jesus Christ and the divine origins of the Book of Mormon. Reason and righteousness require it. Joseph Smith must be accepted either as a prophet of God or else as a charlatan of the first order, but no one should tolerate any ludicrous, even laughable middle ground about the wonderful contours of a young boy's imagination or his remarkable facility for turning a literary phrase. That is an unacceptable position to take—morally, literarily, historically, or theologically.

As the word of God has always been—and I testify again that is purely and precisely what the Book of Mormon is—this record is "quick and powerful, sharper than a two-edged sword, to the dividing asunder of both joints and marrow."[4] The Book of Mormon is that quick and is that powerful. And it certainly is that sharp. Nothing in our history or our message cuts to the chase faster than our uncompromising declaration that Joseph Smith saw the Father and the Son and that the Book of Mormon is the word of God. A recent critic said that our account of and devotion to the Book of Mormon and, by implication, Joseph Smith's role in producing it, is "the most cherished and unique Mormon belief."[5] I could not agree more, so long as we are allowed to maintain that is so because the Book of Mormon affirms our yet higher and more sublime belief that Jesus is the Christ, the Son of the Living God, the Savior and Redeemer of the world.

Consider the withering examination the Book of Mormon and its admittedly extraordinary claims have withstood. Has anyone presently reading these words ever tried to write anything of spiritual, redeeming, genuinely inspiring substance? With university degrees and libraries and computers and research assistants and decades of time, have you ever tried to write anything that anyone could read without tedium or apathy? And if one could produce even a few such inspiring pages, would that slim volume be anything anyone would want to read more than once, to say nothing of scores of times—marking it and pondering it, cross-referencing and quoting it, taking thousands of public sermons and a heart full of personal solace from it? Would it be good enough for people to weep over, to say it changed their lives, or saved their lives, or became something they were willing to give up fortune and future for—and then did just that?

What if your literary piece created enemies for you? What if it were left in the public arena, open to the criticism of your most hostile and learned opponents, for more than 150 years? What if it were pulled apart and minutely examined and held up to the light of history, literature, anthropology, and religion with no other purpose than to discredit it and denounce you? Could what you have written be *that* good? Would you still be willing to say that it was an inspired piece of work, let alone hold to your assertion that it was divinely revealed and that its contents were *eternally* important—that in a very real sense the whole future of the world was linked to your little volume? By this time would either you or your piece still be standing? Would anyone still be reading it?

If Joseph Smith did not translate the Book of Mormon as a work of ancient origin, then I would move heaven and earth to meet the "real" nineteenth-century author. After one hundred and fifty years, no one can come up with a credible alternative candidate, but if the book were false, surely there must be someone willing to step forward—if no one else, at least the descendants of the "real" author—claiming credit for such a remarkable document and all that has transpired in its wake. After all, a writer that can move millions can make millions. Shouldn't someone have come forth then or now to cashier the whole phenomenon?

And what of the witnesses, the three and the eight, who forever affixed their signatures to the introductory pages of the Book of Mormon declaring they had, respectively, seen an angel and handled the plates of gold? Each of the three and several of the eight had difficulty with the institutional Church during their lifetimes, including years of severe disaffection from Joseph Smith personally. Nevertheless, none of them—even in hours of emotional extremity or days of public pressure—ever disavowed his testimony of the divinity of the Book of Mormon.

Late in his life David Whitmer said "as sure as there is a God in heaven," he had indeed seen the angel Moroni and did know the Book of Mormon was true. Fifty years after the experience, he could still readily identify the month, the year, even the time of day ("It was approximately 11 A.M.," he said) when the angel appeared in "a dazzlingly brilliant light" and brought "a sensation of joy absolutely indescribable."

Martin Harris was asked in the last year of his life if he "believed the Book of Mormon was true." He answered "No," then reassured his initially surprised interrogator that he "knew" the book was true, which was greater than belief. "I know what I know. I have seen what I have seen, and I have heard what I have heard," he said. "I saw the angel and the plates from which the Book of Mormon was translated and heard the voice of God declare it was translated correctly."

Oliver Cowdery, who served as scribe as well as witness in this remarkable translation process and whose unique role in the early years of the Church is all the more poignant in light of his later fall from such sacred and significant responsibilities, said (while excommunicated from the Church), "I wrote with my own pen the entire Book of Mormon (save a few pages) as it fell from the lips of the Prophet, as he translated it by the gift and power of God. . . . I beheld with my eyes, and handled with my hands, the gold plates from which it was translated. . . . That book is true." Thirty-seven years after Oliver called his family to his deathbed to yet once more bear his testimony of the Book of Mormon, his wife Elizabeth wrote, "From the hour when the glorious vision of the Holy Messenger revealed to mortal eyes the

hidden prophecies which God had promised his faithful followers should come forth in due time, until the moment when he
passed away from earth, he always without one doubt or
shadow of turning affirmed the divinity and truth of the Book of
Mormon."[6]

No other origin for the Book of Mormon has ever come to
light because no other account than the one Joseph Smith and
these witnesses gave can truthfully be given. There is no other
clandestine "author," no elusive ghostwriter still waiting in the
wings after a century and a half for the chance to stride forward
and startle the religious world. Indeed, that any writer—Joseph
Smith or anyone else—could create the Book of Mormon out of
whole cloth would be an infinitely greater miracle than that
young Joseph translated it from an ancient record by "the gift
and power of God."

On occasion this young prophet dictated his translation at
white-hot speed, turning out as many as ten present-day pages
in a sitting and ultimately producing the whole manuscript in
something less than ninety working days. Those who have ever
translated *any* text will understand what this means, especially
when remembering it took fifty English scholars seven years
(using generally superb and readily available translations for a
starting point) to produce the King James Bible at the rate of one
page per day.

It is not insignificant that Joseph Smith did virtually all of
this work in the midst of seemingly endless distractions and in
the face of sometimes open hostility. Nevertheless, following
those breaks in the translation effort he apparently never looked
at the previously dictated material nor had any portion of it read
back to him for context or continuity. Furthermore, he was never
known to have consulted any reference book of any kind during
the whole of the translation experience.

I endorse with all my heart and the holy office I now hold,

indeed with my very life itself, the declaration of John Taylor, who took four rounds, full bore, from the Prophet Joseph Smith's enemies who stormed Carthage Jail that fateful day in June 1844. Brother Taylor's life was spared, and he lived to say of his leader, "Joseph Smith, the Prophet and Seer of the Lord, has done more, save Jesus only, for the salvation of men in this world, than any other man that ever lived in it. . . . He lived great, and he died great in the eyes of God and his people; and like most of the Lord's anointed . . . has sealed his mission and his works with his own blood." Then, including the beloved Hyrum Smith's life as a second witness, Brother Taylor said, "The testators are now dead, *and their testament is in force.*"[7]

That testament which is now in force, sealed with the blood of its translator, is primarily and principally the Book of Mormon. A great many of the judgments passed against Joseph Smith over the years have been made from far more comfortable quarters than the second floor of the Carthage Jail, where John Taylor tried so valiantly to defend his prophet with nothing more than a hickory walking stick. I was not there, but I would offer to be there—then or now or ever—in defense of the truthfulness of the Book of Mormon, its prophet-translator, the gospel of Jesus Christ they teach, and the Church which takes that message to the world.

I have read a reasonable number of books in my life, and I hope to read many more. I am not steeped in scholarship, but I can recognize profundity in print, especially when I see it page after page. In a lifetime of reading, the Book of Mormon stands preeminent in my intellectual and spiritual life, the classic of all classics, a reaffirmation of the Holy Bible, a voice from the dust, a witness for Christ, the word of the Lord unto salvation. I testify of that as surely as if I had, with the Three Witnesses, seen the angel Moroni or, with the Three and the Eight Witnesses, seen and handled the plates of gold.

The Book of Mormon is the sacred expression of Christ's great last covenant with mankind. It is a new covenant, a new testament from the New World to the entire world. Reading it was the beginning of my light. It was the source of my first spiritual certainty that God lives, that he is my Heavenly Father, and that a plan of happiness was outlined in eternity for me. It led me to love the Holy Bible and the rest of the Standard Works of the Church. It taught me to love the Lord Jesus Christ, to glimpse his merciful compassion, and to consider the grace and grandeur of his atoning sacrifice for my sins and the sins of all men, women, and children from Adam to the end of time. The light I walk by is his light. His mercy and magnificence lead me in my witness of him to the world.

As Mormon said to Moroni in one of their most demanding times, so I say to the family of mankind, who must prepare for the coming of our King of Kings: "Be faithful in Christ; and may . . . [he] lift thee up. . . . May his sufferings and death, and the showing his body unto our fathers, and his mercy and long-suffering, and the hope of his glory and of eternal life, rest in your mind forever.

"And may the grace of God the Father, whose throne is high in the heavens, and our Lord Jesus Christ, who sitteth on the right hand of his power . . . be, and abide with you forever."[8]

TITLES FOR CHRIST

ollowing are some of the titles for Christ as found in the Book of Mormon. The scripture entries denote the first occurrence of the titles:

Almighty (2 Nephi 23:6)

Almighty God (Jacob 2:10)

Alpha and Omega (3 Nephi 9:18)

Being (Mosiah 4:19)

Beloved (2 Nephi 31:15)

Beloved Son (2 Nephi 31:11)

Christ (2 Nephi 10:3)

Christ Jesus (Alma 5:44)

Christ the Son (Alma 11:44)

Counselor (2 Nephi 19:6)

Creator (2 Nephi 9:5)

Eternal Father (Mosiah 15:4)

Eternal God (1 Nephi 12:18)

Eternal Head (Helaman 13:38)

Eternal Judge (Moroni 10:34)

Everlasting Father (2 Nephi 19:6)

Everlasting God (1 Nephi 15:15)

Father (Jacob 7:22)

Father of heaven (1 Nephi 22:9)

Father of heaven and of earth (Helaman 14:12)

Founder of peace (Mosiah 15:18)

God (2 Nephi 1:22)

God of Abraham (1 Nephi 19:10)

God of Abraham, and Isaac, and Jacob (Mosiah 7:19)

God of Abraham, and of Isaac, and the God of Jacob (1 Nephi 19:10)

God of Isaac (Alma 29:11)
God of Israel (1 Nephi 19:7)
God of Jacob (2 Nephi 12:3)
God of miracles (2 Nephi 27:23)
God of nature (1 Nephi 19:12)
God of the whole earth (3 Nephi 11:14)
Good shepherd (Alma 5:38)
Great Creator (2 Nephi 9:5)
Great Spirit (Alma 18:2)
Head (Jacob 4:17)
Holy Child (Moroni 8:3)
Holy God (2 Nephi 9:39)
Holy Messiah (2 Nephi 2:6)
Holy One (2 Nephi 2:10)
Holy One of Israel (1 Nephi 19:14)
Holy One of Jacob (2 Nephi 27:34)
Husband (3 Nephi 22:5)
Immanuel (2 Nephi 18:8)
Jehovah (Moroni 10:34)
Jesus (2 Nephi 31:10)
Jesus Christ (2 Nephi 25:19)
Keeper of the gate (2 Nephi 9:41)
King (2 Nephi 16:5)
King of heaven (2 Nephi 10:14)
Lamb (1 Nephi 13:35)
Lamb of God (1 Nephi 10:10)
Lord (1 Nephi 10:14)

Lord God (2 Nephi 1:5)
Lord God Almighty (2 Nephi 9:46)
Lord God Omnipotent (Mosiah 3:21)
Lord God of Hosts (2 Nephi 13:15)
Lord Jehovah (2 Nephi 22:2)
Lord Jesus (Moroni 6:6)
Lord Jesus Christ (Mosiah 3:12)
Lord of Hosts (1 Nephi 20:2)
Lord of the vineyard (Jacob 5:8)
Lord Omnipotent (Mosiah 3:5)
Maker (2 Nephi 9:40)
Man (3 Nephi 11:8)
Master (Jacob 5:4)
Mediator (2 Nephi 2:28)
Messiah (1 Nephi 1:19)
Mighty God (2 Nephi 6:17)
Mighty One of Israel (1 Nephi 22:12)
Mighty One of Jacob (1 Nephi 21:26)
Most High (2 Nephi 24:14)
Most High God (Alma 26:14)
Only Begotten of the Father (2 Nephi 25:12)
Only Begotten Son (Jacob 4:5)
Prince of Peace (2 Nephi 19:6)
Prophet (1 Nephi 22:20)
Rabbanah (Alma 18:13)
Redeemer (1 Nephi 10:6)

Redeemer of Israel (1 Nephi 21:7)

Redeemer of the world (1 Nephi 10:5)

Rock (1 Nephi 15:15)

Savior (2 Nephi 31:13)

Savior Jesus Christ (3 Nephi 5:20)

Savior of the world (1 Nephi 10:4)

Shepherd (1 Nephi 13:41)

Son (2 Nephi 31:13)

Son of God (1 Nephi 10:17)

Son of Righteousness (Ether 9:22)

Son of the Eternal Father (1 Nephi 11:21)

Son of the everlasting God (1 Nephi 11:32)

Son of the living God (2 Nephi 31:16)

Son of the most high God (1 Nephi 11:6)

Stone (Jacob 4:16)

Supreme Being (Alma 11:22)

Supreme Creator (Alma 30:44)

True and living God (1 Nephi 17:30)

True Messiah (2 Nephi 1:10)

True shepherd (Helaman 15:13)

True vine (1 Nephi 15:15)

Well Beloved (Helaman 5:47)

Wonderful (2 Nephi 19:6)

(With appreciation to Susan Easton Black for her work in *Finding Christ through the Book of Mormon* [Salt Lake City: Deseret Book Co., 1987], pp. 16–18.)

BOOK OF MORMON REFERENCES TO ISAIAH

Book of Mormon Reference	Bible Reference
1 Nephi 10:8	Isaiah 40:3
1 Nephi 20	Isaiah 48
1 Nephi 21	Isaiah 49
2 Nephi 6:7, 16–18	Isaiah 49:23–26
2 Nephi 7	Isaiah 50
2 Nephi 8	Isaiah 51
2 Nephi 8:24–25	Isaiah 52:1–2
2 Nephi 9:50–51	Isaiah 55:1–2
2 Nephi 12	Isaiah 2
2 Nephi 13	Isaiah 3
2 Nephi 14	Isaiah 4
2 Nephi 15	Isaiah 5
2 Nephi 16	Isaiah 6
2 Nephi 17	Isaiah 7
2 Nephi 18	Isaiah 8
2 Nephi 19	Isaiah 9
2 Nephi 20	Isaiah 10
2 Nephi 21	Isaiah 11
2 Nephi 22	Isaiah 12
2 Nephi 23	Isaiah 13

Book of Mormon Reference	Bible Reference
2 Nephi 24	Isaiah 14
2 Nephi 26:15–18	Isaiah 29:3–5
2 Nephi 27:2–35	Isaiah 29:6–24
2 Nephi 28:30	Isaiah 28:10
2 Nephi 30:9–16	Isaiah 11:4–9
Mosiah 12:21–24	Isaiah 52:7–10
Mosiah 14	Isaiah 53
Mosiah 15:29–31	Isaiah 52:8–10
3 Nephi 16:18–20	Isaiah 52:8–10
3 Nephi 20:32–45	Isaiah 52:1–3, 6–15
3 Nephi 22	Isaiah 54

(With appreciation to Monte S. Nyman for his work in *Great Are the Words of Isaiah* [Salt Lake City: Bookcraft, 1980], pp. 283–85.)

THE FATHER AND THE SON: A DOCTRINAL EXPOSITION BY THE FIRST PRESIDENCY AND THE TWELVE

he scriptures plainly and repeatedly affirm that God is the Creator of the earth and the heavens and all things that in them are. In the sense so expressed, the Creator is an Organizer. God created the earth as an organized sphere; but He certainly did not create, in the sense of bringing into primal existence, the ultimate elements of the materials of which the earth consists, for "the elements are eternal" (D&C 93:33).

So also life is eternal, and not created; but life, or the vital force, may be infused into organized matter, though the details of the process have not been revealed unto man. For illustrative instances see Genesis 2:7; Moses 3:7; and Abraham 5:7. Each of these scriptures states that God breathed into the body of man the breath of life. See further Moses 3:19, for the statement that God breathed the breath of life into the bodies of the beasts and birds. God showed unto Abraham "the intelligences that were organized before the world was"; and by "intelligences" we are to understand personal "spirits" (Abraham 3:22, 23); nevertheless, we are expressly told that "Intelligence" that is, "the light of truth, was not created or made, neither indeed can be" (D&C 93:29).

The term "Father" as applied to Deity occurs in sacred writ with plainly different meanings. Each of the four significations specified in the following treatment should be carefully segregated.

1. "Father" as Literal Parent—Scriptures embodying the ordinary signification—literally that of Parent—are too numerous and specific to require citation. The purport of these scriptures is to the effect that God the Eternal Father, whom we designate by the exalted name-title "Elohim," is the literal Parent of our Lord and Savior Jesus Christ, and of the spirits of the human race. Elohim is the Father in every sense in which Jesus Christ is so designated, and distinctively He is the Father of spirits. Thus we read in the Epistle to the Hebrews: "Furthermore we have had fathers of our flesh which corrected us, and we gave them reverence: shall we not much rather be in subjection unto the Father of spirits, and live?" (Hebrews 12:9). In view of this fact we are taught by Jesus Christ to pray: "Our Father which art in heaven, Hallowed be thy name."

Jesus Christ applies to Himself both titles, "Son" and "Father." Indeed, he specifically said to the brother of Jared: "Behold, I am Jesus Christ. I am the Father and the Son" (Ether 3:14). Jesus Christ is the Son of Elohim both as spiritual and bodily offspring; that is to say, Elohim is literally the Father of the spirit of Jesus Christ and also of the body in which Jesus Christ performed His mission in the flesh, and which body died on the cross and was afterward taken up by the process of resurrection, and is now the immortalized tabernacle of the eternal spirit of our Lord and Savior. No extended explanation of the title "Son of God" as applied to Jesus Christ seems necessary.

2. "Father" as Creator—A second scriptural meaning of "Father" is that of Creator, e.g., in passages referring to any one of the Godhead as "The Father of the heavens and of the earth

and all things that in them are" (Ether 4:7; see also Alma 11:38, 39 and Mosiah 15:4).

God is not the Father of the earth as one of the worlds in space, nor of the heavenly bodies in whole or in part, nor of the inanimate objects and the plants and the animals upon the earth, in the literal sense in which He is the Father of the spirits of mankind. Therefore, scriptures that refer to God in any way as the Father of the heavens and the earth are to be understood as signifying that God is the Maker, the Organizer, the Creator of the heavens and the earth.

With this meaning, as the context shows in every case, Jehovah who is Jesus Christ the Son of Elohim, is called "the Father," and even "the very eternal Father of heaven and of earth" (see passages before cited, and also Mosiah 16:15). With analogous meaning Jesus Christ is called "The Everlasting Father" (Isaiah 9:6; compare 2 Nephi 19:6). The descriptive titles "Everlasting" and "Eternal" in the foregoing texts are synonymous.

That Jesus Christ, whom we also know as Jehovah, was the executive of the Father, Elohim, in the work of creation is set forth in the book Jesus the Christ, chapter 4. Jesus Christ, being the Creator, is consistently called the Father of heaven and earth in the sense explained above; and since His creations are of eternal quality He is very properly called the Eternal Father of heaven and earth.

3. Jesus Christ the "Father" of Those Who Abide in His Gospel—A third sense in which Jesus Christ is regarded as the "Father" has reference to the relationship between Him and those who accept His Gospel and thereby become heirs of eternal life. Following are a few of the scriptures illustrating this meaning.

In the fervent prayer offered just prior to His entrance into Gethsemane, Jesus Christ supplicated His Father in behalf of those whom the Father had given unto Him, specifically the apostles, and, more generally, all who would accept and abide in the Gospel through the ministry of the apostles. Read in the Lord's own words the solemn affirmation that those for whom He particularly prayed were His own, and that His Father had given them unto Him: "I have manifested thy name unto the men which thou gavest me out of the world: thine they were, and thou gavest them me; and they have kept thy word. Now they have known that all things whatsoever thou hast given me are of thee. For I have given unto them the words which thou gavest me; and they have received them, and have known surely that I came out from thee, and they have pray for them: I pray not for the world, but for them which thou hast given me; for they are thine. And all mine are thine, and thine are mine; and I am glorified in them. And now I am no more in the world, but these are in the world, and I come to thee. Holy Father, keep through thine own name those whom thou hast given me, that they may be one as we are. While I was with them in the world, I kept them in thy name: those that thou gavest me I have kept, and none of them is lost, but the son of perdition; that the scripture might be filled" (John 17:6–12).

And further: "Neither pray I for these alone, but for them also which shall believe on me through their word; That they all may be one; as thou, Father, art in me, and I in thee, that they also may be one in us: that the world may believe that thou hast sent me. And the glory which thou gavest me I have given them; that they may be one, even as we are one: I in them, and thou in me, that they may be made perfect in one, and that the world may know that thou hast sent me, and hast loved them, as thou hast loved me. Father, I will that they also, whom thou hast given me, be with me where I am; that they may behold my glory, which thou hast given me: for thou lovedst me before the foundation of the world" (John 17:20–24).

To His faithful servants in the present dispensation the Lord has said:"Fear not, little children, for you are mine, and I have overcome the world, and you are of them that my Father hath given me" (D&C 50:41).

Salvation is attainable only through compliance with the laws and ordinances Hearken and listen to the voice of him who is from all eternity to all eternity, the Great I AM, even Jesus Christ—The light and the life of the world; a light which shineth in darkness and the darkness comprehendeth it not; The same which came in the meridian of time unto mine own, and mine own received me not; But to as many as received me, gave I power to become my sons; and even so will I give unto as many as will receive me, power to become my sons" (D&C 39:1–4). In a revelation given through Joseph Smith in March, 1831, we read: "For verily I say unto you that I am Alpha and Omega, the beginning and the end, the light and the life of the world—a light that shineth in darkness and the darkness comprehendeth it not. I came unto mine own, and mine own received me not; but unto as many as received me, gave I power to do many miracles, and to become the sons of God, and even unto them that believed on my name gave I power to obtain eternal life" (D&C 45:7–8).

A forceful exposition of this relationship between Jesus Christ as the Father and those who comply with the requirements of the Gospel as His children was given by Abinadi, centuries before our Lord's birth in the flesh: "And now I say unto you, who shall declare his generation? Behold, I say unto you, that when his soul has been made an offering for sin, he shall see his seed. And now what say ye? And who shall be his seed? Behold I say unto you, that whosoever has heard the words of the prophets, yea, all the holy prophets who have prophesied concerning the coming of the Lord—I say unto you, that all those who have hearkened unto their words, and believed that the Lord would redeem his people, and have looked forward to that

day for a remission of their sins, I say unto you, that these are his
seed, or they are the heirs of the kingdom of God. For these are
they whose sins he has borne; these are they for whom he has
died to redeem them from their transgressions. And now, are
they not his seed? Yea, and are not the prophets, every one that
has opened his mouth to prophesy, that has not fallen into transgression, I mean all the holy prophets ever since the world
began? I say unto you that they are his seed" (Mosiah 15:10–13).

In tragic contrast with the blessed state of those who become
children of God through obedience to the Gospel of Jesus Christ
is that of the unregenerate, who are specifically called the children of the devil. Note the words of Christ, while in the flesh, to
certain wicked Jews who boasted of their Abrahamic lineage: "If
ye were Abraham's children, ye would do the works of
Abraham. * * * Ye do the deeds of your father * * * If God were
your Father, ye would love me. * * * Ye are of your father the
devil, and the lusts of your father ye will do" (John 8:39, 41, 42,
44). Thus Satan is designated as the father of the wicked, though
we cannot assume any personal relationship of parent and children as existing between him and them. A combined illustration
showing that the righteous are the children of God and the
wicked the children of the devil appears in the parable of the
Tares: "The good seed are the children of the kingdom; but the
tares are the children of the wicked one" (Matthew 13:38).

Men may become children of Jesus Christ by being born
anew—born of God, as the inspired word states: "He that committeth sin is of the devil; for the devil sinneth from the beginning. For this purpose the Son of God was manifested, that he
might destroy the works of the devil. Whosoever is born of God
doth not commit sin; for his seed remaineth in him: and he cannot sin, because he is born of God. In this the children of God are
manifest, and the children of the devil: whosoever doeth not

righteousness is not of God, neither he that loveth not his brother" (1 John 3:8–10).

Those who have been born unto God through obedience to the Gospel may by valiant devotion to righteousness obtain exaltation and even reach the status of godhood. Of such we read: "Wherefore, as it is written, they are gods, even the sons of God" (D&C 76:58; compare 132:20, and contrast paragraph 17 in same section; see also paragraph 37). Yet, though they be gods they are still subject to Jesus Christ as their Father in this exalted relationship; and so we read in the paragraph following the above quotation: "and they are Christ's, and Christ is God's" (76:59).

By the new birth—that of water and the Spirit—mankind may become children of Jesus Christ, being through the means by Him provided "begotten sons and daughters unto God" (D&C 76:24). This solemn truth is further emphasized in the words of the Lord Jesus Christ given through Joseph Smith in 1833: "And now, verily I say unto you, I was in the beginning with the Father, and am the Firstborn; And all those who are begotten through me are partakers of the glory of the same, and are the church of the Firstborn" (D&C 93:21, 22). For such figurative use of the term "begotten" in application to those who are born unto God see Paul's explanation: "for in Christ Jesus I have begotten you through the gospel" (1 Corinthians 4:15). An analogous instance of sonship attained by righteous service is found in the revelation relating to the order and functions of Priesthood, given in 1832: "For whoso is faithful unto the obtaining of these two priesthoods of which I have spoken, and the magnifying their calling, are sanctified by the Spirit unto the renewing of their bodies. They become the sons of Moses and of Aaron and the seed of Abraham, and the church and kingdom, and the elect of God" (D&C 84:33, 34).

If it be proper to speak of those who accept and abide in the Gospel as Christ's sons and daughters—and upon this matter the scriptures are explicit and cannot be gainsaid nor denied—it is consistently proper to speak of Jesus Christ as the Father of the righteous, they having become His children and He having been made their Father through the second birth—the baptismal regeneration.

4. Jesus Christ the "Father" by Divine Investiture of Authority—A fourth reason for applying the title "Father" to Jesus Christ is found in the fact that in all His dealings with the human family Jesus the Son has represented and yet represents Elohim His Father in power and authority. This is true of Christ in His pre-existent, antemortal, or unembodied state, in the which He was known as Jehovah; also during His embodiment in the flesh; and during His labors as a disembodied spirit in the realm of the dead; and since that period in His resurrected state. To the Jews He said: "I and my Father are one" (John 10:30; see also 17:11, 22); yet He declared "My Father is greater than I" (John 14:28); and further, "I am come in my Father's name" (John 5:43; see also 10:25). The same truth was declared by Christ Himself to the Nephites (see 3 Nephi 20:35 and 28:10), and has been reaffirmed by revelation in the present dispensation (D&C 50:43). Thus the Father placed His name upon the Son; and Jesus Christ spoke and ministered in and through the Father's name; and so far as power, authority, and Godship are concerned His words and acts were and are those of the Father.

We read, by way of analogy, that God placed His name upon or in the Angel who was assigned to special ministry unto the people of Israel during the exodus. Of that Angel the Lord said: "Beware of him, and obey his voice, provoke him not; for he will not pardon your transgressions: for my name is in him" (Exodus 23:21).

The ancient apostle, John, was visited by an angel who ministered and spoke in the name of Jesus Christ. As we read: "The Revelation of Jesus Christ, which God gave unto him, to shew unto his servants things which must shortly come to pass; and he sent and signified it by his angel unto his servant John" (Revelation 1:1). John was about to worship the angelic being who spoke in the name of the Lord Jesus Christ, but was forbidden: "And I John saw these things, and heard them. And when I had heard and seen, I fell down to worship before the feet of the angel which shewed me these things. Then saith he unto me, See thou do it not: for I am thy fellowservant, and of thy brethren the prophets, and of them which keep the sayings of this book: worship God" (Revelation 22:8, 9). And then the angel continued to speak as though he were the Lord Himself: "And, behold, I come quickly; and my reward is with me, to give every man according as his work shall be. I am Alpha and Omega, the beginning and the end, the first and the last" (verses 12, 13). The resurrected Lord, Jesus Christ, who had been exalted to the right hand of God His Father, had placed His name upon the angel sent to John, and the angel spoke in the first person, saying "I come quickly," "I am Alpha and Omega" though he meant that Jesus Christ would come, and that Jesus Christ was Alpha and Omega.

None of these considerations, however, can change in the least degree the solemn fact of the literal relationship of Father and Son between Elohim and Jesus Christ. Among the spirit children of Elohim the firstborn was and is Jehovah or Jesus Christ to whom all others are juniors. Following are affirmative scriptures bearing upon this great truth. Paul, writing to the Colossians, says of Jesus Christ: "Who is the image of the invisible God, the firstborn of every creature: For by him were all things created, that are in heaven, and that are in earth, visible and invisible, whether they be thrones, or dominions, or principalities, or powers; all things were created by him, and for him: And he is before all things, and by him all things consist. And he is the head of the body, the church: who is the beginning, the firstborn from the dead; that in all things he might have the preeminence. For it pleased the Father that in him should all fulness dwell" (Colossians 1:15–19). From this scripture we learn that Jesus Christ was "the firstborn of every creature" and it is evident that the seniority here expressed must be with respect to antemortal existence, for Christ was not the senior of all mortals in the flesh. He is further designated as "the firstborn from the dead," this having reference to Him as the first to be resurrected from the dead, or as elsewhere written "the firstfruits of them that slept" (1 Corinthians 15:20, see also verse 23); and "the first begotten of the dead" (Revelation 1:5; compare Acts 26:23). The writer of the Epistle to the Hebrews affirms the status of Jesus Christ as the firstborn of the spirit children of His Father, and extols the preeminence of the Christ when tabernacled in flesh: "And again, when he bringeth in the firstbegotten into the world, he saith, And let all the angels of God worship him" (Hebrews 1:6; read the preceding verses). That the spirits who were juniors to Christ were predestined to be born in the image of their Elder Brother is thus attested by Paul: "And we know that all things work together for good to them that love God, to them who are the called according to his purpose. For whom he did foreknow, he also did predestinate to be conformed to the image of his Son, that he might be the firstborn among many brethren" (Romans 8:28, 29). John the Revelator was commanded to write to the head of the Laodicean church, as the words of the Lord Jesus Christ: "These things saith the Amen, the faithful and true witness, the beginning of the creation of God" (Revelation 3:14). In the course of a revelation given through Joseph Smith in May, 1833, the Lord Jesus Christ said as before cited: "And now, verily I say unto you, I was in the beginning with the Father, and am the Firstborn" (D&C 93:21). A later verse makes plain the fact that human beings generally were similarly existent in spirit state prior to their embodiment in the flesh: "Ye were also in the beginning with the Father; that which is Spirit, even the Spirit of truth" (verse 23).

There is no impropriety, therefore, in speaking of Jesus Christ as the Elder Brother of the rest of human kind. That He is by spiritual birth Brother to the rest of us is indicated in Hebrews: "Wherefore in all things it behoved him to be made like unto his brethren, that he might be a merciful and faithful high priest in things pertaining to God, to make reconciliation for the sins of the people" (Hebrews 2: 17). Let it not be forgotten, however, that He is essentially greater than any and all others, by reason (1) of His seniority as the oldest or firstborn; (2) of His unique status in the flesh as the offspring of a mortal mother and of an immortal, or resurrected and glorified, Father; (3) of His selection and foreordination as the one and only Redeemer and Savior of the race; and (4) of His transcendent sinlessness.

Jesus Christ is not the Father of the spirits who have taken or yet shall take bodies upon this earth, for He is one of them. He is The Son, as they are sons and daughters of Elohim. So far as the stages of eternal progression and attainment have been made known through divine revelation, we are to understand that only resurrected and glorified beings can become parents of spirit offspring. Only such exalted souls have reached maturity in the appointed course of eternal life; and the spirits born to them in the eternal worlds will pass in due sequence through the several stages or estates by which the glorified parents have attained exaltation.

The First Presidency

and the Council of the Twelve Apostles

of The Church of Jesus Christ

of Latter-day Saints

[June 1916]

COMPARISON OF THE SERMON AT THE TEMPLE AND THE SERMON ON THE MOUNT

The Sermon at the Temple *(Book of Mormon)*	*The Sermon on the Mount* *(New Testament)*
3 Nephi 12:1	*Matthew 5:1*
And it came to pass that when Jesus had spoken these words unto Nephi, and to those who had been called, (now the number of them who had been called, and received power and authority to baptize, was twelve) and behold, he stretched forth his hand unto the multitude, and cried unto them, saying: Blessed are ye if ye shall give heed unto the words of these twelve whom I have chosen from among you to minister unto you, and to be your servants; and unto them I have given power that they may baptize you with water;	And seeing the multitudes, he went up into a mountain: and when he was set, his disciples came unto him:

and after that ye are baptized with water, behold, I will baptize you with fire and with the Holy Ghost; therefore blessed are ye if ye shall believe in me and be baptized, after that ye have seen me and know that I am.

3 Nephi 12:2

And again, more blessed are they who shall believe in your words because that ye shall testify that ye have seen me, and that ye know that I am. Yea, blessed are they who shall believe in your words, and come down into the depths of humility and be baptized, for they shall be visited with fire and with the Holy Ghost, and shall receive a remission of their sins.

Matthew 5:2

And he opened his mouth, and taught them, saying,

3 Nephi 12:3

Yea, blessed are the poor in spirit who come unto me, for theirs is the kingdom of heaven.

Matthew 5:3

Blessed are the poor in spirit: for theirs is the kingdom of heaven.

3 Nephi 12:4

And again, blessed are all they that mourn, for they shall be comforted.

Matthew 5:4

Blessed are they that mourn: for they shall be comforted.

3 Nephi 12:5

And blessed are the meek, for they shall inherit the earth.

Matthew 5:5

Blessed are the meek: for they shall inherit the earth.

3 Nephi 12:6

And blessed are all they who do hunger and thirst after righteousness, for they shall be filled with the Holy Ghost.

Matthew 5:6

Blessed are they which do hunger and thirst after righteousness: for they shall be filled.

3 Nephi 12:7

And blessed are the merciful, for they shall obtain mercy.

Matthew 5:7

Blessed are the merciful: for they shall obtain mercy.

3 Nephi 12:8

And blessed are all the pure in heart, for they shall see God.

Matthew 5:8

Blessed are the pure in heart: for they shall see God.

3 Nephi 12:9

And blessed are all the peacemakers, for they shall be called the children of God.

Matthew 5:9

Blessed are the peacemakers: for they shall be called the children of God.

3 Nephi 12:10

And blessed are all they who are persecuted for my name's sake, for theirs is the kingdom of heaven.

Matthew 5:10

Blessed are they which are persecuted for righteousness' sake: for theirs is the kingdom of heaven.

3 Nephi 12:11

And blessed are ye when men shall revile you and persecute, and shall say all manner of evil against you falsely, for my sake;

Matthew 5:11

Blessed are ye, when men shall revile you, and persecute you, and shall say all manner of evil against you falsely, for my sake.

3 Nephi 12:12	*Matthew 5:12*
For ye shall have great joy and be exceedingly glad, for great shall be your reward in heaven; for so persecuted they the prophets who were before you.	Rejoice, and be exceeding glad: for great is your reward in heaven: for so persecuted they the prophets which were before you.

3 Nephi 12:13	*Matthew 5:13*
Verily, verily, I say unto you, I give unto you to be the salt of the earth; but if the salt shall lose its savor wherewith shall the earth be salted? The salt shall be thenceforth good for nothing, but to be cast out and to be trodden under foot of men.	Ye are the salt of the earth: but if the salt have lost his savour, wherewith shall it be salted? it is thenceforth good for nothing, but to be cast out, and to be trodden under foot of men.

3 Nephi 12:14	*Matthew 5:14*
Verily, verily, I say unto you, I give unto you to be the light of this people. A city that is set on a hill cannot be hid.	Ye are the light of the world. A city that is set on an hill cannot be hid.

3 Nephi 12:15	*Matthew 5:15*
Behold, do men light a candle and put it under a bushel? Nay, but on a candlestick, and it giveth light to all that are in the house;	Neither do men light a candle, and put it under a bushel, but on a candlestick; and it giveth light unto all that are in the house.

3 Nephi 12:16

Therefore let your light so shine before this people, that they may see your good works and glorify your Father who is in heaven.

Matthew 5:16

Let your light so shine before men, that they may see your good works, and glorify your Father which is in heaven.

3 Nephi 12:17

Think not that I am come to destroy the law or the prophets. I am not come to destroy but to fulfil;

Matthew 5:17

Think not that I am come to destroy the law, or the prophets: I am not come to destroy, but to fulfil.

3 Nephi 12:18

For verily I say unto you, one jot nor one tittle hath not passed away from the law, but in me it hath all been fulfilled.

Matthew 5:18

For verily I say unto you, Till heaven and earth pass, one jot or one tittle shall in no wise pass from the law, till all be fulfilled.

3 Nephi 12:19

And behold, I have given you the law and the command- ments of my Father, that ye shall believe in me, and that ye shall repent of your sins, and come unto me with a broken heart and a contrite spirit. Behold, ye have the command- ments before you, and the law is fulfilled.

Matthew 5:19

Whosoever therefore shall break one of these least com- mandments, and shall teach men so, he shall be called the least in the kingdom of heaven: but whosoever shall do and teach them, the same shall be called great in the kingdom of heaven.

3 Nephi 12:20

Therefore come unto me and be ye saved; for verily I say unto you, that except ye shall keep my commandments, which I have commanded you at this time, ye shall in no case enter into the kingdom of heaven.

Matthew 5:20

For I say unto you, That except your righteousness shall exceed the righteousness of the scribes and Pharisees, ye shall in no case enter into the kingdom of heaven.

3 Nephi 12:21

Ye have heard that it hath been said by them of old time, and it is also written before you, that thou shalt not kill, and whosoever shall kill shall be in danger of the judgment of God;

Matthew 5:21

Ye have heard that it was said by them of old time, Thou shalt not kill; and whosoever shall kill shall be in danger of the judgment:

3 Nephi 12:22

But I say unto you, that whosoever is angry with his brother shall be in danger of his judgment. And whosoever shall say to his brother, Raca, shall be in danger of the council; and whosoever shall say, Thou fool, shall be in danger of hell fire.

Matthew 5:22

But I say unto you, That whosoever is angry with his brother without a cause shall be in danger of the judgment: and whosoever shall say to his brother, Raca, shall be in danger of the council: but whosoever shall say, Thou fool, shall be in danger of hell fire.

3 Nephi 12:23

Therefore, if ye shall come unto me, or shall desire to come unto me, and rememberest that thy brother hath aught against thee—

Matthew 5:23

Therefore if thou bring thy gift to the altar, and there rememberest that thy brother hath ought against thee;

3 Nephi 12:24

Go thy way unto thy brother, and first be reconciled to thy brother, and then come unto me with full purpose of heart, and I will receive you.

Matthew 5:24

Leave there thy gift before the altar, and go thy way; first be reconciled to thy brother, and then come and offer thy gift.

3 Nephi 12:25

Agree with thine adversary quickly while thou art in the way with him, lest at any time he shall get thee, and thou shalt be cast into prison.

Matthew 5:25

Agree with thine adversary quickly, whiles thou art in the way with him; lest at any time the adversary deliver thee to the judge, and the judge deliver thee to the officer, and thou be cast into prison.

3 Nephi 12:26

Verily, verily, I say unto thee, thou shalt by no means come out thence until thou hast paid the uttermost senine. And while ye are in prison can ye pay even one senine? Verily, verily, I say unto you, Nay.

Matthew 5:26

Verily I say unto thee, Thou shalt by no means come out thence, till thou hast paid the uttermost farthing.

3 Nephi 12:27

Behold, it is written by them of old time, that thou shalt not commit adultery;

Matthew 5:27

Ye have heard that it was said by them of old time, Thou shalt not commit adultery:

3 Nephi 12:28

But I say unto you, that whosoever looketh on a woman, to lust after her, hath committed adultery already in his heart.

Matthew 5:28

But I say unto you, That whosoever looketh on a woman to lust after her hath committed adultery with her already in his heart.

3 Nephi 12:29

Behold, I give unto you a commandment, that ye suffer none of these things to enter into your heart;

Matthew 5:29

And if thy right eye offend thee, pluck it out, and cast it from thee: for it is profitable for thee that one of thy members should perish, and not that thy whole body should be cast into hell.

3 Nephi 12:30

For it is better that ye should deny yourselves of these things, wherein ye will take up your cross, than that ye should be cast into hell.

Matthew 5:30

And if thy right hand offend thee, cut it off, and cast it from thee: for it is profitable for thee that one of thy members should perish, and not that thy whole body should be cast into hell.

3 Nephi 12:31

It hath been written, that whosoever shall put away his wife, let him give her a writing of divorcement.

Matthew 5:31

It hath been said, Whosoever shall put away his wife, let him give her a writing of divorcement:

3 Nephi 12:32

Verily, verily, I say unto you, that whosoever shall put away his wife, saving for the cause of fornication, causeth her to commit adultery; and whoso shall marry her who is divorced committeth adultery.

Matthew 5:32

But I say unto you, That whosoever shall put away his wife, saving for the cause of fornication, causeth her to commit adultery: and whosoever shall marry her that is divorced committeth adultery.

3 Nephi 12:33

And again it is written, thou shalt not forswear thyself, but shalt perform unto the Lord thine oaths;

Matthew 5:33

Again, ye have heard that it hath been said by them of old time, Thou shalt not forswear thyself, but shalt perform unto the Lord thine oaths:

3 Nephi 12:34

But verily, verily, I say unto you, swear not at all; neither by heaven, for it is God's throne;

Matthew 5:34

But I say unto you, Swear not at all; neither by heaven; for it is God's throne:

3 Nephi 12:35

Nor by the earth, for it is his footstool;

Matthew 5:35

Nor by the earth; for it is his footstool: neither by Jerusalem; for it is the city of the great King.

3 Nephi 12:36

Neither shalt thou swear by thy head, because thou canst not make one hair black or white;

Matthew 5:36

Neither shalt thou swear by thy head, because thou canst not make one hair white or black.

3 Nephi 12:37

But let your communication be Yea, yea; Nay, nay; for whatsoever cometh of more than these is evil.

Matthew 5:37

But let your communication be, Yea, yea; Nay, nay: for whatsoever is more than these cometh of evil.

3 Nephi 12:38

And behold, it is written, an eye for an eye, and a tooth for a tooth;

Matthew 5:38

Ye have heard that it hath been said, An eye for an eye, and a tooth for a tooth:

3 Nephi 12:39

But I say unto you, that ye shall not resist evil, but whosoever shall smite thee on thy right cheek, turn to him the other also;

Matthew 5:39

But I say unto you, That ye resist not evil: but whosoever shall smite thee on thy right cheek, turn to him the other also.

3 Nephi 12:40

And if any man will sue thee at the law and take away thy coat, let him have thy cloak also;

Matthew 5:40

And if any man will sue thee at the law, and take away thy coat, let him have thy cloke also.

3 Nephi 12:41

And whosoever shall compel thee to go a mile, go with him twain.

Matthew 5:41

And whosoever shall compel thee to go a mile, go with him twain.

3 Nephi 12:42

Give to him that asketh thee, and from him that would borrow of thee turn thou not away.

Matthew 5:42

Give to him that asketh thee, and from him that would borrow of thee turn not thou away.

3 Nephi 12:43

And behold it is written also, that thou shalt love thy neighbor and hate thine enemy;

Matthew 5:43

Ye have heard that it hath been said, Thou shalt love thy neighbour, and hate thine enemy.

3 Nephi 12:44

But behold I say unto you, love your enemies, bless them that curse you, do good to them that hate you, and pray for them who despitefully use you and persecute you;

Matthew 5:44

But I say unto you, Love your enemies, bless them that curse you, do good to them that hate you, and pray for them which despitefully use you, and persecute you;

3 Nephi 12:45

That ye may be the children of your Father who is in heaven; for he maketh his sun to rise on the evil and on the good.

Matthew 5:45

That ye may be the children of your Father which is in heaven: for he maketh his sun to rise on the evil and on the good, and sendeth rain on the just and on the unjust.

3 Nephi 12:46

Therefore those things which were of old time, which were under the law, in me are all fulfilled.

Matthew 5:46

For if ye love them which love you, what reward have ye? do not even the publicans the same?

3 Nephi 12:47

Old things are done away, and all things have become new.

Matthew 5:47

And if ye salute your brethren only, what do ye more than others? do not even the publicans so?

3 Nephi 12:48	Matthew 5:48
Therefore I would that ye should be perfect even as I, or your Father who is in heaven is perfect.	Be ye therefore perfect, even as your Father which is in heaven is perfect.

3 Nephi 13:1	Matthew 6:1
Verily, verily, I say that I would that ye should do alms unto the poor; but take heed that ye do not your alms before men to be seen of them; otherwise ye have no reward of your Father who is in heaven.	Take heed that ye do not your alms before men, to be seen of them: otherwise ye have no reward of your Father which is in heaven.

3 Nephi 13:2	Matthew 6:2
Therefore, when ye shall do your alms do not sound a trumpet before you, as will hypocrites do in the synagogues and in the streets, that they may have glory of men. Verily I say unto you, they have their reward.	Therefore when thou doest thine alms, do not sound a trumpet before thee, as the hypocrites do in the synagogues and in the streets, that they may have glory of men. Verily I say unto you, They have their reward.

3 Nephi 13:3	Matthew 6:3
But when thou doest alms let not thy left hand know what thy right hand doeth;	But when thou doest alms, let not thy left hand know what thy right hand doeth:

3 Nephi 13:4	Matthew 6:4
That thine alms may be in secret; and thy Father who seeth in secret, himself shall reward thee openly.	That thine alms may be in secret: and thy Father which seeth in secret himself shall reward thee openly.

3 Nephi 13:5

And when thou prayest thou shalt not do as the hypocrites, for they love to pray, standing in the synagogues and in the corners of the streets, that they may be seen of men. Verily I say unto you, they have their reward.

Matthew 6:5

And when thou prayest, thou shalt not be as the hypocrites are: for they love to pray standing in the synagogues and in the corners of the streets, that they may be seen of men. Verily I say unto you, They have their reward.

3 Nephi 13:6

But thou, when thou prayest, enter into thy closet, and when thou hast shut thy door, pray to thy Father who is in secret; and thy Father, who seeth in secret, shall reward thee openly.

Matthew 6:6

But thou, when thou prayest, enter into thy closet, and when thou hast shut thy door, pray to thy Father which is in secret; and thy Father which seeth in secret shall reward thee openly.

3 Nephi 13:7

But when ye pray, use not vain repetitions, as the heathen, for they think that they shall be heard for their much speaking.

Matthew 6:7

But when ye pray, use not vain repetitions, as the heathen do: for they think that they shall be heard for their much speaking.

3 Nephi 13:8

Be not ye therefore like unto them, for your Father knoweth what things ye have need of before ye ask him.

Matthew 6:8

Be not ye therefore like unto them: for your Father knoweth what things ye have need of, before ye ask him.

3 Nephi 13:9

After this manner therefore pray ye: Our Father who art in heaven, hallowed be thy name.

Matthew 6:9

After this manner therefore pray ye: Our Father which art in heaven, Hallowed be thy name.

3 Nephi 13:10

Thy will be done on earth as it is in heaven.

Matthew 6:10

Thy kingdom come. Thy will be done in earth, as it is in heaven.

3 Nephi 13:11

And forgive us our debts, as we forgive our debtors.

Matthew 6:11

Give us this day our daily bread.

3 Nephi 13:12

And lead us not into temptation, but deliver us from evil.

Matthew 6:12

And forgive us our debts, as we forgive our debtors.

3 Nephi 13:13

For thine is the kingdom, and the power, and the glory, forever. Amen.

Matthew 6:13

And lead us not into temptation, but deliver us from evil: For thine is the kingdom, and the power, and the glory, for ever. Amen.

3 Nephi 13:14

For, if ye forgive men their trespasses your heavenly Father will also forgive you;

Matthew 6:14

For if ye forgive men their trespasses, your heavenly Father will also forgive you:

3 Nephi 13:15

But if ye forgive not men their trespasses neither will your Father forgive your trespasses.

Matthew 6:15

But if ye forgive not men their trespasses, neither will your Father forgive your trespasses.

3 Nephi 13:16

Moreover, when ye fast be not as the hypocrites, of a sad countenance, for they disfigure their faces that they may appear unto men to fast. Verily I say unto you, they have their reward.

Matthew 6:16

Moreover when ye fast, be not, as the hypocrites, of a sad countenance: for they disfigure their faces, that they may appear unto men to fast. Verily I say unto you, They have their reward.

3 Nephi 13:17

But thou, when thou fastest, anoint thy head, and wash thy face;

Matthew 6:17

But thou, when thou fastest, anoint thine head, and wash thy face;

3 Nephi 13:18

That thou appear not unto men to fast, but unto thy Father, who is in secret; and thy Father, who seeth in secret, shall reward thee openly.

Matthew 6:18

That thou appear not unto men to fast, but unto thy Father which is in secret: and thy Father, which seeth in secret, shall reward thee openly.

3 Nephi 13:19

Lay not up for yourselves treasures upon earth, where moth and rust doth corrupt, and thieves break through and steal;

Matthew 6:19

Lay not up for yourselves treasures upon earth, where moth and rust doth corrupt, and where thieves break through and steal:

3 Nephi 13:20

But lay up for yourselves treasures in heaven, where neither moth nor rust doth corrupt, and where thieves do not break through nor steal.

Matthew 6:20

But lay up for yourselves treasures in heaven, where neither moth nor rust doth corrupt, and where thieves do not break through nor steal:

3 Nephi 13:21

For where your treasure is, there will your heart be also.

Matthew 6:21

For where your treasure is, there will your heart be also.

3 Nephi 13:22

The light of the body is the eye; if, therefore, thine eye be single, thy whole body shall be full of light.

Matthew 6:22

The light of the body is the eye: if therefore thine eye be single, thy whole body shall be full of light.

3 Nephi 13:23

But if thine eye be evil, thy whole body shall be full of darkness. If, therefore, the light that is in thee be darkness, how great is that darkness!

Matthew 6:23

But if thine eye be evil, thy whole body shall be full of darkness. If therefore the light that is in thee be darkness, how great is that darkness!

3 Nephi 13:24

No man can serve two masters; for either he will hate the one and love the other, or else he will hold to the one and despise the other. Ye cannot serve God and Mammon.

Matthew 6:24

No man can serve two masters: for either he will hate the one, and love the other; or else he will hold to the one, and despise the other. Ye cannot serve God and mammon.

3 Nephi 13:25

And now it came to pass that when Jesus had spoken these words he looked upon the twelve whom he had chosen, and said unto them: Remember the words which I have spoken. For behold, ye are they whom I have chosen to

Matthew 6:25

Therefore I say unto you, Take no thought for your life, what ye shall eat, or what ye shall drink; nor yet for your body, what ye shall put on. Is not the life more than meat, and the body than raiment?

minister unto this people. Therefore I say unto you, take no thought for your life, what ye shall eat, or what ye shall drink; nor yet for your body, what ye shall put on. Is not the life more than meat, and the body than raiment?

3 Nephi 13:26

Behold the fowls of the air, for they sow not, neither do they reap nor gather into barns; yet your heavenly Father feedeth them. Are ye not much better than they?

Matthew 6:26

Behold the fowls of the air: for they sow not, neither do they reap, nor gather into barns; yet your heavenly Father feedeth them. Are ye not much better than they?

3 Nephi 13:27

Which of you by taking thought can add one cubit unto his stature?

Matthew 6:27

Which of you by taking thought can add one cubit unto his stature?

3 Nephi 13:28

And why take ye thought for raiment? Consider the lilies of the field how they grow; they toil not, neither do they spin;

Matthew 6:28

And why take ye thought for raiment? Consider the lilies of the field, how they grow; they toil not, neither do they spin:

3 Nephi 13:29

And yet I say unto you, that even Solomon, in all his glory, was not arrayed like one of these.

Matthew 6:29

And yet I say unto you, That even Solomon in all his glory was not arrayed like one of these.

3 Nephi 13:30

Wherefore, if God so clothe the grass of the field, which today is, and tomorrow is cast into the oven, even so will he clothe you, if ye are not of little faith.

Matthew 6:30

Wherefore, if God so clothe the grass of the field, which to day is, and to morrow is cast into the oven, shall he not much more clothe you, O ye of little faith?

3 Nephi 13:31

Therefore take no thought, saying, What shall we eat? or, What shall we drink? or, Wherewithal shall we be clothed?

Matthew 6:31

Therefore take no thought, saying, What shall we eat? or, What shall we drink? or, Wherewithal shall we be clothed?

3 Nephi 13:32

For your heavenly Father knoweth that ye have need of all these things.

Matthew 6:32

(For after all these things do the Gentiles seek:) for your heavenly Father knoweth that ye have need of all these things.

3 Nephi 13:33

But seek ye first the kingdom of God and his righteousness, and all these things shall be added unto you.

Matthew 6:33

But seek ye first the kingdom of God, and his righteousness; and all these things shall be added unto you.

3 Nephi 13:34

Take therefore no thought for the morrow, for the morrow shall take thought for the things of itself. Sufficient is the day unto the evil thereof.

Matthew 6:34

Take therefore no thought for the morrow: for the morrow shall take thought for the things of itself. Sufficient unto the day is the evil thereof.

3 Nephi 14:1

And now it came to pass that when Jesus had spoken these words he turned again to the multitude, and did open his mouth unto them again, saying: Verily, verily, I say unto you, Judge not, that ye be not judged.

Matthew 7:1

Judge not, that ye be not judged.

3 Nephi 14:2

For with what judgment ye judge, ye shall be judged; and with what measure ye mete, it shall be measured to you again.

Matthew 7:2

For with what judgment ye judge, ye shall be judged: and with what measure ye mete, it shall be measured to you again.

3 Nephi 14:3

And why beholdest thou the mote that is in thy brother's eye, but considerest not the beam that is in thine own eye?

Matthew 7:3

And why beholdest thou the mote that is in thy brother's eye, but considerest not the beam that is in thine own eye?

3 Nephi 14:4

Or how wilt thou say to thy brother: Let me pull the mote out of thine eye—and behold, a beam is in thine own eye?

Matthew 7:4

Or how wilt thou say to thy brother, Let me pull out the mote out of thine eye; and, behold, a beam is in thine own eye?

3 Nephi 14:5

Thou hypocrite, first cast the beam out of thine own eye; and then shalt thou see clearly to cast the mote out of thy brother's eye.

Matthew 7:5

Thou hypocrite, first cast out the beam out of thine own eye; and then shalt thou see clearly to cast out the mote out of thy brother's eye.

3 Nephi 14:6

Give not that which is holy unto the dogs, neither cast ye your pearls before swine, lest they trample them under their feet, and turn again and rend you.

Matthew 7:6

Give not that which is holy unto the dogs, neither cast ye your pearls before swine, lest they trample them under their feet, and turn again and rend you.

3 Nephi 14:7

Ask, and it shall be given unto you; seek, and ye shall find; knock, and it shall be opened unto you.

Matthew 7:7

Ask, and it shall be given you; seek, and ye shall find; knock, and it shall be opened unto you:

3 Nephi 14:8

For every one that asketh, receiveth; and he that seeketh, findeth; and to him that knocketh, it shall be opened.

Matthew 7:8

For every one that asketh receiveth; and he that seeketh findeth; and to him that knocketh it shall be opened.

3 Nephi 14:9

Or what man is there of you, who, if his son ask bread, will give him a stone?

Matthew 7:9

Or what man is there of you, whom if his son ask bread, will he give him a stone?

3 Nephi 14:10

Or if he ask a fish, will he give him a serpent?

Matthew 7:10

Or if he ask a fish, will he give him a serpent?

3 Nephi 14:11

If ye then, being evil, know how to give good gifts unto your children, how much more shall your Father who is in heaven give good things to them that ask him?

Matthew 7:11

If ye then, being evil, know how to give good gifts unto your children, how much more shall your Father which is in heaven give good things to them that ask him?

3 Nephi 14:12	Matthew 7:12
Therefore, all things whatsoever ye would that men should do to you, do ye even so to them, for this is the law and the prophets.	Therefore all things whatsoever ye would that men should do to you, do ye even so to them: for this is the law and the prophets.

3 Nephi 14:13	Matthew 7:13
Enter ye in at the strait gate; for wide is the gate, and broad is the way, which leadeth to destruction, and many there be who go in thereat;	Enter ye in at the strait gate: for wide is the gate, and broad is the way, that leadeth to destruction, and many there be which go in thereat:

3 Nephi 14:14	Matthew 7:14
Because strait is the gate, and narrow is the way, which leadeth unto life, and few there be that find it.	Because strait is the gate, and narrow is the way, which leadeth unto life, and few there be that find it.

3 Nephi 14:15	Matthew 7:15
Beware of false prophets, who come to you in sheep's clothing, but inwardly they are ravening wolves.	Beware of false prophets, which come to you in sheep's clothing, but inwardly they are ravening wolves.

3 Nephi 14:16	Matthew 7:16
Ye shall know them by their fruits. Do men gather grapes of thorns, or figs of thistles?	Ye shall know them by their fruits. Do men gather grapes of thorns, or figs of thistles?

3 Nephi 14:17

Even so every good tree bringeth forth good fruit; but a corrupt tree bringeth forth evil fruit.

Matthew 7:17

Even so every good tree bringeth forth good fruit; but a corrupt tree bringeth forth evil fruit.

3 Nephi 14:18

A good tree cannot bring forth evil fruit, neither a corrupt tree bring forth good fruit.

Matthew 7:18

A good tree cannot bring forth evil fruit, neither can a corrupt tree bring forth good fruit.

3 Nephi 14:19

Every tree that bringeth not forth good fruit is hewn down, and cast into the fire.

Matthew 7:19

Every tree that bringeth not forth good fruit is hewn down, and cast into the fire.

3 Nephi 14:20

Wherefore, by their fruits ye shall know them.

Matthew 7:20

Wherefore by their fruits ye shall know them.

3 Nephi 14:21

Not every one that saith unto me, Lord, Lord, shall enter into the kingdom of heaven; but he that doeth the will of my Father who is in heaven.

Matthew 7:21

Not every one that saith unto me, Lord, Lord, shall enter into the kingdom of heaven; but he that doeth the will of my Father which is in heaven.

3 Nephi 14:22

Many will say to me in that day: Lord, Lord, have we not prophesied in thy name, and in thy name have cast out devils, and in thy name done many wonderful works?

Matthew 7:22

Many will say to me in that day, Lord, Lord, have we not prophesied in thy name? and in thy name have cast out devils? and in thy name done many wonderful works?

3 Nephi 14:23	Matthew 7:23
And then will I profess unto them: I never knew you; depart from me, ye that work iniquity.	And then will I profess unto them, I never knew you: depart from me, ye that work iniquity.

3 Nephi 14:24	Matthew 7:24
Therefore, whoso heareth these sayings of mine and doeth them, I will liken him unto a wise man, who built his house upon a rock—	Therefore whosoever heareth these sayings of mine, and doeth them, I will liken him unto a wise man, which built his house upon a rock:

3 Nephi 14:25	Matthew 7:25
And the rain descended, and the floods came, and the winds blew, and beat upon that house; and it fell not, for it was founded upon a rock.	And the rain descended, and the floods came, and the winds blew, and beat upon that house; and it fell not: for it was founded upon a rock.

3 Nephi 14:26	Matthew 7:26
And every one that heareth these sayings of mine and doeth them not shall be likened unto a foolish man, who built his house upon the sand—	And every one that heareth these sayings of mine, and doeth them not, shall be likened unto a foolish man, which built his house upon the sand:

3 Nephi 14:27	Matthew 7:27
And the rain descended, and the floods came, and the winds blew, and beat upon that house; and it fell, and great was the fall of it.	And the rain descended, and the floods came, and the winds blew, and beat upon that house; and it fell: and great was the fall of it.

3 Nephi 15:1

And now it came to pass that when Jesus had ended these sayings he cast his eyes round about on the multitude, and said unto them: Behold, ye have heard the things which I taught before I ascended to my Father; therefore, whoso remembereth these sayings of mine and doeth them, him will I raise up at the last day.

Matthew 7:28

And it came to pass, when Jesus had ended these sayings, the people were astonished at his doctrine:

3 Nephi 15:2

And it came to pass that when Jesus had said these words he perceived that there were some among them who marveled, and wondered what he would concerning the law of Moses; for they understood not the saying that old things had passed away, and that all things had become new.

Matthew 7:29

For he taught them as one having authority, and not as the scribes.

NOTES

Chapter One
"THE NEW COVENANT, EVEN THE BOOK OF MORMON"

1. D&C 84:57. In her book *Finding Christ through the Book of Mormon* (Salt Lake City: Deseret Book Co., 1987), Susan Easton Black calculates that some form of Christ's name is used 3,925 times in the Book of Mormon, a figure that averages out to one reference for every 1.7 verses; some 101 different names are used to describe the Only Begotten Son of God. See appendix A.

2. Moses 5:9.

3. Book of Mormon Title Page.

4. 1 Nephi 13:23.

5. 1 Nephi 13:23–28.

6. 1 Nephi 13:26–29.

7. 1 Nephi 13:29.

8. 1 Nephi 13:34–36.

9. 1 Nephi 13:40–41.

10. Moroni 10:4.

11. See Moses 5.

12. D&C 84:49.

13. Jacob 5:77.

14. 2 Nephi 2:8–9.

15. 2 Nephi 31:19–21.

16. Mormon 8:35.

17. Joseph Smith, *History of the Church* 4:461.

Chapter Two
RENDING THE VEIL OF UNBELIEF

1. See Ezekiel 37:15–28; 1 Nephi 13:41; 2 Nephi 3:12.

2. Alma 34:2.

3. Ether 2:13.

4. Ether 2:14.

5. Ether 2:16–17.

6. Ether 2:21–22.

7. Genesis 18:14.

8. Ether 2:23–25; emphasis added here and in other scriptures throughout this book.

9. Ether 3:2–3.

10. Ether 3:4–5.

11. Ether 3:6.

12. Ether 3:7–11.

13. See Ether 3:6–13.

14. Ether 3:14–16.

15. 2 Nephi 9:20; see also D&C 38:1–2.

16. Genesis 3:9, 13.

17. See Genesis 22.

18. Ether 3:9, 15.

19. See D&C 107:53–55.

20. Moses 7:4.

21. Genesis 6:8–9.

22. See Genesis 5:24.

23. Ether 3:15, 20.

24. Ether 3:9.

25. Ether 3:17.

26. Ether 3:16.

27. Ether 3:17.

28. Ether 3:19–20.

29. Ether 3:25.

30. Ether 3:26.

31. Ether 3:25.

32. See Moses 1:27–29.

33. Ether 4:4.

34. Ether 4:4.

35. Ether 4:7.

36. See Ether 3:14.

37. See Ether 3:14.

38. Ether 3:14.

39. See Moses 7:47; Revelation 13:8.

40. Ether 3:6.

41. Ether 3:16.

42. See Ether 3:16.

43. See Ether 3:14; 4:7.

44. Ether 3:24.

45. See Ether 3:23; D&C 17:1.

46. See Ether 3:25.

47. Ether 3:14.

48. Ether 3:13.

49. Alma 40:8.

50. Mosiah 16:6.

51. See Ether 4:7.

52. Ether 4:8.

53. Ether 4:9.

54. Ether 4:11.

55. Ether 4:12.

56. See Ether 4:12.

57. See Ether 4:12.

58. See Ether 4:12.

59. Ether 4:13.

60. Ether 4:15.

61. Ether 4:14.

62. Ether 4:15.

63. Ether 4:16.

64. See Ether 4:18.

65. See Ether 4:18.

66. Ether 4:19.

67. Ether 4:13–15.

68. Ether 3:4.

Chapter Three
THREE EARLY WITNESSES: NEPHI

1. 2 Corinthians 13:1.

2. Ether 5:3–4.

3. See D&C 3, 10.

4. 2 Nephi 11:2–3.

5. 2 Nephi 11:4, 6.

6. 2 Nephi 31:21.

7. See heading to D&C 3.

8. 1 Nephi 1:9.

9. 1 Nephi 1:10, 14, 19.

10. 1 Nephi 10:4–6.

11. 1 Nephi 10:9–10.

12. 1 Nephi 10:11, 17.

13. 2 Nephi 1:15.

14. 1 Nephi 10:17; 11:6–7.

15. Genesis 49:22.

16. 1 Nephi 11:6.

17. See 1 Nephi 11:13.

18. 1 Nephi 11:15.

19. 1 Nephi 11:19.

20. 1 Nephi 11:18.

21. 1 Nephi 11:21.

22. See 1 Nephi 11:20.

23. 1 Nephi 11:22–23; 15:36.

24. See 1 Nephi 11:27.

25. 1 Nephi 11:24, 28.

26. 1 Nephi 11:29, 34.

27. 1 Nephi 11:31.

28. 1 Nephi 11:32–33.

29. 1 Nephi 12:4.

30. 1 Nephi 12:6, 1.

31. 1 Nephi 12:7–9.

32. 1 Nephi 12:7, 10.

33. 1 Nephi 13:34.

34. 1 Nephi 13:24, 26, 28.

35. See 1 Nephi 13:35.

36. 1 Nephi 13:39.

37. 1 Nephi 13:40.

38. 1 Nephi 13:41.

39. 1 Nephi 13:42.

40. 1 Nephi 14:1.

41. 1 Nephi 14:2.

42. 1 Nephi 14:7.

43. 1 Nephi 14:10.

44. 1 Nephi 14:12, 14.

45. 1 Nephi 14:13.

46. 1 Nephi 14:14.

47. 1 Nephi 14:17.

48. 1 Nephi 19:7.

49. 1 Nephi 19:9.

50. 1 Nephi 17:30.

51. 1 Nephi 19:10.

52. 1 Nephi 19:11–12.

53. 1 Nephi 19:13–14.

54. 1 Nephi 19:15, 17.

55. Deuteronomy 18:15, 17–19; see 1 Nephi 22:20.

56. 1 Nephi 22:21, 24–25.

57. See Malachi 4:2.

58. See John 10:1–16.

59. Elder Bruce R. McConkie proposed that both Nephi and Malachi were quoting the prophet Zenos. See *A New Witness for the Articles of Faith* (Salt Lake City: Deseret Book Co., 1985), pp. 558, 563.

60. 2 Nephi 25:12–13.

61. 2 Nephi 25:16–19.

62. See Numbers 21:6–9.

63. See Exodus 17:6–7.

64. 2 Nephi 25:20.

65. 2 Nephi 25:22–29.

66. 2 Nephi 26:8–9.

67. 2 Nephi 26:24.

68. 2 Nephi 26:25–27, 30, 33.

69. 2 Nephi 31:1–2.

70. Articles of Faith 1:4.

71. 2 Nephi 31:2.

72. 2 Nephi 31:12.

73. 2 Nephi 31:10.

74. 2 Nephi 31:7, 9–10.

75. 2 Nephi 31:13.

76. 2 Nephi 31:17.

77. Joseph Smith–History 1:19.

78. 2 Nephi 31:13.

79. 2 Nephi 31:11.

80. 2 Nephi 31:12.

81. 2 Nephi 31:5.

82. 2 Nephi 31:6–7.

83. 2 Nephi 31:9.

84. 2 Nephi 31:13.

85. See Matthew 3:16; 2 Nephi 31:12.

86. 2 Nephi 31:13.

87. 2 Nephi 31:17.

88. 2 Nephi 31:13.

89. 2 Nephi 31:14.

90. 2 Nephi 31:15–16.

91. 2 Nephi 31:19–20.

92. 2 Nephi 31:21.

93. 2 Nephi 32:1.

94. 2 Nephi 31:20; 32:3.

95. 2 Nephi 32:5.

96. 2 Nephi 32:6, 4.

97. 2 Nephi 32:7; see also 2 Nephi 33:3.

98. 2 Nephi 33:4, 6.

99. 2 Nephi 33:7–9.

100. 2 Nephi 33:10–15.

Chapter Four
THREE EARLY WITNESSES: JACOB

1. 2 Nephi 2:1–2.

2. 2 Nephi 2:3–4.

3. Jacob 7:5, 12.

4. See 2 Nephi 10:3.

5. Jacob 1:1–2, 4.

6. D&C 18:10–14.

7. Jacob 1:6–8.

8. Jacob 4:3–5, 13.

9. Jacob 4:6.

10. Jacob 4:11–12.

11. 2 Nephi 2:26–27.

12. 2 Nephi 2:6–9.

13. 2 Nephi 6:3.

14. 2 Nephi 6:9.

15. 2 Nephi 6:11.

16. See 2 Nephi 6:12.

17. 2 Nephi 6:14.

18. 2 Nephi 6:17–18.

19. 2 Nephi 9:1–3.

20. See 2 Nephi 9:5.

21. 2 Nephi 9:5.

22. 2 Nephi 9:6.

23. See 2 Nephi 9:6–7.

24. 2 Nephi 9:8–9.

25. 2 Nephi 9:11–12.

26. See 2 Nephi 9:7, 13.

27. 2 Nephi 9:13; see D&C 88:15.

28. 2 Nephi 9:14.

29. See 2 Nephi 9:15.

30. 2 Nephi 9:16.

31. 2 Nephi 9:18.

32. See 2 Nephi 9:19.

33. 2 Nephi 9:20; see D&C 38:1–2.

34. 2 Nephi 9:21.

35. 2 Nephi 9:22.

36. 2 Nephi 9:23–24.

37. 2 Nephi 9:25–26.

38. 2 Nephi 9:27.

39. See 2 Nephi 10:3.

40. See 2 Nephi 25:19.

41. See 2 Nephi 10:3–4.

42. See 2 Nephi 10:5.

43. 2 Nephi 10:7.

44. 2 Nephi 10:8.

45. 2 Nephi 10:24.

46. 2 Nephi 9:43, 41–42, 50, 53; 10:25.

47. Jacob 7:11.

48. Jacob 1:5; 2:3.

49. See Jacob 2:8.

50. Jacob 2:7.

51. 2 Nephi 9:44–45.

52. Jacob 4:5.

53. The prevalence of messianic types and shadows will be discussed in chapters 7 and 8 of this book.

54. Jacob 4:14–16.

55. For a detailed reference to this allegory, see chapter 8, including the notes for that chapter.

56. Jacob 6:7–8, 12.

57. Jacob 4:11–12.

Chapter Five
THREE EARLY WITNESSES: ISAIAH

1. 1 Nephi 19:18, 23.

2. When accounting for several of the same verses quoted more than once and a few verses clearly drawn from Isaiah but not identified as such in the text, the total number of Book of Mormon verses from Isaiah may run as high as 446. See appendix B and Monte C. Nyman, *Great Are the Words of Isaiah* (Salt Lake City: Bookcraft, 1980), pp. 283–87.

3. See Nyman, *Great Are the Words of Isaiah*, p. 7.

4. Personal conversation with Donald Parry.

5. 2 Nephi 25:4–5, 8.

6. 2 Nephi 6:4.

7. 3 Nephi 23:1–2.

8. 2 Nephi 11:2–3, 8; see also 2 Nephi 16:1–5.

9. 2 Nephi 17:14–15.

10. See 1 Nephi 11:13, 15, 18, 20; Alma 7:10; Matthew 1:21–23.

11. 2 Nephi 19:6–7.

12. 2 Nephi 13:13.

13. D&C 45:3–5.

14. See Mosiah 3:10; Moroni 10:34; Moses 6:57.

15. Mosiah 13:28; see also Mosiah 13:34; 15:1; Alma 42:15.

16. See Mosiah 5:7.

17. 1 Nephi 21:6–9.

18. See 1 Peter 3:19–20.

19. Isaiah 61:1–3.

20. 1 Nephi 19:23.

21. 1 Nephi 21:13–16.

22. See Zechariah 13:6; Luke 24:39–40; 3 Nephi 11:14–15; D&C 45:52.

23. 2 Nephi 7:1–2.

24. 3 Nephi 22:8.

25. 2 Nephi 21:1–5.

26. See 2 Nephi 30:9–11.

27. See D&C 113.

28. Joseph Smith–History 1:40.

29. I am indebted to Professor Donald Parry for the Hebrew translation, which has "shoot" a more literal rendering than "rod," and "stump" more literal than "stem."

30. Zechariah 3:7–10.

31. Zechariah 6:12–13.

32. Bruce R. McConkie, *The Promised Messiah* (Salt Lake City: Deseret Book Co., 1978), pp. 193–95.

33. 2 Nephi 30:9.

34. 2 Nephi 21:6–10, 12.

35. 2 Nephi 12:2–5.

36. See Luke 4:16–21.

37. 2 Nephi 7:5–7.

38. See Mosiah 14.

39. Isaiah 53:2.

40. See 2 Nephi 21:1, 10; D&C 113:5–6; Revelation 22:16.

41. See 1 Nephi 11:21–22; Acts 5:30.

42. Isaiah 53:2.

43. Luke 4:22.

44. Isaiah 53:3–4.

45. Matthew 27:46.

46. Isaiah 53:5–6.

47. See Romans 3:23.

48. See Alma 7:11–12.

49. Isaiah 53:7.

50. Matthew 26:63.

51. Luke 23:9.

52. John 19:9.

53. See Exodus 12:21–30.

54. Isaiah 53:8–9.

55. Luke 23:34.

56. Isaiah 53:10.

57. See Mosiah 15:11–12.

58. See D&C 138:11–19.

59. Isaiah 53:11–12.

60. Matthew 26:37–38.

61. Luke 22:44.

62. D&C 19:18.

63. See D&C 84:38; see also D&C 76:55, 58–59, 94–95.

64. Mosiah 15:11; see also vv. 10 and 12.

Chapter Six
"WE KNEW OF CHRIST"

1. See Alma 34:2.

2. 1 Nephi 19:18–21.

3. See 2 Nephi 10:3; 25:19.

4. 2 Nephi 25:19.

5. Jacob 4:4–6.

6. Jacob 6:8.

7. Jacob 7:2.

8. Jacob 7:3–4, 6–7.

9. Jacob 7:10–11.

10. Jacob 7:17, 19.

11. Enos 1:8.

12. Jarom 1:11.

13. Omni 1:25–26.

14. Mosiah 3:1.

15. Mosiah 3:5.

16. Mosiah 3:5–6.

17. Mosiah 3:7.

18. See Mosiah 3:7.

19. See Mosiah 3:8.

20. See Mosiah 3:8.

21. See Mosiah 3:9.

22. Mosiah 3:10.

23. Mosiah 3:10.

24. Mosiah 3:11.

25. Mosiah 3:12.

26. Mosiah 3:15.

27. Mosiah 3:17.

28. Mosiah 3:18.

29. Mosiah 3:19–21.

30. Mosiah 3:13.

31. Mosiah 4:2–3. As noted throughout the Book of Mormon, the timeless, infinite, eternal nature of

the Atonement provides promise of a remission of sins to the faithful, whether they live before Christ's advent, during his earthly ministry, or after his death and resurrection. This is a reminder of the eternal reach of the Atonement, each dispensation (including those before Christ's advent) making their covenants, obtaining their blessings, and working out their salvation. These prophets, priests, and teachers labored to teach people the intent for which the Law of Moses had been given, "persuading them to look forward unto the Messiah, and believe in him to come as though he already was." (Jarom 1:11.)

32. Mosiah 5:2, 5.

33. Mosiah 5:7.

34. Mosiah 5:8, 12, 15.

35. Mosiah 6:1–2.

36. Mosiah 13:33–35.

37. Mosiah 13:28; see also Mosiah 13:34; 15:1; 17:8; Alma 42:15.

38. See Mosiah 15:2–7.

39. See Mosiah 13:31; 16:14.

40. See Mosiah 15:5.

41. See Mosiah 15:5.

42. Mosiah 15:6–7.

43. Mosiah 15:8–9.

44. See Mosiah 15:9.

45. Mosiah 15:11–12.

46. See Mosiah 15:19.

47. Mosiah 15:21–25.

48. See Mosiah 15:26.

49. Mosiah 15:11.

50. Mosiah 16:6–9, 15.

51. See Mosiah 18:8.

52. See Mosiah 18:8.

53. See Mosiah 18:8.

54. See Mosiah 18:9.

55. See Mosiah 18:9.

56. See Mosiah 18:9.

57. See Mosiah 18:10.

58. See Hugh Nibley, *An Approach to the Book of Mormon*, 3rd ed. (Salt Lake City: Deseret Book Co. and Provo, Utah: FARMS, 1988), pp. 157–66; Mosiah 25:21–23; 18:17.

59. Mosiah 18:20–29.

60. Mosiah 26:18, 22–24, 26.

61. Mosiah 27:20.

62. Mosiah 27:24–31.

63. Alma 36:12, 14–15.

64. Alma 36:17–18.

65. Alma 36:20–21, 24–26.

66. Alma 36:3.

67. Alma 36:27.

68. Mosiah 27:30.

69. Alma 5:14–15, 21, 27, 38, 44, 48.

70. Alma 6:8.

71. Alma 7:7.

72. Alma 7:9.

73. Alma 7:11–13.

74. Alma 7:14–15.

75. Psalm 23:3, 6.

76. Alma 9:26.

77. See Alma 9:26.

78. See Alma 9:27.

79. Alma 11:37; Helaman 5:10.

80. Alma 11:39.

81. Alma 11:40.

82. Alma 11:41.

83. Alma 11:43–44.

84. Alma 11:43.

85. Alma 11:45.

86. See Alma 12:14.

87. Alma 12:16–17.

88. See Alma 12:18.

89. Alma 12:24; see also v. 22.

90. Alma 12:26.

91. Alma 12:30.

92. See Alma 12:32.

93. Alma 12:33.

94. Alma 12:36–37.

95. Alma 13:1; see also vv. 2–3, 7–11, 16–18.

96. Alma 13:23.

97. See Alma 13:24–26.

98. Alma 14:26, 28.

99. Alma 15:6–12.

100. Alma 16:16, 19–20.

101. Alma 18:39.

102. Alma 18:41.

103. Alma 19:13.

104. Alma 19:29.

105. Alma 19:6.

106. Alma 21:7–9.

107. Alma 22:13–14.

108. Alma 24:10.

109. Alma 24:13.

110. Alma 27:27–28.

111. Alma 30:6, 12–13, 15.

112. Alma 30:16–17; 30:31, 27; see also vv. 28–30.

113. Alma 30:22.

114. Alma 30:39, 41; 2 Nephi 11:4.

115. Alma 31:1, 22, 18, 17, 23, 19.

116. Alma 31:30–34.

117. Alma 31:38.

118. Alma 33:11.

119. Alma 33:14–19, 22–23.

120. Alma 34:2, 5–6.

121. See Alma 8:20, 27; 10:6–10.

122. Alma 34:4; see also 32:28–43; 33:19, 23.

123. Alma 34:8.

124. See Alma 34:8.

125. Alma 34:9.

126. Alma 34:10.

127. See Alma 34:11.

128. Alma 34:14.

129. See Alma 34:13.

130. Alma 34:14.

131. Alma 34:15–16.

132. See Alma 34:17.

133. Alma 34:28–29.

134. Alma 34:36.

135. Alma 34:30.

136. Alma 34:37–38.

137. Alma 37:33.

138. Alma 38:8–9.

139. Alma 39:15–19.

140. Alma 44:3–4.

141. Alma 46:13–16, 18, 21, 39.

142. Helaman 3:28–30.

143. Helaman 3:35.

144. Helaman 5:12; see also v. 9.

145. Helaman 8:13–20, 22–23.

146. Helaman 13:4.

147. Helaman 13:6.

148. See 3 Nephi 1:4–21.

149. Helaman 14:3–6.

150. Helaman 14:12–13, 15–16.

151. Helaman 14:18.

152. Helaman 14:20.

153. Helaman 15:2; see also 14:20–31.

154. 1 Nephi 19:12.

155. Helaman 16:4.

156. Helaman 16:12.

157. Helaman 16:15, 17–18.

158. Helaman 16:20.

159. Helaman 16:16, 21–22.

160. Jacob 4:4; Helaman 8:18.

161. 1 Nephi 11:22–23; Jacob 4:4; 1 Nephi 11:35, 36; 12:18.

Chapter Seven
TYPES AND SHADOWS: THE LAW OF MOSES

1. 2 Nephi 5:10; 11:4.

2. 2 Nephi 25:24–27, 30; 26:1.

3. See Galatians 3:24.

4. John 3:30.

5. Hosea 12:10.

6. Hebrews 8:5.

7. Moses 1:6.

8. See Genesis 1:26–27.

9. Deuteronomy 18:15, 17–19.

10. 1 Nephi 22:21.

11. 3 Nephi 20:23. See McConkie, *The Promised Messiah*, pp. 445–48, for an extended discussion of the similitude between Moses and Christ.

12. John 5:39, 43, 45–47.

13. 2 Nephi 25:28.

14. 2 Nephi 25:25.

15. See 1 Nephi 5:11.

16. Mosiah 13:29–30.

17. 2 Nephi 25:25.

18. McConkie, *The Promised Messiah*, p. 427.

19. D&C 84:14–15, 19–22.

20. D&C 84:23.

21. D&C 84:24–27.

22. For the definitive work on the Joseph Smith Translation of the Bible, see Robert J. Matthews, "*A Plainer Translation*": *Joseph Smith's Translation of the Bible, a History and Commentary* (Provo, Utah: Brigham Young University Press, 1995).

23. See Galatians 3:17–25.

24. Jacob 7:7.

25. Jacob 7:19.

26. Jarom 1:11.

27. Mosiah 3:15; see also vv. 5–14.

28. Mosiah 12:19.

29. Mosiah 12:27–29, 31–32.

30. Mosiah 12:33.

31. Compare Mosiah 13:5 with Exodus 34:29, 35. In a discussion of types, the parallel to Moses' story, including the riotous behavior of King Noah's court, is not coincidental.

32. Mosiah 13:25–26.

33. Mosiah 13:27–31.

34. Mosiah 13:33–34.

35. See chapter 5 for an examination of these passages from Isaiah.

36. See Mosiah 15:15–18; compare Mosiah 12:21–24 and Isaiah 52:7–10.

37. Mosiah 16:12–15.

38. See chapter 8.

39. Alma 25:15–16.

40. Alma 34:7.

41. Alma 34:13–14.

42. 3 Nephi 1:24–25.

43. 3 Nephi 9:15–20.

44. 3 Nephi 12:17–19, 46–47; compare Matthew 5.

45. 3 Nephi 15:2, 4–10.

46. Mosiah 13:27.

47. 2 Nephi 25:27.

48. JST Galatians 3:24.

49. 4 Nephi 1:12–13.

Chapter Eight
Types and Shadows: All Things Are the Typifying of Christ

1. 2 Nephi 11:4.

2. Bruce W. Jorgensen was among the first to give serious typological consideration to the Book of Mormon generally and the Tree of Life image specifically. See his "The Dark Way to the Tree: Typological Unity in the Book of Mormon," *Encyclia*, vol. 54, part 2, 1977, pp. 16–24.

3. 1 Nephi 8:11–12.

4. 1 Nephi 11:7.

5. 1 Nephi 11:21.

6. 1 Nephi 11:8; see also vv. 7, 9, 21–22.

7. 1 Nephi 11:25.

8. John 3:16; see also Ether 12:33.

9. 1 Nephi 8:22–23.

10. 1 Nephi 8:24–25, 28.

11. 1 Nephi 8:30.

12. 1 Nephi 10:14.

13. 1 Nephi 15:14.

14. Truman Madsen, "The Olive Press: A Symbol of Christ," in *The Allegory of the Olive Tree*, ed. Stephen D. Ricks and John W. Welch (Salt Lake City: Deseret Book Co. and Provo, Utah: FARMS, 1994), p. 2. Professor Madsen's essay provides useful background and context for the observations that follow.

15. See Jacob 4:14–18.

16. Jacob 5:61, 74; see also 1 Nephi 8:12; 11:22; 15:36.

17. See M. Catherine Thomas, "Jacob's Allegory: The Mystery of Christ," in *The Allegory of the Olive Tree*, pp. 11–20.

18. John S. Tanner, "Jacob and His Descendants as Authors," in *Rediscovering the Book of Mormon*, edited by John L. Sorenson and Melvin J. Thorne (Salt Lake City: Deseret Book Co. and Provo, Utah: FARMS, 1991), p. 61.

19. Jacob 5:73–74.

20. Jacob 6:4–5, 8.

21. See 1 Nephi 17:41.

22. See Numbers 21:8.

23. 2 Nephi 25:20.

24. Helaman 8:13–15.

25. 1 Nephi 8:11.

26. Alma 32:28, 30, 34.

27. Alma 32:37–43.

28. Alma 32:42.

29. Alma 33:19, 21–23.

30. Alma 34:2, 4.

31. Acts 5:30; see also 10:39.

32. 3 Nephi 27:14–15.

33. Mosiah 13:10.

34. Mosiah 13:31.

35. Mosiah 16:14; see chapter 7.

36. D&C 107:3.

37. Alma 13:7; see also D&C 84:17.

38. See Hebrews 4:5.

39. Alma 13:9.

40. Alma 13:1–2, 16.

41. See Alma 13:3.

42. See Alma 13:3.

43. See Alma 13:3.

44. See Alma 13:4.

45. See Alma 13:3.

46. See Alma 13:6.

47. See Alma 13:8.

48. See Alma 13:9.

49. See Alma 13:11.

50. See Alma 13:12.

51. See Alma 13:12.

52. Alma 13:14.

53. See Alma 13:17.

54. See Alma 13:17.

55. See Alma 13:18.

56. Alma 13:18.

57. See Alma 13:18.

58. See Alma 13:18.

59. See Alma 13:18.

60. Alma 13:19.

61. See Jacob 4:5.

62. 1 Nephi 16:10.

63. 1 Nephi 16:27.

64. 1 Nephi 16:28–29.

65. Alma 37:39–41.

66. Alma 37:43–45; compare 33:19.

Chapter Nine
THE FATHER AND THE SON

1. *Teachings of the Prophet Joseph Smith*, selected by Joseph Fielding Smith (Salt Lake City: Deseret Book Co., 1938), p. 370.

2. Matthew 3:16–17; for additional commentary from the Father on the baptism of his Son, see 2 Nephi 31:11–15.

3. Joseph Smith–History 1:17.

4. 2 Nephi 31:21.

5. Alma 11:44.

6. 3 Nephi 11:27, 36.

7. Mormon 7:5–7.

8. Alma 11:38.

9. Alma 11:39–40.

10. See Mosiah 15:2–7.

11. Mosiah 15:3.

12. This doctrine outlining the relationship between the Father and the Son is of such significance that in June 1916 the First Presidency issued a definitive doctrinal statement on this subject. See appendix C.

13. D&C 84:38.

14. Mosiah 3:5, 8.

15. Mosiah 5:15.

16. Mosiah 4:2.

17. Mosiah 26:22–23.

18. Mosiah 27:24, 30–31.

19. Helaman 14:12.

20. 3 Nephi 9:15.

21. Ether 3:14.

22. Mosiah 5:7.

23. Mosiah 15:10–12.

24. Mosiah 27:24–26, 28.

25. Alma 36:18–20, 23–26.

26. Alma 5:14.

27. Mosiah 7:26–28.

28. Mosiah 13:28, 34; 15:1.

29. Mosiah 15:2–9.

30. 2 Nephi 2:8.

31. 2 Nephi 2:28–29.

32. 3 Nephi 1:14.

33. See also D&C 93:4.

34. Luke 22:42; see also D&C 19:16–19.

Chapter Ten
THE ATONEMENT

1. Alma 42:8.

2. *Teachings of the Prophet Joseph Smith*, p. 121.

3. Mormon 9:12–13.

4. See 2 Nephi 2:1–3.

5. 2 Nephi 2:4.

6. See 1 Nephi 10, especially verse 18.

7. 1 Corinthians 15:45.

8. Romans 5:14.

9. 1 Peter 1:20.

10. Revelation 13:8.

11. Mosiah 4:7; see also v. 6.

12. Alma 12:25; see also v. 30.

13. Alma 22:13.

14. Ether 3:14; for other representative Book of Mormon examples of this commonly taught doctrine, see Mosiah 15:19; 18:13; Alma 42:26.

15. 2 Nephi 2:25–26.

16. 2 Nephi 2:5.

17. 2 Nephi 2:8–10. Note how repeatedly the Book of Mormon teaches simple truths that so effortlessly counter what would become the erroneous beliefs of many in the post-Messianic era. Lehi repeated three times that Christ would make intercession for *all* the children of men and that *all* would stand before God. The blessings of redemption and the invitation to eternal life were to be for *all* who came to earth. From start to finish, the Book of Mormon clearly opposes the later doctrines of reformed theology, predicated upon, among other things, an erroneous view of predestination. Such error would teach selective redemption for a limited few alone who, through no choice or effort of their own, would be given the privilege of embracing salvation and its eternal blessings.

18. See Revelation 12:7–17; Moses 4:1–4.

19. 2 Nephi 2:16, 26–27.

20. 2 Nephi 2:11.

21. 2 Nephi 2:12.

22. 2 Nephi 2:11.

23. Moses 5:10.

24. Moses 5:11.

25. Mosiah 16:3.

26. 2 Nephi 2:25, 23; see also Moses 5:11.

27. 2 Nephi 2:22–23; 19–20.

28. Mosiah 3:16.

29. Mosiah 3:19.

30. Mosiah 16:3–5.

31. Ether 3:2.

32. Ether 3:2.

33. See Mosiah 3:26.

34. 2 Nephi 2:24.

35. 2 Nephi 2:21.

36. Alma 12:24, 28–30, 32–33.

37. 2 Nephi 2:26–27.

38. Romans 3:23.

39. 2 Nephi 2:28–29, 27.

40. 2 Nephi 2:30.

41. 2 Nephi 2:8.

42. 2 Nephi 9:5–7.

43. Alma 34:8–10, 12.

44. 2 Nephi 9:21–22.

45. See Articles of Faith 1:2.

46. 2 Nephi 9:8–10.

47. 2 Nephi 9:27.

48. 2 Nephi 9:9–11.

49. 2 Nephi 9:13, 19–21.

50. 2 Nephi 9:25–26.

51. See D&C 68:25; 29:46–47.

52. Moroni 8:8.

53. Moroni 8:9–12, 14, 19, 22–23.

54. Mosiah 3:16, 18, 21.

55. Matthew 19:14.

56. 2 Nephi 9:23–24, 27.

57. Moroni 8:25–26.

58. Mosiah 3:19.

59. Mosiah 4:2; see Helaman 12:7–8 for Mormon's commentary on the disobedience and willfulness of mortals that makes them "less than the dust of the earth."

60. Mosiah 4:2.

61. Mosiah 4:6–8.

62. Mosiah 5:7–9.

63. Alma 5:7.

64. Alma 5:14, 27, 38, 48.

65. Mosiah 27:24–26, 28.

66. Alma 36:5, 24, 26.

67. Alma 7:13–14.

68. Alma 7:11–12.

69. See Luke 15:5.

70. Isaiah 40:29, 31.

71. Alma 7:15; Matthew 11:28–29.

72. D&C 88:6, 13.

73. D&C 133:53.

74. D&C 122:9.

75. See Alma 42:13, 22, 25.

76. Alma 42:14; see also v. 12.

77. Alma 42:19–20.

78. Alma 42:25.

79. Mosiah 2:36–39.

80. Jacob 6:10; see also 1 Nephi 12:18.

81. Mosiah 3:10; Alma 11:41, 44.

82. Alma 12:1, 7.

83. Mosiah 15:27.

84. See Alma 42:13, 22, 25.

85. Alma 12:15.

86. Alma 42:15.

87. See Mosiah 13:28, 34; 15:1.

88. Alma 34:11.

89. Alma 42:15.

90. See Mosiah 15:8.

91. Alma 42:13–14, 22–24.

92. Mosiah 15:9.

93. John Taylor, *Mediation and Atonement* (Salt Lake City: Deseret News Co., 1882), pp. 148–49.

94. Alma 42:23–24.

95. Alma 34:15–16.

96. Mosiah 16:12.

97. 1 Corinthians 6:20.

98. 2 Nephi 9:5.

99. 2 Nephi 9:41.

100. 2 Nephi 9:51.

101. 2 Nephi 26:24–25, 27–28, 33.

102. Alma 12:34; 24:10.

103. Alma 24:15.

104. Alma 18:41.

105. Alma 19:29.

106. Alma 33:4–11. Were it not for the Book of Mormon, no one would even know of the prophet Zenos, nor would there be recorded such an eloquent prayer of thanksgiving and salvation as this jewel of personal supplication.

107. Alma 36:17–21.

108. Alma 38:8.

109. Alma 42:27.

110. Alma 42:30–31.

111. 2 Nephi 10:24.

112. Alma 22:14.

113. 2 Nephi 2:8.

114. 2 Nephi 31:19.

115. Mosiah 13:28.

116. 2 Nephi 10:23–25.

117. Moroni 10:32–33.

118. 2 Nephi 25:23.

119. 2 Nephi 2:8.

120. Moroni 10:34.

121. Mosiah 26:2.

122. Mosiah 16:6–7.

123. Helaman 14:25; see also Matthew 27:52–53.

124. See 3 Nephi 23:7–13.

125. Mosiah 15:21, 24, 26.

126. Alma 40:3; 12:8–9.

127. Alma 40:4; see also vv. 3 and 5–8.

128. Alma 40:15.

129. Alma 40:20.

130. See Alma 40:21.

131. Alma 40:11–14; see also 1 Peter 3:19.

132. Alma 40:23.

133. Alma 11:43–44.

134. Alma 41:9.

135. Alma 41:10–15.

136. Alma 11:45.

137. For example see 2 Nephi 9:8–9, previously cited.

138. D&C 93:33–34.

139. D&C 88:15–16.

140. 2 Nephi 9:13.

141. 2 Nephi 9:14.

142. D&C 132:19.

143. 2 Nephi 9:9.

144. 2 Nephi 9:19.

145. "I Stand All Amazed," *Hymns of The Church of Jesus Christ of Latter-day Saints* (Salt Lake City: The Church of Jesus Christ of Latter-day Saints, 1985), no. 193.

Chapter Eleven
CHRIST IN THE NEW WORLD: THE FIRST DAY

1. *Nature*, 1836, Section 1.

2. See 3 Nephi 8:5–19.

3. See 1 Nephi 19:10–12.

4. 3 Nephi 8:20–23.

5. 3 Nephi 11:7.

6. 3 Nephi 11:10.

7. 3 Nephi 11:11.

8. 3 Nephi 11:12.

9. 3 Nephi 1:8.

10. 3 Nephi 1:9.

11. 3 Nephi 1:10–11, 14; see also vv. 12–13 and chapter 9 on the Father and the Son.

12. 3 Nephi 1:19, 21.

13. 3 Nephi 1:24.

14. 3 Nephi 2:1–2.

15. 3 Nephi 5:1–3.

16. 3 Nephi 6:5; see also v. 10.

17. 3 Nephi 6:14.

18. 3 Nephi 6:18.

19. 3 Nephi 6:20.

20. 3 Nephi 7:15, 18–20.

21. 3 Nephi 8:5.

22. 3 Nephi 9:2, 13–14.

23. 3 Nephi 9:15–22.

24. See 3 Nephi 9:15.

25. 3 Nephi 9:15.

26. See 3 Nephi 9:15.

27. See 3 Nephi 9:15.

28. See 3 Nephi 9:15.

29. See 3 Nephi 9:16.

30. See 3 Nephi 9:16.

31. See 3 Nephi 9:17.

32. See 3 Nephi 9:17.

33. See 3 Nephi 9:17.

34. See 3 Nephi 9:17.

35. See 3 Nephi 9:18.

36. See 3 Nephi 9:18.

37. See 3 Nephi 9:19.

38. See 3 Nephi 9:20.

39. See 3 Nephi 9:20.

40. See 3 Nephi 9:21.

41. 3 Nephi 9:22.

42. See 3 Nephi 10:4–7.

43. 3 Nephi 11:14.

44. Zechariah 13:6; see also D&C 45:52.

45. 3 Nephi 11:14–17.

46. See 3 Nephi 11:18–21; *History of the Church* 4:538; D&C 20:38.

47. 3 Nephi 11:22–28.

48. 3 Nephi 11:29–30, 32–35, 37–40.

49. See 2 Nephi 31.

50. For a verse-by-verse comparison of these two sermons, see Appendix D.

51. See 2 Nephi 31:18–21.

52. 3 Nephi 12:1–2.

53. 3 Nephi 12:3.

54. 3 Nephi 12:6.

55. The definitive LDS work on the sermon at the temple and its relationship to covenant making people, including temple covenants, is John W. Welch's, *The Sermon at the Temple and the Sermon on the Mount* (Salt Lake City: Deseret Book Co. and Provo, Utah: FARMS, 1990). See especially pp. 14–15. For several non-LDS scholars' views of the covenantal aspect of the Sermon on the Mount, see Welch's citations of Betts, Jeremias, Stendahl, Davies, and others, pp. 6–7ff.

56. 3 Nephi 13:25–34.

57. 3 Nephi 14:1.

58. 3 Nephi 15:4–5.

59. 3 Nephi 15:9–10.

60. 3 Nephi 15:12–15.

61. 3 Nephi 15:18.

62. John 16:12.

63. 3 Nephi 15:20–24.

64. 3 Nephi 16:1–5.

65. 3 Nephi 16:9–11.

66. 3 Nephi 17:1–3.

67. 3 Nephi 17:4.

68. 3 Nephi 17:5–7, 9–10.

69. 3 Nephi 17:14.

70. 3 Nephi 17:15–17.

71. 3 Nephi 17:21–23.

72. 3 Nephi 17:24–25.

73. 3 Nephi 18:5–7.

74. 3 Nephi 18:9–11.

75. 3 Nephi 11:39–41.

76. 3 Nephi 18:12–14.

77. 3 Nephi 18:15–16.

78. 3 Nephi 18:18–21.

79. 3 Nephi 18:22, 24.

80. See 3 Nephi 11:14–15.

81. 3 Nephi 18:34.

Chapter Twelve
CHRIST IN THE NEW WORLD: THE SECOND DAY

1. 3 Nephi 19:1.

2. 3 Nephi 19:2.

3. 3 Nephi 19:3.

4. 3 Nephi 19:8–9.

5. *History of the Church* 4:42.

6. See Moses 6:65; Mosiah 18:14; Joseph Smith–History 1:73.

7. 3 Nephi 19:13.

8. See 3 Nephi 19:13–18.

9. 3 Nephi 19:19–23.

10. See John 17.

11. 3 Nephi 19:22.

12. 3 Nephi 19:24.

13. Romans 8:26.

14. 3 Nephi 19:25.

15. 3 Nephi 19:25–26.

16. 3 Nephi 19:28–29.

17. 3 Nephi 19:30–31.

18. 3 Nephi 19:32.

19. 3 Nephi 19:34.

20. 3 Nephi 19:35.

21. 3 Nephi 20:1.

22. 3 Nephi 20:6–7.

23. Luke 4:28–30.

24. 3 Nephi 20:8.

25. See 3 Nephi 18:4–5, 9.

26. 3 Nephi 20:9.

27. 3 Nephi 20:10.

28. 3 Nephi 20:13, 21.

29. 3 Nephi 20:22; see also v. 14.

30. 3 Nephi 20:23; compare Deuteronomy 18:15–22.

31. See Joseph Smith–History 1:40; Acts 3:22–23.

32. 3 Nephi 20:25–27.

33. 3 Nephi 20:30–33.

34. 3 Nephi 20:34–35.

35. 3 Nephi 20:39–40.

36. See Mosiah 15:18–19.

37. 3 Nephi 20:40.

38. 3 Nephi 20:44.

39. 3 Nephi 20:46.

40. 3 Nephi 21:3.

41. 3 Nephi 21:5, 7.

42. 3 Nephi 21:9.

43. 3 Nephi 21:10.

44. 3 Nephi 20:16; see also 3 Nephi 21:12–21; 20:17–20, 28.

45. 3 Nephi 21:22–26.

46. 3 Nephi 21:26–28.

47. Isaiah 54:1–3.

48. Isaiah 54:3; D&C 115:6.

49. Isaiah 54:4–6.

50. Isaiah 54:7–10.

51. Isaiah 54:11–12.

52. See Revelation 21:18–21.

53. Isaiah 54:13–14.

54. Isaiah 54:15–17.

55. See D&C 71:9–10; 109:25.

56. I am indebted to Professor Victor L. Ludlow for this insight. See his *Isaiah: Prophet, Seer, and Poet* (Salt Lake City: Deseret Book Co., 1982), p. 462.

57. 3 Nephi 23:1–2.

58. 3 Nephi 23:4–5, 11–12.

59. 3 Nephi 24:1; 26:2.

60. Joseph Smith–History 1:36.

61. Malachi 3:1.

62. See D&C 110.

63. Malachi 3:2–3.

64. D&C 128:24.

65. See *Teachings of the Prophet Joseph Smith* (Salt Lake City: Deseret Book Co., 1938), pp. 172–73; *Doctrines of Salvation,* 3 vols., compiled by Bruce R. McConkie (Salt Lake City: Bookcraft, 1954–56) 3:94.

66. D&C 124:39.

67. D&C 13:1.

68. Malachi 3:5–10.

69. Malachi 3:13–18.

70. 3 Nephi 12:45.

71. Malachi 4:1.

72. Malachi 4:5–6.

73. D&C 2:2–3.

74. D&C 110:14.

75. 3 Nephi 26:2–3.

76. 3 Nephi 26:6–7; see also vv. 1–5.

77. 3 Nephi 26:8.

78. 3 Nephi 26:11.

79. 3 Nephi 26:14.

80. 3 Nephi 26:15.

Chapter Thirteen
CHRIST IN THE NEW WORLD: THE THIRD DAY AND BEYOND

1. 3 Nephi 26:13.

2. 3 Nephi 26:16.

3. Matthew 19:14.

4. 3 Nephi 26:18–20.

5. 3 Nephi 27:1.

6. 3 Nephi 27:2.

7. See D&C 115:4.

8. 3 Nephi 27:7.

9. 3 Nephi 27:8.

10. 3 Nephi 27:10.

11. D&C 115:4.

12. 3 Nephi 27:7, 9.

13. 3 Nephi 27:14–15.

14. See 3 Nephi 19:13; 20:9.

15. 3 Nephi 27:16–17, 19.

16. 3 Nephi 27:20; Mosiah 3:19.

17. 3 Nephi 27:21, 27.

18. 3 Nephi 27:28–29.

19. 3 Nephi 28:1.

20. 3 Nephi 28:7.

21. 3 Nephi 28:15.

22. See Matthew 17:1–13 and *Teachings of the Prophet Joseph Smith,* pp. 170–71, 158.

23. 3 Nephi 28:13–14.

24. 3 Nephi 28:15.

25. 3 Nephi 28:38–39.

26. 3 Nephi 28:8, 40.

27. See 3 Nephi 28:25.

28. See 3 Nephi 28:26.

29. See Mormon 8:11.

30. 3 Nephi 28:30, 31.

31. 3 Nephi 28:12.

32. 3 Nephi 28:33.

33. 3 Nephi 29:1.

34. 3 Nephi 30:1–2.

Chapter Fourteen
THE HEAVENLY GIFT AND THE SINS OF THE WORLD

1. 4 Nephi 1:1.

2. 4 Nephi 1:2–3.

3. 4 Nephi 1:5.

4. 4 Nephi 1:11.

5. 4 Nephi 1:12.

6. 4 Nephi 1:15.

7. 4 Nephi 1:16–18.

8. 4 Nephi 1:20.

9. 4 Nephi 1:24–26.

10. 4 Nephi 1:27.

11. 4 Nephi 1:28.

12. 4 Nephi 1:34.

13. 4 Nephi 1:43.

14. 4 Nephi 1:44.

15. 4 Nephi 1:46.

16. 2 Nephi 25:21.

17. Moroni 10:27.

Chapter Fifteen
A HEART FILLED WITH SORROW

1. Mormon 2:18–19.

2. Mormon 1:2.

3. Mormon 1:7.

4. Mormon 1:13–14.

5. Mormon 1:15.

6. Mormon 2:10.

7. Mormon 2:13–14.

8. Mormon 2:15.

9. Mormon 2:26.

10. Mormon 3:2–3.

11. Mormon 3:11–12.

12. Mormon 3:16, 19–21.

13. Mormon 5:8–9, 11.

14. Mormon 5:15–16, 17.

15. Mormon 6:17–20.

16. Mormon 7:5–7; see also vv. 1–4.

17. Mormon 7:8–10.

Chapter Sixteen
MORONI'S THREE WITNESSES: A CRY FOR FAITH, HOPE, AND CHARITY

1. See Mormon 8 and 9.

2. Mormon 8:6, 3–4.

3. Mormon 8:10–11.

4. Mormon 8:31.

5. Mormon 8:26.

6. Mormon 8:35.

7. Mormon 8:38–41.

8. Mormon 9:5–8.

9. Mormon 9:12–14.

10. Mormon 9:30.

11. Mormon 9:27, 21, 26–27, 29, 37.

12. Ether 12:3.

13. Ether 12:4.

14. Ether 12:4, 6.

15. Ether 12:6.

16. Ether 12:7; see also v. 12.

17. Ether 12:8.

18. Ether 12:10; compare Alma 13:3.

19. Ether 12:11.

20. See Ether 12:12.

21. See Ether 12:13; compare Alma 14:27.

22. Ether 12:14; compare Helaman 5:45.

23. See Ether 12:15; Alma 17–26.

24. See Ether 12:16, 18.

25. Ether 12:17; compare 3 Nephi 28:7.

26. Ether 12:19.

27. Ether 12:20–21.

28. Ether 12:22.

29. See Ether 12:9.

30. Ether 12:26–28.

31. Ether 12:29–34.

32. Ether 12:38–41.

33. Moroni 1:1, 3.

34. Moroni 7:3–4.

35. Moroni 7:12, 16.

36. Moroni 7:18–19.

37. Moroni 7:22, 24.

38. Moroni 7:25.

39. Moroni 7:26–28, 33.

40. Moroni 7:33–34.

41. Moroni 7:38.

42. Moroni 7:40.

43. Ether 12:9.

44. Moroni 7:41.

45. Moroni 7:42.

46. Moroni 7:45. The fact that Paul uses comparable language without having the benefit of Mormon and Moroni's text suggests the possibility of an ancient source available to both Book of Mormon and New Testament writers. It may also simply be another evidence that the Holy Ghost can reveal a truth in essentially the same words to more than one person.

47. Moroni 7:46.

48. 1 Corinthians 13:1–2, 13.

49. 1 Corinthians 13:4–5, 7–8; Moroni 7:48.

50. 2 Nephi 9:9.

51. Ether 12:33–34.

52. Moroni 7:46, 48.

53. Moroni 10:20–21.

54. Moroni 10:24, 30–31.

55. D&C 88:75, 85.

56. Moroni 10:32–33.

57. Moroni 10:34.

58. See Revelation 14:6.

Chapter Seventeen
WITNESS

1. D&C 107:23.

2. D&C 135:3; see also Book of Mormon Title Page.

3. George Q. Cannon, in Andrew Jenson, *Historical Record* 6:174.

4. D&C 6:2.

5. Bill McKeever, quoted in Daniel C. Peterson, "Editors' Introduction," *Review of Books on the Book of Mormon*, vol 6, no. 1 (Provo, Utah: FARMS, 1994), p. v.

6. A great deal of contemporary research continues to provide valuable information about the Book of Mormon witnesses, but the most readable single source is still Richard Lloyd Anderson's *Investigating the Book of Mormon Witnesses* (Deseret Book Company: Salt Lake City, 1981). The above quotations are drawn from that work.

7. D&C 135:3, 5.

8. Moroni 9:25–26.

SCRIPTURE INDEX

SUBJECT INDEX

CHRIST
AND THE NEW COVENANT
JEFFREY R. HOLLAND

n *Christ and the New Covenant,*
Elder Jeffrey R. Holland, a member of the Quorum of the Twelve Apostles, features the role of Jesus Christ as "the principal and commanding figure" in the Book of Mormon, from first chapter to last. Brother Holland's comprehensive study documents why this ancient Nephite record is truly "another testament of Jesus Christ."

The author takes his title from another book of modern scripture in which the Lord called upon "the whole church [to] remember the new covenant, even the Book of Mormon." (D&C 84:55, 57.) In his warm and thoughtful style Elder Holland writes, "The Book of Mormon is the sacred expression of Christ's full and final covenant with mankind. It is a new covenant, a new testament from the New World to the entire world. More than any other book it has taught me to love the Lord Jesus Christ and to consider the full wonder and grandeur, the eternally resonating power of the atoning sacrifice he made for us."

Elder Jeffrey R. Holland was sustained as a member of the Quorum of the Twelve Apostles of The Church of Jesus Christ of Latter-day Saints on October 1, 1994. A native of St. George, Utah, he has spent most of his professional life in Church education. He received his bachelor's and master's degrees from Brigham Young University, and a master's degree and Ph.D. in American Studies from Yale University.

In 1974 he became Dean of Religious Instruction at BYU. Two years later, he was named Church Commissioner of Education. In 1980 he was appointed president of BYU, the position in which he was serving when sustained as a member of the First Quorum of the Seventy in 1989.

Elder Holland and his wife, Patricia Terry Holland, are the parents of three children.

Deseret Book®

ISBN 1-57345-235-1
SKU 3316845
U.S. $23.95

52395

9 781573 452359

ISBN 1-57345-235-1
SKU 3316845